John Wayne's World

John Wayne's World

TRANSNATIONAL MASCULINITY IN THE FIFTIES

By Russell Meeuf

University of Texas Press ⟁ *Austin*

Portions of the Introduction and Chapter 4 were originally published as "Shouldering the Weight of the World: The Sensational and Global Appeal of John Wayne's Body," *Journal of Popular Film and Television* 39, no. 2 (2011). Reprinted by permission of the publisher, Taylor and Francis, Ltd.

Portions of Chapter 6 originally published as "John Wayne's Japan: International Production, Global Trade, and John Wayne's Diplomacy in *The Barbarian and the Geisha*," in *Transnational Stardom: International Celebrity in Film and Popular Culture*, edited by Russell Meeuf and Raphael Raphael (New York: Palgrave Macmillan, 2013). Reproduced by permission of the publisher.

First edition, 2013
First paperback edition, 2014

Requests for permission to reproduce material from this work should be sent to:
Permissions
University of Texas Press
P.O. Box 7819
Austin, TX 78713-7819
http://utpress.utexas.edu/index.php/rp-form

⊗ The paper used in this book meets the minimum requirements of ANSI/NISO Z39.48-1992 (R1997) (Permanence of Paper).

LIBRARY OF CONGRESS CATALOGING-IN-PUBLICATION DATA
Meeuf, Russell, 1981–
   John Wayne's world : transnational masculinity in the fifties / by Russell Meeuf. — First edition.
      pages   cm
   Includes bibliographical references and index.
   ISBN 978-0-292-74746-3 (cl. : alk. paper)
   ISBN 978-1-4773-0218-7 (paperback)
   1. Wayne, John, 1907–1979.   2. Motion picture industry—United States—History—20th century.   3. Masculinity in motion pictures.   4. Motion pictures and globalization.   5. Nineteen fifties.   I. Title.
      PN2287.W454M445   2013
      791.4302′8092—dc23
                                                    2012044368

doi:10.7560/747463

For Ryanne

Contents

Acknowledgments

THIS PROJECT HAS ITS ROOTS IN AN UNDERGRADUATE honors seminar I took while a student at Pacific University in Forest Grove, Oregon, which first got me thinking about John Wayne in the context of globalization and U.S. power in the 1950s. So my first thanks should go to Jeffrey Barlow, who taught that course, and my professors at Pacific who helped me decide to be a researcher and teacher: Pauline Beard, Johanna Hibbard, Mike Steele, and Doyle Walls.

As my interest in John Wayne slowly developed into a dissertation topic and then a book, I was blessed with amazing support from my mentors at the University of Oregon: Kathleen Karlyn, Mike Aronson, and Sangita Gopal, all of whom have graciously submitted to watching some obscure John Wayne films. Their feedback and support was essential to this project, as was the work of my other dissertation committee members, Janet Wasko at the University of Oregon and Jon Lewis of Oregon State University. I had the privilege of conducting this research amid a wonderful community of film and media scholars whose intellectual, moral, and emotional support has made me a better scholar and helped this book come to fruition: Daisuke Miyao, Julie Lesage, Priscilla Ovalle, Tres Pyle, Carter Soles, Steve Rust, Kom Kunyosying, Jeong Chang, and Erica Elliot, among others. Several colleagues at the University of Idaho have provided feedback as this project has developed, including David Sigler, John Mihelich, and Traci Craig.

Research for this project was supported by a number of grants, including the University of Oregon Center on Diversity and Community/Center for the Study of Women and Society Summer Research Grant, a Charles A. Reed Fellowship through the University of Oregon College of Arts and Sciences, the University of Oregon Graduate School Summer Research Grant, and a University of Oregon Center for Asian and Pacific Studies Small Professional Grant. Thanks to all those organizations for helping make this project possible.

Archival research was conducted at the Academy of Motion Picture Arts and Sciences' Margaret Herrick Library and the University of Southern California's Warner Bros. Archive. Special thanks to Barbara Hall and Sandra Joy Lee Aguilar for helping me find traces of John Wayne's international circulation in the archives.

I would also like to thank the anonymous readers at the University of Texas Press who helped shape this project tremendously as it developed, and Jim Burr for his patience as the manuscript took shape.

I'm not sure my family understands why I've spent so much time writing about John Wayne, but they have not let that fact dampen their excitement for my research. Special thanks to Ron Meeuf, Toni Meeuf, Marcia Pilgeram, and Casey Pilgeram for their many years of support. And thanks to Alden, who knows more about John Wayne than any other five-year-old, and Will, who will become an expert on the topic of my next book. I probably could have written the book faster without you two, but it would not have been nearly as fun.

And finally, thanks to my wife, Ryanne. It would be impossible to list everything you have done to help me get to this point, so let me simply say thank you.

Introduction

REEXAMINING JOHN WAYNE

DESPITE SOME FORMAL SIMILARITIES, THE FRENCH and U.S. posters advertising the 1953 classic western *Hondo* offer radically different visions of John Wayne. In the French version, Wayne stands centered in the poster in "Warnercolor" splendor, rifle in one hand and pistol in the other, amid the empty frontier in a moment of indecision, yet poised for action. Over one shoulder, Indians charge on the warpath, and over the other armed cowboys creep out from behind a craggy outcrop. But in the foreground stands Geraldine Page, hand on hip, beckoning Wayne's character, Hondo Lane, to a life of domestic and paternal responsibilities. In the U.S. poster, on the other hand, that colorful backdrop is erased: Wayne is simply put against a white background as he draws near to Page, anticipating a romantic interlude. In the French poster, Wayne's body is tensed, on the verge of heroic action but also caught in the dilemma dramatized in the film between, on the one hand, the pull of domesticity, fatherhood, and daily labor and, on the other, the lure of violent, nomadic roaming that *"l'homme du desert"* (the man of the desert) has grown accustomed to. But in the U.S. poster, rather than positioning Wayne between the mortal danger of the open, competitive spaces of the frontier and the appeal of a domestic existence, he is simply the rugged object of Page's gaze, an interpretation supported by the poster's text, which describes Hondo as "hot blooded with the heat of the plains." The poster notes of Page's character: "First she was afraid he'd stay—then she was afraid he wouldn't." In the French poster, Wayne is a figure caught tensely in the middle not only of the violent competition for a heterogeneous frontier but also of competing visions of masculinity (and in fact it is not even really Wayne, but a sketch, an imagined construction of a heroic but troubled masculinity). But in the U.S. poster that colorful and anxious context is missing, offering instead a much smaller

FIGURES I.1 AND I.2. *French and U.S. posters advertising* Hondo *(1953). Source: Heritage Auction Galleries.*

and relaxed Wayne, stripped of his guns, limited to his role within the gendered discourses of romance.

This literal erasure of the colorful and revealing material context offered by the French poster mirrors the process of obfuscation that has narrowly defined the cultural significance of John Wayne in the United States. Thirty years after his death, we continue to see Wayne in simplified terms: as a nostalgic icon of right-wing, white American masculinity. Wayne has become a cultural myth more than a movie star, a name invoked to signify an ideal, patriotic, conservative manhood. In part because of his association with the western genre (a genre widely connected with mythologies of U.S. national identity and U.S. colonialism), in part because of his associations with Hollywood's anticommunist crusade in the 1950s (he served for several terms as president of the Motion Picture Alliance for the Preservation of American Ideals, Hollywood's primary anticommunist organization), and in part because of Wayne's very public support of the Vietnam War both on- and offscreen, his "star text"— the range of meanings circulated in the culture pertaining to Wayne—is dominated by a relatively narrow set of meanings tied to ideas about patriotism and conservatism.

As a teacher, I often poll my students about the Wayne movies they have seen and what they know about John Wayne. Despite the fact that only two or three students have usually seen a John Wayne film (thanks to their film professors showing them *The Searchers* or their grandparents making them watch *Mc-Lintock!*), every student is able to explain clearly the values that Wayne represents: toughness, patriotism, militarism. Although most of these students know next to nothing about Wayne's films, the specter of John Wayne continues to linger in their imaginations as the pinnacle of American masculinity, the flawed and outmoded yardstick that remains a potent force in their definitions of masculinity and U.S. values.

These seemingly self-evident conceptions of Wayne are perhaps why film scholarship and the culture at large have been so reluctant to closely examine the complexities of Wayne and his global cultural significance. As Jonathan Lethem points out, "thinking about his politics" offers "a way out of really looking at John Wayne" ("Darkest Side of Wayne"). Because of how Wayne came to symbolize hard-line conservative politics in the 1960s and 1970s, he became a political symbol deployed by those on both the right and the left: either he was a patriotic American hero, an always righteous man's man who nostalgically suggested a necessary but benevolent patriarchal and national authority, or he was a racist, sexist totalitarian who represented all of U.S. culture's oppressive past—in Lethem's words, a "political ignoramus, a warmongering hypocrite who never served in the armed services." Academics and cultural critics, Lethem argues, find it easier to scoff and dismiss Wayne's "brute Republicanism" than to plumb "the dark, highly sexual depths of the Wayne image." As Wayne became a political symbol within U.S. culture, the real complexities of his star persona and the global circulation of his image starting in the late 1940s have remained relatively unexamined, with most of the scholarship on Wayne affirming the assumption that he offers an uncomplicated masculinity that is uniquely American.[1]

But as the French poster for *Hondo* reveals, Wayne was a star whose complex signification of masculine identity amid the heterogeneous and modernizing spaces of the cinematic frontier resonated beyond the national and cultural borders of the United States. In this instance within the international marketing of the film, we see Wayne's anxious relationship to heterosexual coupling and the kinds of nuclear-family domesticity becoming a prominent part of modern definitions of masculinity, capturing Wayne at the moment he must choose between an emerging construction of masculine behavior and an alternate vision of masculinity tied to mobility and often-violent competition. For those responsible for marketing Wayne to international audiences, it would seem that Wayne as Hondo dramatized a whole set of conflicts and anxieties surrounding modern masculinity, its relationship to the domestic world of the nuclear family, and the lure of a dangerous world of intense, even violent, individualism, not necessarily a limited and straightforward expression of U.S. cultural values and masculinity.

Both the U.S. poster and the dominant U.S. conceptions of Wayne, therefore, perform the same fallacy, turning a blind eye to the broad historical backdrop of Wayne's global stardom and ambivalent construction of his masculinity. This erasure has meant that the world's most popular movie star in the 1950s and beyond, a star with mythic significance around the world who continues to resonate today, a star who emerged at a key historical moment, when U.S. global power was expanded and redefined, has been largely ignored and oversimplified within film and media studies, resulting in an incomplete vision of 1950s masculinity and Hollywood's relationship to international markets.

John Wayne was a crucial figure in articulating the boundaries and anxieties of a modern, capitalist, transnational masculinity in the 1950s, providing an important and resonant fantasy of male identity in a world being transformed by international social, economic, and political forces. Situating Wayne and his complex representation of masculinity within the international context of the global spread of capitalism and modernization that emerged in the years following World War II, this project explores the construction of John Wayne and a particular vision of transnational masculinity in Hollywood films of the fifties. As movie audiences around the world experienced the often-disturbing social and economic changes of capitalism becoming increasingly global, as well as pressures to conform to a particular form of Western modernity, Wayne was the world's most popular movie star, offering an appealing image of modern manhood managing those social changes. This project, therefore, uncovers and analyzes a history of John Wayne's stardom that has been both internationally ubiquitous and yet most often invisible, examining the global context central to understanding a star who has been so stubbornly defined only within the bounds of U.S. culture.

Wayne, after all, was a star with a near-global fan base whose image resonated well beyond the borders of the United States. In 1953 fans in more than fifty countries in a poll conducted by the Hollywood Foreign Press Association voted Wayne the most popular film star in the world (*Hollywood Reporter*, "Hayward, Wayne Win Foreign Poll"). Wayne was perhaps even more popular in Europe than he was in America. Emanuel Levy reports that Wayne was immensely popular in England, particularly in small towns, and those fans voted Wayne the top western star in the UK in 1952, over Alan Ladd, Randolph Scott, Roy Rogers, and Jimmy Stewart (*John Wayne: Prophet*, 228). In France, New Wave directors and critics exalted Wayne and his work with Ford and Hawks well before American critics and scholars began to appreciate such work. The French moviegoing public shared that critical admiration; in 1950 the French awarded Wayne the Grand Prix-Film de Français Award for being the most popular foreign star in France (*Hollywood Reporter*, "French Award to Wayne"). And in Germany, Wayne's popularity was "unprecedented," according to Levy. The German director Wim Wenders, in fact, described Wayne as "the most popular American actor ever to appear on the screen in Germany," citing Wayne's "physical and mental strength" as appealing to German audiences, and claiming that his love of Wayne's westerns and other American films prompted him to become a film director (quoted in Levy, *John Wayne: Prophet*, 229). Several of Wayne's commercial failures in the U.S. market were immense hits in Germany, such as *The Big Trail* (1929) and *The Alamo* (1960) (229–230).

Outside Europe, Wayne experienced enormous popularity, particularly in Japan, a large market for Hollywood films. According to the Japanese actress Teruko Akatsuki, Wayne was the most popular American actor in Japan in the early 1950s, particularly among the "Tokyo movie colony" (*Citizen-News*, "Wayne Most Popular in Japan"), and Levy reports that even Wayne's war films, which typically rely on dehumanizing, racist representations of the Japanese and other Asians, were a huge hit in Japan. Charles Miller, a *Los Angeles Times* reporter, captured this near-global appeal during extensive traveling before and just after Wayne's death in 1979, as Levy explains:

> In Australia, a farmer asked him when the next John Wayne movie would come out, and in Burma, he saw pictures of the star in restaurants and other public places. A shop owner in Afghanistan said, in response to the question of how life has changed under the new pro-Soviet regime, that the John Wayne movies had gone. In Eastern Turkey, upon telling a nomad that he was from America, the latter reached to his side in a mock draw and with a big grin exclaimed: "John Wayne." And a South African tourist in America asked Miller whether he knew Wayne had died; he had heard the news from a Frenchman. (*John Wayne: Prophet*, 230–31)

After Wayne's death, he was eulogized on the front pages of newspapers around the world, including the *London Evening Standard*, the major papers in Tokyo, and *Noticias*, of Lima, Peru, which ran the story under the headline "Goodbye Cowboy" (231). As this outpouring of remembrance suggests, throughout the 1950s, 1960s, and 1970s, Wayne enjoyed a global fan base and remained a top box-office draw in Europe, Asia, and Latin America (228–231). Wayne even enjoyed popularity in the Soviet bloc countries: in the midst of the Cold War, Nikita Khrushchev declared Wayne his favorite movie star.

Wayne's construction as uniquely American and his global popularity are not mutually exclusive; his international pervasiveness might easily be seen as the dominating imposition of U.S. culture and ideologies on audiences around the world via the oligopolistic hegemony of the Hollywood studios in international markets. Just as Wayne on-screen is often a dominating and imposing figure, the international popularity of his films might be understood as the imposing presence of Hollywood, sitting tall in the saddle, pushing around those weaker than it and forcing its products on them. But such narratives of Hollywood's success can go only so far, overlooking the power and resonance of different films as well as the cultural and emotional appeal of spectacles such as Wayne. After all, while the Hollywood studios and their international distribution networks circulated images of Wayne around the world, it is perhaps more appropriate to say that Wayne's international drawing power and the transnational appeal of his body in action helped circulate Hollywood globally in the 1950s.

Wayne's rise to superstardom, in fact, coincided with the transformation of Hollywood studios in the years after World War II as they faced the challenges of governmental regulation and declining domestic attendance. During the first decade of John Wayne's international superstardom, from roughly 1948 through the early 1960s, Hollywood studios put themselves on a path toward what we would describe today as the globalization of the industry. As Thomas Guback documented in 1969 in an underappreciated and out-of-print study of the industry, throughout the post–World War II years the Hollywood studios became increasingly global in their operations, becoming more like transnational corporations than dominant "American" companies (*International Film Industry*). As the studio system began to fall apart after the forced separation of production and exhibition in the United States was mandated by the *Paramount* decision (1948), and as television and suburbanization dramatically shrank the U.S. theatrical market, Hollywood studios became increasingly reliant on international revenue. Guback estimates that in the 1950s, 40 percent of the industry's theatrical revenue came from international markets, and by the early 1960s it accounted for around 53 percent ("Hollywood's International Market," 481). Throughout the 1950s, furthermore, it became clear to the industry that revenues from the U.S. market were not sufficient to allow the studios to recoup production costs. In a presentation to a U.S. Senate committee, a United Artists representative reported that without international revenue, "the industry would soon face insolvency and bankruptcy" (quoted in Guback, *International Film Industry*, 10–11). In response to such challenges and the increasing importance of international revenue, Hollywood studios quickly integrated themselves further into the international film industry, circumventing protectionist trade policies by pursuing international productions and coproductions and investing heavily in international film industries while continuing to dominate international distribution.[2]

For Hollywood in the fifties, then, the U.S. market increasingly became merely one node in a vast, global network of distribution and consumption, suggesting that the international popularity of John Wayne should be understood not as the imposition of U.S. cultural values but as part of cross-cultural negotiations in which Hollywood relied on the international appeal of stars like Wayne.[3] Indeed, Hollywood's internationalization during this period indicates that the very concept of "U.S. cultural values" that are somehow separate from the international operations of the American government or American corporations is meaningless in the context of global U.S. power. The international expansion of U.S. cultural industries such as Hollywood is only one example of the broader spread of U.S. power and influence after World War II. In the words of one scholar, the United States "expanded its influence and its reach so profoundly as to belie any attempts to understand 'Americanness' outside that expansion" (McAlister, *Epic Encounters*, 4). To talk of Hollywood's or John Wayne's Americanness in this period obscures the ways that both Hollywood and Wayne were active participants in the expansion of U.S.-inspired global capitalism and of a system of modernization privileging international trade and consumption.

These histories of Hollywood's internationalization and the global nature of U.S. culture complicate the typical either-or debate that usually accompanies a discussion of U.S. mass culture abroad: either such cultural products are foisting U.S. culture and values on other nations and cultures, or international audiences function as autonomous agents and simply pick and choose the meanings and interpretations from U.S. mass culture that best fit their worldviews.[4] But the complex reality of transnational media lies somewhere in the middle: local audiences exercise interpretive autonomy, and yet U.S. mass culture helps transform international cultures into a vision of global modernity. These complicated histories have been best understood in the context of Hollywood's relationship to Europe. Robert Rydell and Rob Kroes's history of U.S. mass culture in the late nineteenth and early twentieth centuries, *Buffalo Bill in Bologna*, explores how the emergence of mass culture not only transformed U.S. culture but also established the central debates concerning culture and industrialization in Europe. Similarly, Victoria de Grazia's *Irresistible Empire* examines the complex relationship between U.S. mass culture and European culture in the twentieth century. Exploring the various ways that the United States created a "Market Empire" based on the promotion of seductive and appealing U.S. goods, de Grazia provides a compelling history of the emergence of a modern and inherently transnational consumerist subjectivity in Europe based on trade with the United States and U.S.-inspired visions of consumerism, culture, and identity.[5] Finally, Vanessa Schwartz's *It's So French!* makes the case that the relationship between Hollywood and France in the 1950s was not an example of Hollywood's Americanizing of France but rather the creation of a cosmopolitan film culture based on cultural exchange and the careful marketing of Frenchness: "Global culture does not simply 'replace' national or local culture.

Instead, global culture becomes an idiom through which an additional identity is formed" (6). Her argument suggests that film has been central to the articulation of a cosmopolitan and global sense of identity that coexists and interacts with the nation as an imagined community.

The global circulation of John Wayne in the fifties, then, is best understood not in the context of Americanization nor through the selective appropriation and reception of local audiences. Instead, understanding Wayne as a global star reveals the role that his image played in the process of cultural globalization — the transformation of culture around the world according to the logic of global capitalism and modernization. Wayne was not a figure of cultural imperialism who simply promoted a conservative U.S. agenda abroad, nor was he an open-ended icon who became incorporated into various local systems of meaning and culture. Instead, Wayne in the fifties provided perhaps the most popular embodiment of the tenets and tensions of male identity within capitalism and modernity, a model of what manhood ought to be as the world came to conform to the U.S. vision of a modern, democratic, and capitalist world. He was also a key figure expressing the gendered tensions of this transition. Throughout the book, therefore, I situate Wayne and the John Wayne western within a series of international historical contexts, examining how he provided a set of globally popular images and styles that dramatized the conditions of global capitalism and uneven modernization. In a period marked by the social transformations resulting from changing patterns of labor emphasizing First World corporatism and Third World wage labor, the increasing migration of populations to big cities and across national borders, the quickening pace of decolonization throughout the 1950s, and the transformation of cross-cultural relations through international trade, John Wayne as a global star provides a site from which to investigate the cultural transformations of the increasingly globalized world of the 1950s. He was a key agent in the globalization of culture as modern male identities were promoted through Hollywood as a global industry.

As this suggests, I focus in particular on Wayne's relationship to the globalization and transformation of gender through the processes of imperialism, modernization, and global capitalism. Most academic discussions of gender and globalization privilege the local and specific as sites of gender construction, but this tendency obscures the fact that "gender is intrinsic to globalizing capitalist processes" (Acker, "Gender, Capitalism, and Globalization," 23) and that through the processes of globalization, we can see the emergence of a "world gender order" (Connell, *Men and Boys*, 40). Geopolitical issues and ideologies such as modernization, global trade, and neoliberalism — as well as the institutions charged with implementing these policies, such as the World Bank, the International Monetary Fund, the World Trade Organization, and the national governments that both support and are affected by them — are often assumed to be (and explicitly claim to be) gender neutral. They are seen as macrolevel political and economic ideologies or institutions that are disconnected from the personal and local realm of gender relations, even if their policies "accidentally" have an unequal impact on the opportunities of men and women. But these institutions and ideologies are highly gendered, operating in ways that contribute to the construction of a world gender order and global gender inequality. As R. W. Connell explains, "International relations, international trade and global markets are inherently, not accidentally, arenas of gender formation and gender politics" (*Men and Boys*, 40). Contrary to the utopian vision of globalization "producing vast unfettered global markets in which all participate on equal terms," the supposed homogenization of globalization has yielded instead a wildly unequal world economy in which the gendered assumptions of Western culture and Western capitalism have unevenly transformed local and national gender relations (41).

Within the construction and perpetuation of global articulations of gender, mass media have played a particularly important role, providing an "obvious vector for the globalization of gender" (Connell, *Men and Boys*, 44). The fantasies and images provided by Hollywood and others within the global media constitute a steady stream of gendered imagery that interacts with local and national conceptions of gender relations. In particular, media stars, especially those like John Wayne, who attain international popularity, often act as vehicles for expressing gender ideologies across national and cultural borders, providing a model of "modern" gendered behavior in international contexts.

I explore here, therefore, the complexities of Wayne's masculinity that are often overlooked by the nostalgic construction of Wayne as an always-righteous, honest, tough, father figure. In contemporary culture, Wayne is often looked back on as an exemplar of an uncomplicated masculinity, a straightforward man's man who rigidly adhered to a moral code that makes his an ideal form of masculinity to aspire to. Yet that conception of Wayne glosses over the real tensions expressed in his films and star text, particularly in the first decade of his superstardom. After all, in two of his most popular and critically acclaimed films of this period—Howard Hawks's *Red River* (1948) and John Ford's *The Searchers* (1956)—Wayne plays highly authoritarian men whose single-minded obsessions drive them toward insanity and megalomania. For a critic such as Lethem, therefore, Wayne's most popular and resonant films do not offer the straightforward, conservative masculinity described by both his supporters and detractors; rather, Wayne depicts "the most persuasive and overwhelming embodiment of our ambivalence about American manhood. His persona gathers in one place the allure of violence, the call away from the frontier, the tortured ambivalence toward women and the home, the dark pleasure of soured romanticism" ("Darkest Side of Wayne").

Wayne's popular articulation of a dark and complex masculinity on the western frontier coincided with the tumultuous international transformations of modernization, development, and the globalization of capitalism. These transformations were "global" discourses and ideologies promoted by policy makers in the First World and were also intensely "local" changes in social structures, bureaucracy, and everyday life. Wayne's projection of modern masculinity, therefore, represents the idealistic vision of cultural globalization pushed by proponents of modernization and global capitalism, along with the perceived tensions of those transformations, as a way of both acknowledging and repressing the contradictions of globalization. Stars' articulation of modern social identities, after all, is deeply embedded within complex and often contradictory ideological systems. As Richard Dyer explains, stars achieve cultural significance because of how they manage ideological tensions, expressing ideological contradictions and yet containing those contradictions, collapsing and erasing the tensions through their powerful presentation of individuality. By offering a pleasurable exploration of the paradoxes and inconsistencies of modern capitalism, stars ironically help repress those disjunctures, resolving such tensions because stars are not ultimately fragmented like the ideologies they signify; they are ordinary yet extraordinary modern individuals (Dyer, *Stars*). Thus, if stars like John Wayne provide compelling models of modern masculine subjectivity in the competitive world of global capitalism, they do so only by also showcasing the anxieties of modernity and capitalism. In the 1950s, therefore, as capitalism globalized and modernization transformed social and cultural relations, stars like John Wayne provided a spectacular representation of the tensions of globalization while still insisting on the unity and pleasures of modern manhood.

The global appeal of John Wayne, therefore, is rooted in his ability and the ability of his films to both express and manage the tensions of the gendered socioeconomic disruptions of the time. The image of John Wayne expresses the cultural changes brought about by modernization and global capitalism while still recognizing the anxieties such changes engender. In other words, as global audiences experienced modernization and global capitalism in ways much darker and more ambivalent than the powerful proponents of such systems imagined, Wayne offered a dark and ambivalent representation of masculinity within a social world being transformed by new technologies, new forms of mobility, and new social structures. By situating Wayne within the global history of the 1950s, then, we can interrogate both the possibilities and restrictions inherent in Hollywood's projection of a capitalist modernity.

As the above summary suggests, rather than relying on a historical analysis of Wayne's reception internationally—which would consider how John Wayne or a specific John Wayne film was received in a particular local or national context (the way *Hondo* was reviewed in France, for example) — this project will use a cultural-studies-inspired textual analysis to understand how the cultural tensions resulting from global capitalism and modernization are structured into the John Wayne star text and John Wayne's films.

There are, after all, limitations to a reception-studies approach. It can analyze only the local rather than the global, and so it primarily offers insight into the local circumstances of reception rather than explaining and analyzing the global popularity of Hollywood and stars like Wayne. As Simon During has pointed out, ethnographic or other types of studies of media consumption in local contexts ultimately can reveal only how a star functions within local or national ideological systems. Such studies cannot explain why stars like Wayne attain global popularity in the first place, why their spectacular depiction of violent masculinity appeals to so many groups of people across so many cultures, or how the representation of such stars relates to the transnational cultural, political, and economic backdrop of their production and reception (During, "Popular Culture").

That said, I hope that my work inspires further historical-reception studies on Hollywood abroad and on John Wayne in international markets in particular. But in this project I use a textual analysis that considers the global historical context as a starting point for considering not local reception but how and why stars like Wayne and genres like the western crossed national borders so easily. As numerous scholars of global media and culture have pointed out, in a globalizing world in which films and other media crisscross national borders and are consumed by mobile audiences, such media become important sites of contestation where audiences negotiate and engage with their sense of the local and their place within a globally capitalist modernity. Transnationally popular films, stars, and other mediated texts within what Arjun Appadurai calls the "mediascape" provide "resources for self-imagining as an everyday project" (*Modernity at Large*, 4). Put another way, the texts constituting what During calls the "global popular" — the set of films, stars, and other media images that are popular almost everywhere in the world at a given historical moment — should "be read in terms of the limited capacities of particular media to provide for individuals' needs and desires, especially male needs and desires, across the various territories that constitute the world image market" ("Popular Culture," 815). A careful reading of such texts, then, can begin to map out the terrain on which this negotiation takes place, defining the key issues and the boundaries of processes of "self-imagining" while also examining the "needs and desires" (as well as the tensions and contradictions) that are structured into globally popular media forms such as the John Wayne western.

To that end, this book analyzes the key films in the construction of the John Wayne star persona throughout the long cultural decade of the fifties, starting with Red *River* (1948) and ending with *The Man Who Shot Liberty Valance* (1962). While not every Wayne film in this period is discussed here—for example, Wayne's airplane disaster films with William Wellman, *Island in the Sky* (1953) and *The High and the Mighty* (1954), were left out but certainly explore the dynamics of Wayne's masculinity—I focus here on the films that most defined John Wayne in this period, many of which were commercially successful "classics" that are often written about in film studies: *Fort Apache* (1948), *Hondo*, *The Searchers*, or *Rio Bravo* (1959). I also discuss several less well-known Wayne films in order to explore Wayne's relationship to different international historical contexts, such as the Cold War, decolonization in Africa, and U.S.-Japanese trade relations.

Given that many of the films at the core of this study are not only star vehicles for Wayne but also the products of some of Hollywood's most famous auteurs—namely, John Ford and Howard Hawks—I examine how such directors helped shape the contours of the John Wayne persona in relation to various international contexts. Figures such as Ford and Hawks used Wayne to explore the construction of masculine leadership in contexts of capitalism and community formation, in the process helping establish the key themes and discourses defining "John Wayne." Thus Wayne's international resonance cannot be fully understood apart from the creative influence of Ford and Hawks as internationally popular storytellers whose narratives and imagery helped facilitate the movement of Wayne's image across national and cultural borders. This is not to say, of course, that either Ford or Hawks saw their work as engaging the set of international contexts I identify here; while both directors were aware of the international appeal of their films, at least as expressed in published interviews, both saw their work as essentially American. But for both directors, the cultural themes they consistently explored in their films with Wayne—primarily the definition of masculinity within the complex and competitive spaces of the frontier—cannot be separated from the contexts of the globalization of capitalism and the social transformations of modernization in this period, contexts that fundamentally link the transformation of postwar "American" masculinity on display in their films with the globalization of U.S. power and the power of international corporations.

Chapter 1 starts by analyzing the emergence of the John Wayne star persona in *Red River* (1948). Most accounts of Wayne's rise to stardom use his role as the Ringo Kid in *Stagecoach* (1939) as the moment of Wayne's arrival as a star, but it wasn't until *Red River* that Wayne became one of Hollywood's most bankable performers. In this chapter, I show how the film establishes the most prevalent aspects of the John Wayne star text. Specifically, I analyze how *Red River* and the Wayne star text manage the tension between an emerging emphasis on homosocial professionalism within international capitalism—this is a film about bringing goods (cattle) to distant markets as part of an emerging economic order—and a restructuring of gender relations that sees heterosexual romance and the nuclear family as the primary means of establishing a "modern" masculine social identity.

Turning to the creative presence of John Ford in the articulation of John Wayne, Chapter 2 examines the Cavalry Trilogy that Wayne made with Ford: *Fort Apache* (1948), *She Wore a Yellow Ribbon* (1949), and *Rio Grande* (1950). All three films tell similar stories about distant cavalry outposts that played important roles in U.S. military ventures while also managing the personal troubles of the forts' communities. In examining Ford's vision of migratory communities and the burdens of life on the frontier, I situate the trilogy within the increasing patterns of population mobility in the 1950s and the subsequent transformation of space and social relations within modernity. Ford's films explore the utopian possibilities of geographically distant but culturally central communities of outsiders and ethnics while sentimentally capturing the (often gendered) personal sacrifices necessary for such communities to succeed, dramatizing some of the spatial tensions and anxieties of a mobile, capitalist world.

Chapter 3 examines Wayne's anticommunist films *Big Jim McLain* (1952) and *Jet Pilot* (1957). Wayne is widely connected with Hollywood's anticommunist campaign of the 1950s, and was very vocal about his personal anticommunist beliefs. But while the anticommunist discourses in the United States in the 1950s were primarily focused on protecting America from foreign communist contagion, both of Wayne's anticommunist projects are more interested in promoting international tourism and consumption as antidotes to communism, celebrating an international consumerist modernity, and protecting the pleasures of tourism from communism.

Focusing on *Hondo* and *The Searchers*—films that use the technologies of 3-D (*Hondo*) and wide-screen Technicolor (*The Searchers*) to showcase Wayne's body in action—Chapter 4 explores how the representation of the male body within a changing frontier displays a growing ambivalence about the social and cultural possibilities of borderlessness and mobility. In analyzing the spectacle of Wayne in action and the body politics of global capitalism, I argue that the sensations and pleasures of watching Wayne reproduce the bodily experiences of global capitalism, in particular the endurance of wage labor, the mobility of labor and migration, and the complex racial politics of a culturally mobile world.

Chapters 5 and 6 examine two of several films Wayne shot abroad in the 1950s, using each one's international production to analyze how U.S. global power was represented and negotiated in different historical contexts. Both films are examples of a larger trend in Hollywood that relied on international productions to explore international relations, a trend that, as Vanessa Schwartz argues, is not an example of Hollywood's international domination but rather an expression of cosmopolitanism and cosmopolitan identity in the 1950s (*It's So French!*, 159–164).

In Chapter 5, I discuss *Legend of the Lost* (1957), a U.S.-Italian coproduction shot in Africa and starring Wayne, Rossano Brazzi, and Sophia Loren. In the film, Wayne plays an American desert guide who leads a wealthy European and a local prostitute into the Sahara in search of treasure. I read the film as an allegory of U.S. and European attitudes regarding decolonization and African autonomy. While dramatizing the different visions of Africa represented by Wayne and Brazzi, *Legend of the Lost* ultimately affirms a U.S. perspective that sees Africa as a space for libertarian, capitalist entrepreneurship.

Wayne's next international project, however, offered a much more nuanced vision of U.S. global power. Chapter 6 situates *The Barbarian and the Geisha* (1958)—a film shot in Japan, with a mostly Japanese cast and crew, in which Wayne plays the first U.S. consul to Japan—within U.S.-Japanese relations in the 1950s and the emerging discourses of modernization theory. Unlike *Legend of the Lost*, however, *Barbarian* complicates the condescending assumptions of modernization theory by foregrounding the retention of traditional beliefs within a modernizing world. Using the trope of a failed Asian-Caucasian romance, the film envisions the possibilities of global economic partnerships based on a U.S. model but leaving some autonomy for local cultures. By placing the usually action-oriented Wayne in the role of a diplomat, the film carefully negotiates the role of the United States in the emerging global economy.

Examining the end of the decade for the Wayne star persona, Chapter 7 emphasizes the closing down of space and mobility in the John Wayne western as a result of irresponsible capitalism or militant despotism. In both *Rio Bravo* (1959) and *The Alamo* (1960), the open spaces and borderlessness typical of the western genre are no longer available to Wayne's homosocial professionalism. Featuring Wayne first as a sheriff under siege by a powerful local rancher and then as Davy Crockett in his doomed last stand against the Mexican army in a small Texas fort, the films explore the construction of masculinity, professional identity, and political leadership among groups of men in dangerous and violent situations. By contextualizing the films' visions of modern masculinity within, respectively, the homosocial structures of capitalist wage labor and the political turmoil of decolonization in the late 1950s and early 1960s, I examine how a maturing John Wayne continued to articulate a vision of masculine subjectivity that managed the global social and cultural transformations of the 1950s.

Finally, the conclusion briefly analyzes *The Man Who Shot Liberty Valance* (1962) as a key text in the transformation of Wayne's persona. It was at this point in Wayne's career that his persona began to trend away from a dynamic model of modern masculinity and became instead an aging figure who signified nostalgia for a time gone by. This transformation of Wayne's signification is explicitly foreshadowed in *Liberty Valance* and its frame narrative highlighting the death of Wayne's character, Tom Doniphon, and the lifestyle he represents. Moreover, the film's exploration of political mythologies, nationalism, and spatial conflict (the "closing" of open spaces through statehood) situates this shift within the broader cultural contexts of the U.S. role in the global economy. So while Wayne continued to be a global star throughout the 1960s and 1970s, his films during that period addressed issues of modernization and global capitalism differently from those of the 1950s.

Throughout this book, I explore how John Wayne and the John Wayne western dramatize the cultural tensions of modernization, global capitalism, and U.S. global power, providing elaborate fantasies of male subjectivity within a modernizing world. My examination of Wayne sheds light on an issue often overlooked or taken for granted within film and media studies: the global consumption of images of a tough, violent, powerful, white masculinity. Such images are most often taken for granted as reflections of Hollywood's imperialistic dominance flexing its muscles economically, culturally, and cinematically. But Hollywood's economic and diplomatic muscle cannot fully explain why diverse audiences around the world are drawn to such images in such powerful ways. The dynamic and sensational spectacle of John Wayne's world, therefore, can reveal the pleasures, anxieties, and histories of the globalizing 1950s.

CHAPTER ONE

The Emergence of "John Wayne"

RED RIVER, GLOBAL MASCULINITY, AND WAYNE'S ROMANTIC ANXIETIES

*I*N A BELGIAN POSTER ADVERTISING HOWARD HAWKS'S *Red River* (1948), two visions of John Wayne are displayed in a spectacular colorful image. To the left stands Wayne as Tom Dunson with Fen (Coleen Gray), his love interest, who early in the film is murdered by a band of Indians. Wayne stares deeply and romantically into her eyes as he slips a bracelet onto her wrist. In the film, this is the same bracelet he would later give to his adopted son, Matthew Garth (Montgomery Clift), who in the poster is taking a hard blow to the face from the other Wayne in the lower right. This other Wayne offers a frantic and frenzied vision of violence, his mouth wide open and screaming, suggesting a release of anger and a loss of control not often seen in representations of Wayne, who is usually taciturn and cool in his violence. All the while, a flaming arrow darts across the poster, hinting at the racialized threat that Native Americans pose to the men and their desperate attempts to keep their cattle enterprise afloat.

This doubling of Wayne in the poster reflects the central problem of the film: the choice between, on one hand, the lure and necessity of heterosexual romantic love and, on the other, a homosocial professional sphere in which men must create and sustain relationships with one another in the context of highly dangerous labor. Of course, the poster attempts to repress this dilemma, implying that the male-male violence between Dunson and Matt is perhaps competitive violence over a woman. But for those familiar with the film, it is clear that the violence and frenzied rage on Wayne's face expresses not a desire to defeat Matt for the love of a woman but rather reveals Dunson's repressed need to replace Fen with Matt, to find some way of expressing his love and intimacy with Matt while recognizing the cultural pressures to embrace heterosexual coupling and romantic love. In essence, Dunson's love for Garth in both the poster and film can be expressed only through a hypermasculinized violence and only when the

FIGURE 1.1. *Belgian poster advertising* Red River *(La Rivière Rouge, 1948). Source: Heritage Auction Galleries.*

specter of heterosexual coupling looms (literally, in the poster) above this emotional display. Like the film, the poster is fraught with contradictions and dilemmas, attempting to reconcile two visions of John Wayne and modern masculinity. But it can do so only in a way that foregrounds the disjunctures between the kinds of male-male intimacy increasingly prominent in a gender-segregated workforce in the 1950s and the modern institutions of romantic love and the nuclear family that have come to dominate modern conceptions of individuality and subjectivity.

The masculine dilemmas on display in both the poster and film, which are central to the global cultural appeal of John Wayne in this period, have their roots in *Red River*. It is in *Red River*, after all, that Wayne established the parameters of his star text, which would remain relatively consistent throughout his career. The typical narrative of Wayne's rise to stardom in Wayne mythology starts with *Stagecoach* (1939), but it was not until *Red River* that Wayne first appeared on the list of Hollywood's top 10 box-office draws. Indeed, John Ford noted that he began to offer Wayne starring roles in the films that would cement Wayne's stardom, such as *Rio Grande* (1950) or *The Searchers* (1956), only after he saw Wayne's performance in *Red River*. While *Stagecoach* rescued Wayne from his roles in the low-budget B westerns that dominated his career in the 1930s, Wayne remained a low-level star throughout the 1940s, often appearing alongside and sharing billing with other stars (Marlene Dietrich, for example) rather than carrying a film by himself. But *Red River*'s immense success propelled Wayne to international popularity and laid the groundwork for the John Wayne star persona that would define the rest of his career. Wayne's role in the film, therefore, is a particularly important site for investigating the emergence of John Wayne as a global star as well as the emergence of the idea of "John Wayne" in the cultural imagination, establishing the key ideas, anxieties, and ideological contradictions that would mark the John Wayne star text throughout the 1950s and beyond.

More specifically, in *Red River* the cultural dilemma between male camaraderie and the intrusions of femininity and family into spheres of professionalism and capitalism became a central component of Wayne's star persona. At a time when the globalization of capitalism meant men around the world were drafted into wage labor and an increasingly homosocial public sphere while at the same time marriage and modern ideas about intimacy and romantic love were insisted on as essential to male identity, Wayne in *Red River* attempted to find a delicate balance between the pleasures and spectacle of men working together and the perceived threat to the all-male world posed by women and marriage. It is in this film that Wayne crafted and fully realized a star persona that explored the possibilities of male intimacy (sometimes homoerotic, sometimes not) inherent in modern empire building and other masculine endeavors while grappling with the challenges posed by femininity and the hegemony of heterosexual romance. In essence, Wayne in *Red River* fully takes on a persona that superficially adheres to the normative desire for heterosexual coupling but consistently finds a way to push such feminization and domestication away and revel in the company of other men.

As established in *Red River*, then, the Wayne star persona throughout the 1950s revolved around this dichotomy, a darkly appealing rejection of femininity and a celebration of intimacy between men in professional contexts. But *Red River* and similar films also masochistically punished Wayne's character for transgressing the hegemony of romantic love or for making too explicit his comfort and closeness with other men. In very few of Wayne's roles in this period could his character be described as happy and emotionally stable. He is instead always somewhat disgruntled, always too hard on and critical of those around him, always struggling to emotionally connect with anyone, male or female. From *Red River* on, Wayne's popularity hinged on a construction of masculinity in which the tensions between a life of homosociality and the cultural imperatives of heterosexual coupling turned characters like Tom Dunson into cynical, abrasive, borderline psychopaths whose stubborn adherence to all-male spheres was simultaneously pleasurable and repugnant. Thus, as definitions of masculinity and its relationship to labor conditions, mobility, and the institutions of marriage and family (among other issues) underwent radical shifts, John Wayne provided an image and a model of modern subjectivity for audiences around the world, but one whose dark contradictions expressed both the frustrations and pleasures of the modernization of gender.[1]

MASCULINITIES, GLOBALIZATION, AND *RED RIVER*

The context of global capitalism is particularly salient for *Red River*, given that its cattle-drive narrative dramatizes not simply the dynamics of men finding relationships with other men but also the cultural dynamics of men laboring with one another within an increasingly mobile and transitory capitalist system. The film tells the story of a Texas rancher, Tom Dunson, and his attempt to move ten thousand head of cattle on a long and dangerous cattle drive. The film opens with a young Dunson breaking away from a westbound wagon train in order to find land to the south. His fiancée, Fen, begs to go with him, using all her feminine charms, but Dunson insists that the journey is too dangerous for women. Leaving her behind, he is joined by his sidekick, Nadine Groot (Walter Brennan), only to see from a distance hours later that Native Americans have attacked the wagon train, killing Fen. Dunson and Groot join up with the lone survivor of the attack, a young boy named Matthew Garth, and the three head south, where Dunson forcibly seizes land from a powerful Mexican rancher and establishes a ranching empire of his own.

Years later, with Matt (Montgomery Clift) back home from the Civil War, Dunson is nearly broke. With the southern economy shattered by the war, the local price of cattle has plummeted, leaving Dunson's massive empire almost worthless. In a last-ditch effort to save the ranch, Dunson, Matt, Groot, and a team of Dunson's cowboys attempt to drive the cattle a thousand miles north to Missouri, where they can get top dollar for their beef and have it shipped around the country. Once the drive is underway, its pressures and dangers torment Dunson, and he slowly becomes harsh and tyrannical, pushing his men to the limit and keeping them from leaving the drive. When he threatens to hang several men who have tried to quit, Matt leads a mutiny, leaving a wounded Dunson behind and changing course to Abilene, Kansas, where there might be a railroad. With Dunson on their trail in search of revenge, Matt leads the drive to Abilene, finding the railhead and falling in love with a gambler named Tess Millay along the way. But in Abilene Dunson catches up, and the two men must face each other in the street. Matt, however, won't draw on Dunson, and Dunson, unwilling to kill Matt unless Matt draws his gun, turns to punches instead of bullets. In a strange ending, the two men settle their differences and show their love for each other in a dusty brawl in the street, reconciling and establishing a family, with Dunson as the patriarch and Matt and Tess (it is implied) marrying and providing an heir for the empire.

The narrative that established the boundaries of "John Wayne" as an idea foregrounds not only different ideas about masculinity and power but also the gendered dynamics of an economic system that closely resembles global capitalism. *Red River* focuses on changing economic conditions in the wake of a major war, conditions in which local markets can no longer support locally produced goods, so producers must distribute their goods long distances via the web of modern communication and transportation. As a major agribusiness enterprise, Dunson's ranch can no longer operate within a specific locality if it is to remain afloat; it must seek out far-flung markets for its goods. Thus, the film centers on the kinds of masculine leadership necessary in this emerging economic order, in which the local must engage with the "global" in order to survive.[2]

In fact, the spatial economic dynamics of the film, with their emphasis on the mobility of goods and the increasing borderlessness of markets, mirrors the relations within what Immanuel Wallerstein refers to as the "world system." As Stanley Corkin pointed out in *Cowboys as Cold Warriors*, his recent discussion of *Red River*, the film explores the economic ideologies of Wallerstein's world systems theory, a theory of global capitalism in which the core (the developed world) relies on the labor and natural resources of the periphery (the developing world) to produce goods and services that will be consumed globally, creating a global division of labor in which the core exploits the periphery. For Corkin, *Red River* displays the ideological underpinnings of the post–World War II U.S. foreign and economic policy that supported this world system, legitimizing U.S. imperialist domination of territory and the necessary incorporation of world markets into a capitalist system dominated by the United States and other developed nations (*Cowboys as Cold Warriors*, 19–50). Corkin suggests that the western frontier dramatized by Hollywood in the 1950s symbolizes the global "periphery" of Africa, Asia, and Latin America and its relationship to the modern, urban United States. A film like *Red River* displays the processes by which the "periphery" is brought into the fold of the capitalist system through the latter's connection to modern technology such as the railroad. Thus *Red River*'s narrative about labor migration and the search for far-flung markets seems to dramatize the tensions of postwar economic shifts not only for developed-world producers who must adapt to new economic conditions of global trade, but also for entrepreneurs around the world who must incorporate into global capitalism.

Moreover, the film concerns itself with the dynamics of mobility and labor, exploring the anxieties of laborers who must adapt to the necessity of labor migrations in order to seek economic opportunities. Dunson's workers, his cowboys, are displaced and dispossessed men without economic opportunities in Texas; they must seek opportunities on the long drive with Dunson if they are to make a living and provide for their families back home. When approaching his men about the drive, he tells them:

> Most of you men have come back to Texas from the war. You came back to nothing. You find your homes gone, your cattle scattered, and your land stolen by carpetbaggers. Well there's no money and no work because there's no market for beef in the South. But there is in Missouri. So we're going to Missouri. Cumberland didn't make it. No one else has. That's the reason I'm here. I want you all to know what you're up against. You probably already know, but I want to make sure you do. We got a thousand miles to go. Ten miles a day'll be good. Fifteen will be luck. It'll be dry country, dry wells when we get to 'em. There'll be wind, rain. There's gonna be Indian Territory—how bad I don't know. When we get to Missouri, there'll be border gangs. It's gonna be a fight all the way. But we'll get there.

When Dunson speaks to his men about the dangers and payoffs of the massive drive, he implies that what is at stake is not simply the economic survival of his ranch but also the economic future of his workers and working people in Texas in general. Returning home to a postwar economy in shambles, the cowboys must adjust to an economic reality in which the only viable option is dangerous work spent transporting goods long distances under harsh conditions. The film dramatizes the spatial dynamics of global capitalism after World War II, exploring the new, deterritorialized economic conditions in which export and the migration of labor are central to economic survival, in which mobility brings the promise of economic survival and yet the threat of unstable and harsh working conditions.

From the beginning of Wayne's superstardom, then, his persona was deeply intertwined with narratives of capitalism, mobility, and the kinds of masculinity necessary for survival in an emerging, global economic order. *Red River*, in fact, acts as a kind of primer describing the relationship between global capitalism and masculinity, using Wayne as Tom Dunson to explore how changing economic conditions produce different masculinities.

As I note in the introduction, the coming of the global economy, which has often been seen as a gender-neutral phenomenon, has yielded massive yet uneven transformations in the construction and definition of gender around the world. From colonialism through other forms of imperialism, including the processes of globalization throughout the second half of the twentieth century, we have seen the emergence of an increasingly unified world gender order in which patriarchal authority and particular forms of masculinity are privileged and empowered. For example, as the sociologist R. W. Connell outlines, globalization and modernization have put more power in the hands of large-scale organizations such as governments and corporations, which are "culturally masculinized and controlled by men," both in the metropole and in decolonized nations, where local elites rely upon their relationship with the metropolitan powers and must balance local and global gender relations and behavior (*Men and Boys*, 42). Additionally, global capitalism has reorganized local gender relations to "produce a male wage-worker/female domestic worker couple," reproducing the associations between masculinity and the public, economic sphere and femininity with the domestic sphere, as in U.S. and European gender systems (42). Globalization has meant the export of gendered institutions from the West such as "armies, states, bureaucracies, corporations, capital markets, labour markets, schools, law courts, [and] transport systems," which have reconstituted gender relations and in particular the definitions of masculinities inherent in the functioning of such institutions (45). Additionally, Joan Acker suggests that the spread of global capitalism has proliferated the ideology of corporate nonresponsibility in international contexts, which encourages a masculinist disregard for women's labor, health, and reproduction ("Gender, Capitalism, and Globalization," 23–28).[3]

Red River's account of Dunson's ranching empire essentially offers a history of these shifting constructions of hegemonic masculinity, particularly the emergence of global patterns of masculinity as described by Connell. Connell's work traces the historical development of different global masculinities as the structures and institutions of imperialism and global capitalism engender new forms of power and gender relations. The earliest set of globalizing masculinities were those of "conquest and settlement," which were associated with the early stages of colonization when the imperial powers violently wrested control of territory from indigenous people, usually through the actions of homosocial groups of men such as "soldiers, sailors, traders, administrators" (*Men and Boys*, 47).

Marked by "an unusual level of violence and egocentric individualism" (47), such patterns of masculinity were tied to the violent imposition of Western gender ideology through the sexual exploitation of indigenous women. After the initial stages of conquest and settlement, the economic and political organization of empire yielded patterns of masculinity based on the perpetuation of the imperial order and the economic exploitation of colonial resources and labor. In imperial centers and colonized lands alike, the restructuring of the global economy through colonization created patterns of masculinity organized around economic self-interest, bureaucracy, scientific expertise, and the selling of one's labor. Finally, the conditions of neoliberal capitalism that emerged in the second half of the twentieth century celebrated the ideal of the "individual," but an individual with the attributes of a particular version of the male entrepreneur. Globally, a particular manifestation of hegemonic masculinity emerged in the last decades of the twentieth century, one associated with the men who control the global economy's primary institutions: "the business executives who operate in global markets, and the political executives who interact (and in many cases merge) with them" (51–52). Connell terms this "transnational business masculinity," a pattern of masculinity marked by "increasing egocentrism, very conditional loyalties (even to the corporation), and a declining sense of responsibility for others (except for purposes of image making)" (52). Transnational business masculinity tends to have "no permanent commitment, except to the idea of accumulation itself" and an "increasingly libertarian sexuality, with a growing tendency to commodify relations with women" through pornography, prostitution, and sex tourism (52).[4]

The transformations that Connell describes, of course, stretch over hundreds of years of the history of imperialism, from its roots in the sixteenth and seventeenth centuries to the dominance of neoliberalism since the 1980s. But the 1950s, amid decolonization, modernization, development, and the increasing internationalism of capitalism, proves an important historical moment in these gendered transformations as the structures of colonialism and explicit dominance gave way and, thanks to increasing U.S. power globally, were slowly replaced by a model of neoliberal corporate power. As colonialism declined over the course of the 1950s and early 1960s and new forms of global capitalism and modernization emerged in the world system, new patterns of masculinity became hegemonic in the transition between the gendered vision of colonization and imperialism (derived from masculinities of violent territorial dominance) and the emerging gender order of transnational capitalism (derived from more flexible masculinities of capitalist accumulation).

As the world's most popular star during this period, Wayne provides a key site for investigating these gendered transformations. On the one hand, it is easy to align Wayne with a straightforward colonialist definition of masculinity rooted in a patriarchal and racist domination of land and indigenous people. And yet, on the other hand, Wayne's nomadic wandering and masculine professionalism in his films seems to equally suggest the capitalistic and competitive mobility of both the emerging transnational business classes and the labor-driven migrations of international working classes in the fifties as both groups increasingly defined their masculinity around the mobility necessary within global capitalism. Wayne's films with Howard Hawks especially develop this emphasis on men and appropriate forms of labor, since Hawks was obsessed with a sense of male professionalism (something I discuss in more detail in Chapter 7). *Red River*, then, explores the possibilities of a transitional masculinity between older forms of colonial dominance and the flexible, capitalist masculinities of modernization and transnational capitalism. In the film, Wayne provides a site where these shifting patterns of masculinity can be negotiated, a site of contradictions where changes in masculinity can be both interrogated and made pleasurable as global capitalism and modernization remake the world gender order.

In fact, *Red River* provides a condensed history of the transformation of masculinity in relation to changing economic conditions, charting the changes in masculinity that Connell describes fairly precisely. Early in the film, a brutal and individualist vision of the "masculinities of settlement and conquest" finds expression in the young Tom Dunson, who breaks away from a wagon train to forge his own destiny, leaving his fiancée behind but taking his friend and partner, Groot, with him to claim land to the south in Texas. After being joined by Matthew Garth, Dunson forcibly and violently lays claim to the land on which he seeks to build his ranching empire, in a bizarre moment of anti-colonial colonialism. When the trio finds the land they want to start ranching on, a pair of Mexican hired guns rides up to tell them that the land they are on belongs to Don Diego, a powerful Mexican rancher who lives hundreds of miles to the South. Groot voices the sentiment that this is "too much land for one man," and Dunson, noting that Don Diego most likely claimed the land by force from the Native peoples, kills one of the gunmen and sends the other south to tell Don Diego that it is Dunson's land now. His violent appropriation of territory is legitimized because his white masculinity is more powerful and brutally efficient than that of his Mexican rivals, revealing his "natural" right to occupy the territory, all under the seemingly progressive logic of redistributing the land and power of a greedy colonialist with too much power (never mind the fact that moments earlier Dunson had drowned a Native American in the Red River as the Native peoples attempted to defend their land from powerful intruders). While masked in the rhetoric of anticolonialism, Dunson's "violence and egocentric individualism" justifies the forcible conquest of land and territorial dominance as the basis for his future empire.

Years after this opening phase of conquest, after Dunson has firmly established his dominance of the local territory, his emphasis shifts to the maintenance of his power and the exploitation of the land and his laborers, exemplifying a rationalist masculinity of empire organized around economic self-interest and the structures of bureaucracy. While the threat of violence still lingers behind his authority, he now primarily exerts a capitalist dominance over his men and property, an authority rooted in the structures of wages, contracts, and ownership. When preparing for the massive drive, he gathers all the cattle he can, regardless of whether they belong to him, bullying his less forceful and less manly neighbor (aptly named Meeker) and putting his brand on Meeker's cattle (and threatening to put his brand on Matthew Garth if he disobeys). While still aggressive and domineering—essentially stealing his neighbor's cattle—Dunson now works within the capitalist logic of accumulation by exploiting his neighbor's shaky financial situation in order to appropriate some of his cattle. He offers Meeker two dollars a head for any of his cattle that have been rounded up into Dunson's herd if they make it to Missouri, cattle that are worth twenty dollars a head if they can get them out of Texas and to the railroad. Older and seeking to salvage his empire, Dunson has replaced the violent masculinity of his youth with a hardened capitalist outlook seeking to manage resources and labor instead of forcibly settling territory.

He also exerts his dominance within the labor hierarchy on the ranch, demonstrating his authority over his hired hands through a signed contract that will later justify his brutal tyranny on the cattle drive. When Dunson approaches the cowboys about the long and dangerous drive, he does so in their quarters, a dark and claustrophobic space in which the men all sit but Dunson stands, occupying the small space with his huge frame, using the size of his body, centered in the foreground of the frame, to illustrate his authority as an owner and empire builder.

Interestingly, this authority begins to erode on the drive when Dunson fails to adapt to changing circumstances, fails to take calculated risks, and ultimately attempts to fall back on the violent masculinity of conquest that was at the core of his actions earlier in the film. When several men try to quit the drive, Dunson tries to hang them for their violation of the contract, using brutality and intimidation to manage his empire and illustrating his disconnection from the appropriate kind of masculine authority in that situation.

What Dunson fails to recognize, then, is that the economic backdrop of the cattle drive—the imperative to move local goods to far-flung markets via modern transportation—has shifted the constructions of hegemonic masculinity, reflecting the emergence of an entrepreneurial masculinity tied to neoliberal economics. Indeed, the transition from a brutally hierarchical and authoritarian vision of masculinity to a more flexible and adaptive masculinity serves as the

FIGURE 1.2. *Dunson (John Wayne) stands while his men sit, his body looming large in the small space, exemplifying his authority as a masculinity of empire in* Red River *(United Artists, 1948).*

film's primary narrative conflict in its allegory of transnational capitalism. As Dunson exerts his extreme and tyrannical authority over the cowboys on the drive, his vision of masculinity is contrasted to that of Matt, who respects the men's labor more and is more willing to change plans and take risks, taking the cattle to Abilene, Kansas, instead of Missouri even though there might not be a railhead in Abilene. As Matt and Groot note before the drive begins, Dunson knows the land and power and cattle, but not the intricacies of money and economics: "He doesn't know who to fight." The changes in the economic structure of the post–Civil War world created a shifting economy of masculine agency and power in which Dunson's violent domination and imperial dominance left him unsure of how to capitalize on the privileges of white masculinity as his accumulation of resources and capital became meaningless in a shattered economy.

The conflict regarding the appropriate construction of masculinity within changing economic conditions is at the core of the film's narrative, with Matt perhaps even offering a vision of modern corporate management. As Corkin notes, "In a film about modern enterprise, Garth telescopes us ahead some forty years to the realm of industrial psychology, as he knows that a happy worker is a productive worker. He allows recreation, manages by coercion rather than by physical domination, and seeks to have his workers obey him out of their belief in him and his position . . . Dunson shouts; Garth almost whispers. Dunson stands or sits upright; Garth slouches. Dunson's face is taut and determined; Garth is relaxed and frequently smiling" (*Cowboys as Cold Warriors*, 46).

So although Clift's Matthew Garth does not exhibit the "conditional loyalties" and corporate "irresponsibility" of Connell's transnational business masculinity, he does offer a flexible and adaptable alternative that better reflects the managerial models of capitalism in the second half of the twentieth century. In fact, his general likability might offer a capitalist fantasy in a period concerned with how men relate to or manage coworkers and subordinates, a utopian vision of management that could be based on violence (the film implies that Matt is faster on the draw than Dunson) but is really based on trust and the well-being of his subordinates.

It is tempting, therefore, to see the forms of masculinity offered by Wayne-Dunson and Clift-Matt as a transition from older forms to newer forms of masculinity, to see Wayne's vision of masculinity here as outdated and outmoded, particularly given the contrast between the young Montgomery Clift and the much older Wayne (who was aged even more in the film with makeup).[5] But it

FIGURE 1.3. *Two models of masculinity: John Wayne's hard authoritarianism and Montgomery Clift's more flexible managerial style in* Red River.

is more accurate to see Dunson and Matt as two interconnected and competing modes of masculinity within the historical moment of the fifties rather than as representing a transition from "old" to "new," with the competition between the two modes negotiating the cultural shifts in gender and masculinity created by global capitalism and modernization. Despite the age difference between the two men, the fact that *Red River* made Wayne a star as much as it did Clift indicates that Wayne offered a viable fantasy of "hard" masculinity in film as much as Clift offered a "soft" one. For Wayne's audiences, there was clearly something "new" and resonant in his construction of masculinity in *Red River*, even if it was an ambivalent pleasure of watching Wayne dominate his men.

Certain aspects of Dunson's construction of masculinity clearly reflect the emerging conditions of global capitalism and its transformation of the world gender order. For example, throughout the film Dunson commodifies his social relations and obligations, usually through contracts. In the opening scenes, as he prepares to leave the wagon train, the leader of the train tells Dunson that he has signed on to go the entire way, but Dunson is insistent that he never physically signed anything, leaving him contractually able to pursue his own self-interest. Dunson, of course, does not make this mistake with his men, requiring them to sign a contract; the contract allows Dunson to rationalize his tyrannical and brutal treatment of his men—they waived their right to quit. Additionally, when Dunson meets with Tess Millay after Matt has left her behind to continue the drive, Dunson offers her half of everything he owns if she will bear him a son, revealing the extent to which Dunson conducts his relationships with others through contracts and exchange, as well as the importance of a male heir to Dunson for the continuation of his capitalist empire. In this way, Dunson expresses several salient characteristics of a modern capitalist masculinity based in the rational calculation of self-interest, the commodification of interpersonal relations, and the exercise of authority rooted in contractual obligation.

The tension between Dunson's and Matt's masculinities, therefore, does not necessitate that Matt's masculinity replace Dunson's, but rather that an equilibrium be found between the two, one that can temper the excesses of Dunson's extreme authority (and what might be considered a form of corporate irresponsibility central to global capitalism) with Matt's flexible and adaptive managerial style. As Corkin points out, when Matt sells the cattle in Abilene, the check is still made out to Dunson, indicating the necessary interconnection between owners such as Dunson and corporate managers such as Matt (*Cowboys as Cold Warriors*, 48). Their different styles of masculinity, then, reflect the shifting nature of masculinity in global capitalism; the dynamics between the two express the gendered changes that were experienced by many of *Red River*'s transnational audiences as different styles of capitalist masculinity became hegemonic in different cultural contexts and then had to negotiate with other forms of masculinity within the capitalist world system. Thus, in this expression of dynamic globalizing masculinities, Dunson provides an ambivalent fantasy, a powerful vision of capitalist masculinity that is appealing yet repugnant, a model of modern masculine identity as well as a warning against the hardness and intractability of this vision of manhood.

HOMOSOCIALITY VERSUS HETEROSEXUAL LOVE

As the tense dynamics between Dunson and Matt suggest, a key component to Wayne's construction of masculinity in *Red River* is the centrality of relationships between men and a concomitant anxiety surrounding heterosexual coupling. As established in *Red River*, Wayne's articulation of masculinity amid the gendered shifts of global capitalism expresses a deep-seated ambivalence about women in general, the kinds of labor they can provide, and their intrusion into the homosocial spheres of capitalism and imperialism.

Of course, throughout the 1950s (and beyond) Wayne's on-screen relationship with heterosexual coupling and the nuclear family is fraught with tension, although that fact is often overlooked in contemporary culture's understanding of Wayne. As Max Westbrook points out, Wayne is "widely credited with being a role model who enacts on the screen the best of American and family values. He has been called [by his daughter Aissa Wayne] 'one of the great defenders of the American nuclear family as a sacred institution,' the 'almost perfect father figure'" ("Flag and Family," 25). And Virginia Wright Wexman notes that while Wayne's persona "was not identified with the kind of erotic charge that characterized most Hollywood leading men," he "stands as a larger-than-life embodiment of the ideal candidate for the roles of husband and father in a hostile world in which struggle, self-protection, and hard physical labor are central realities" (*Creating the Couple*, 69, 84).[6] He is frequently paired with younger men in his films and offered up as a paternal role model for acceptable masculine behavior, cementing his construction within the popular imagination as an ideal father figure.

As Westbrook notes, however, this popular conception of Wayne as an ideal husband and father is the result of a kind of amnesia — or even a kind of ideological collusion — on the part of Wayne's fans and the culture at large. After all, Wayne most often plays men who are separate from or even resistant to romantic love and heterosexual coupling, men who actively shirk their fatherly responsibilities to their children, even if they reluctantly teach their vision of masculinity to younger men. Throughout his roles in the 1950s, 1960s, and even in the 1970s, when his role as a benevolent American patriarch was being established in the U.S. popular imagination, Wayne played roles that positioned his characters outside the realm of the nuclear family and romantic love. As Deborah Thomas notes, throughout Wayne's most popular films "there are surprisingly few actively sexual relationships between Wayne's characters and women (though there are numerous past marriages broken by death or separation). Where they exist, Wayne often treats his female partners as overgrown children (displaying what seems less like sexual tenderness or passion than playful boisterousness or protectiveness: spanking them, carrying them in his arms like a child) and seems most comfortable outside the sexual fray" ("John Wayne's Body," 78). Westbrook notes that of Wayne's most popular westerns of the 1950s, 1960s, and 1970s, in only two of twenty-nine films does Wayne's character father and raise his own children ("Flag and Family," 29). This rejection of the duties associated with the nuclear family (often a rejection necessitated by Wayne's characters' commitment to grand masculine ventures in the context of imperialism or capitalism) leads Westbrook to claim that audiences actively collude with the ideologies of Wayne's films, accepting that his characters' irresponsible actions regarding the family were done for love of family and the "greater good," despite the abundant on-screen examples of Wayne's poor fathering and uninterest in romantic love (30).

So while Wayne's characters often claim to be fighting for families (either their own or others'), they most often resist the feminization of family, preferring the glory and camaraderie of all-male worlds. At the same time, the intractability and violence of Wayne's masculinity make his presence within the structures of romantic love and domestic nuclear families undesirable. At the core of Wayne's masculinity, then, is an inherent tension between his violent and often misogynist masculinity and its relationship to a nuclear-family domesticity that it must appear to desire but in reality does not, a domesticity that needs the violence and protection of Wayne to sustain itself but cannot stomach his masculinist brutality, especially when compared to the "soft" masculinity of younger men who actively embrace romance and fatherhood. This tense relationship with marriage, the nuclear family, and romantic love was established in *Red River* and persisted in almost all of Wayne's films, providing one of the most salient characteristics of Wayne's construction of a modern masculinity.

Such anxieties dramatize and manage the ideological tensions produced by changes in the world gender order and the transnational construction of masculinity. At a time when romantic love and fatherhood were increasingly positioned as a means of performing modern social identities (both in the United States and internationally) yet labor conditions necessitated a spatially segregated, gendered division of labor, Wayne offered a vision of modern masculinity based in homosociality and professionalism, a dark and tortured vision that acknowledged the presence and appeal of love, domesticity, and femininity but always managed to reject or be rejected by them.

In U.S. culture, these tensions in Wayne's relationship with the ideals of family life and romantic love have been situated within changes in popular definitions of masculinity and the rising hegemony of the nuclear family in the 1950s. The demobilization of U.S. troops after World War II sparked a popular discourse regarding a crisis in masculinity as anxieties about the atom bomb, the traumas of shell-shocked troops, and the emerging Cold War contributed to the "culture's self-evaluation, directed at the imperiled state of American manhood" (Cohan, *Masked Men*, x). With the war over and won, the necessity of a hardened and violent vision of masculinity was coming into question, even as fears of unavoidable conflict with the Soviets became more prevalent. Additionally, the perceived crisis in masculinity was rooted in significant shifts in the social structure and culture of post–World War II America. As Cohan notes, "Demobilization required restoration of the gender relations that World War II had disturbed both in the home and the workplace" (xi–xii). Yet in the workplace there emerged a new masculine ideal associated with white-collar labor: "This corporate setting ended up relocating masculinity in what had previously been considered a 'feminine' sphere, primarily by valuing a man's domesticity (and consumption) over his work (and production) as the means through which he fulfilled societal expectations of what it took to be 'manly'" (xii).

As Cohan's observation suggests, one of the primary manifestations of the new masculinity was the nuclear family. According to Stephanie Coontz, "For the first time men as well as women were encouraged to root their identity and self-image in familial or parental roles" (*Way We Never Were*, 27). As soldiers returned home from the war and entered the booming middle class, "the most salient symbol and immediate beneficiary of their newfound prosperity was the nuclear family" (25). The emphasis on domesticity, far from being traditional, "was a qualitatively new phenomenon" (25). The new American male was increasingly rooting his manhood in his participation in the nuclear family. For masculinity, the merger of Cold War anxieties and nuclear-family ideologies resulted in a dilemma: "Cold War politics further complicated the picture by projecting contradictory ideals for American manhood, requiring a 'hard' masculinity as the standard when defending the nation, yet insisting upon a 'soft' masculinity as the foundation of an orderly, responsible home life" (Cohan, *Masked Men*, xii). Thus, Wayne's complicated relationship with heterosexual coupling and the nuclear family manages the tensions within this U.S. cultural dilemma regarding "hard" and "soft" masculinities (Meeuf, "Wayne as Supercrip'").

These changes in U.S. culture regarding masculinity and the nuclear family were not isolated and unique — they were part of a global gender order in which global capitalism, the international push to modernize, the transnational demobilization of troops after World War II, and the remobilization of hardened and violent masculinities for the Cold War and anticolonial struggles transformed definitions of masculinity and the role of the family within those definitions. For example, as noted above, the spread of global capitalism throughout the twentieth century meant the imposition of a male wageworker–female domestic worker structure on the family around the world, essentially necessitating a restructuring of the nuclear family that equates masculinity with the (increasingly white-collar, for some) public sphere of wage labor, and femininity with the domestic, private sphere of the single-family home (Connell, *Men and Boys*, 42).

Additionally, as capitalism re-formed the basic structure of the heterosexual couple and the family, it also reimagined the basis of such coupling, replacing notions of love based on kinship, obligation, or duty with modern conceptions of romantic love based on intimacy, companionship, and self-fulfillment. As Mark B. Padilla and his coeditors pointed out, the processes of globalization throughout the second half of the twentieth century meant that "macro-level political-economic transformations" interacted with "the various cultural and psychosocial meanings of love, intimacy, and sexuality" (*Love and Globalization*, xii). For example, Jennifer Hirsch, referring to Anthony Giddens's *The Transformation of Intimacy*, points out that capitalism, by creating the modern individual, has provided the groundwork for the revolution of heterosexual (and the articulation of homosexual) coupling around the ideal of romantic love as self-fulfillment. Around the world, Hirsch argues, the processes of globalization are transforming young people's conceptions of love as they reject the duty-based obligations of their parents and embrace a vision of affective bonds, companionship, and intimacy ("'Love Makes a Family,'" 100). While the ideal of romantic love has existed for centuries, with different manifestations in different cultures, the "transformation of intimacy" by a reflexive modernity in the late twentieth century has made a companionate model of love based on individual satisfaction and intimate emotional ties the basis for identity formation in ways that differ from older models of love. This has led Hirsch, Padilla, and others to see modern romantic love and companionate sexuality as means of enacting modern social identities: "Love—and the practices of affective consumption that surround it—has become a strategy for affective mobility, and a very individually oriented technique for framing oneself as a modern subject" (*Love and Globalization*, xviii; see also Hirsch, "'Love Makes a Family,'" 99).

Hirsch and Padilla situate these changes in the global gender order within the most recent, accelerated phase of globalization in the 1980s, 1990s, and 2000s, but as Cohan's and Coontz's discussions of shifting gender and family ideologies in the 1950s suggest, the increasingly prevalent "soft" masculinity of that period, which was rooted in domesticity and an emotional engagement as a husband and father, functions as a precursor to the transformations of modern love and intimacy in an age of contemporary globalization. After all, as Coontz points out, while the idea of romantic love has a long history, the idea that people ought to marry for love is a "radical" and relatively recent idea that emerged unevenly throughout the twentieth century, becoming normalized only in the 1950s ("Radical Idea"). In *Between Sex and Power*, Göran Therborn meticulously documents how the institution of marriage was transformed around the world in the second half of the twentieth century as modernization interacted with traditional ideas about marriage and the family. Within 1950s modernization, therefore, conceptions of intimacy, romantic love, and the nuclear family began to transform the global gender order as those ideologies interacted with and unevenly affected traditional constructions of masculinity, marriage, and the family in the period.[7]

The tension between this vision of intimacy-based heterosexual coupling as a form of modern identity formation and the increasing prevalence of a gender-segregated workforce is supposed to be managed by the public-private split in modern social relations, which dictates that different constructions of masculinity be applied in different spheres. In the public sphere of capitalist labor and national or imperial ambitions, masculinity can be structured around a "hard," competitive, and most often homosocial individualism, while masculinity in the private sphere can be structured around romance, marriage, fatherhood, and a commitment to the social values of the nuclear family. Because of the dominance of the public-private split in organizing social relations in the developed world, along with its increasing prevalence in other contexts of modernization around the world, these competing forms of masculinity are often not seen as contradictory. In fact, certain Hollywood stars of the period, such as Cary Grant or Jimmy Stewart, collapsed these distinctions by balancing a commitment to the public world of capitalism or national duty with a commitment to the values of heterosexual romance and the nuclear family, commitments that were often constructed as intensely interrelated in Hollywood films.

But in the case of John Wayne and the John Wayne western, the tensions between the public and private spheres are accentuated rather than obscured. Rather than finding fulfillment and a stable subjectivity in the domestic, private sphere, Wayne's characters after *Red River* stubbornly cling to the public sphere, where a "hard" masculinity is valued and where a kind of intimacy between men can be cultivated as central to one's identity. The private sphere, with its increasing emphasis on male participation in the nuclear family, became a marker of feminization, of weakness, and so Wayne sought emotional intimacy and self-identity in the company of other men, all under the guise of economic, national, or imperial crises that legitimated his rejection of heterosexual coupling and the nuclear family. In essence, Wayne's star persona became a vision of masculinity that only superficially desires the social structures of heterosexual love and the family but always conveniently finds a way to reject or be rejected by those structures, offering his global audiences an indulgent but necessarily ambivalent celebration of male camaraderie and the masculinist endeavors of the public sphere.[8]

So even though *Red River* is essentially a film about men and masculinity, the film interrogates the gendered dynamics of the emerging global economic system that are dramatized in the narrative, structuring itself around the question of women's roles within its vision of capitalism from the very start. After all, the film starts with Dunson's disastrous decision that Fen stay behind with the wagon train, which ultimately leads to her death.

In this scene Fen pleads to go with Dunson, insisting on the importance of women in his venture, both for the domestic labor that she would provide and the sexual comforts she could offer him. She tells him that he will need what a woman can offer as he builds his ranching empire, indicating the kinds of labor that women in agriculture have always provided and yet tend to be invisible within a public-private split that values only the masculine labor of the public sphere. Moreover, Fen conflates this reference to domestic labor (cooking, housekeeping, tending to animals) with the kinds of sexual labor and comfort she would provide for Dunson, suggestively asking Dunson to feel her body and decide for himself whether it is too weak for the road ahead of them. In this way Fen clearly troubles the lived experience of a public-private split and its gendered vision of labor, openly acknowledging that in practice the labor and services a woman brings to marriage—even one based in the ideals of romantic love—are foundational to capitalism at large. Essentially, she offers a vision of a modern companionate marriage that is nevertheless still based on the economic necessity of the male wageworker–female domestic worker split central to modern capitalism.

Dunson, however, sees the tasks ahead of him through a spatial gender split. The establishment of his cattle empire requires a mobile and hard masculinity that can confront the dangers of migration and open space. Once that space has been made safe for a settled domestic existence, then he will send for Fen, apparently overlooking the fact that as a member of a cross-country wagon train, Fen is already facing the dangers of mobility and migration (and indeed is proved to be very inadequately "safe" when she is killed only hours later). Dunson prioritizes the spatial dynamics of feminine-settled and masculine-mobile inherent in 1950s global suburbanization, while Fen more appropriately recognizes the mobility of women's labor and prioritizes her romantic connection to Dunson. As Wayne's characters did throughout the fifties, Dunson stubbornly clings to a model of masculinity and gender relations that is clearly at odds with the complex reality of the cultural context, thereby providing a dark spectacle of male camaraderie amid a dangerous capitalist world.

FIGURES 1.4 AND 1.5. *Fen (Coleen Gray) pleading to go with Dunson (John Wayne) in* Red River. *Though offering her labor and sexuality, she is left behind, ultimately to die.*

Indeed, how could Dunson not realize that Fen was no safer with the wagon train than she would be with him? The frame narrative explicitly asks the audience to question Dunson's adherence to this masculinist vision of the world even as we wallow for several hours in the melodrama of male bonding and at times violent action. In fact, the narrative conveniently erases the necessity of Fen's domestic labor by miraculously offering Dunson a son as young Matt, the wagon train's sole survivor, wanders out of the wilderness, immediately erasing the need for women as reproductive partners in the all-male world that dominates the rest of the film.

Because of Dunson's mistake, the rest of the film focuses on the homosocial world he creates with Groot and Matt and the future of such a world, particularly when Matt repeats Dunson's mistake and leaves Tess Millay behind for the cattle drive and when Dunson contemplates the future of his empire without Matt as his apparent heir. Recognizing that the changing social and economic conditions have put him at odds with Matt, since such conditions value the kinds of masculine leadership that Matt can offer but Dunson cannot, Dunson realizes that the homosocial world he constructed is falling apart. Not only has the kind of male-male intimacy that he built with Matt and Groot faltered (through Matt's rebellion and his newfound intimacy with Cherry Valance, a gunslinger who joins the drive), but Matt intends to disrupt that world further by bringing Tess and femininity permanently into it. (Interestingly, the film makes it clear which betrayal carries more weight—Dunson unceremoniously kills Cherry Valance, his male rival for Matt's love—while suggesting that Dunson and Matt's bond can grow stronger despite the presence of Tess).

When Dunson finally meets Tess as he tracks down Matt on his murderous quest for revenge, the scene becomes an exaggerated inversion of his last meeting with Fen (and in fact these are the only two scenes in the film where Wayne interacts with women at all). Having learned his lesson from Fen about the important labor women provide, Dunson transforms Fen's delicate balance between romantic connection and economic necessity into a blunt capitalist transaction, offering Tess half of his empire if she would bear him a son. In his self-interested, capitalist, and all-male world, all social relations are commodified, although here he is really only making explicit the implicit economic basis of marriage and the nuclear family. Such actions, however, yield only humiliation for Dunson, as suggested by the blocking of the scene. Earlier in the film when Dunson approached his men in their quarters about engaging in a contractual obligation to finish the drive with him, Dunson stood while the men sat, emphasizing Wayne's size and the "natural" dominance of his masculinity. But in this discussion of contracts, Dunson sits while Tess stands, suggesting her power in their interaction. In the masculinist logic of the film, this inversion of the character blocking punishes Dunson and his vision of masculinity, literally making him stoop, perhaps because he brought attention to the ideological contradictions of the modern institution of marriage — the tension between ideals of love and the economic nature of the institution — or perhaps simply because Dunson had to finally acknowledge that women might have an economic role in his grand masculine ventures, even if it is only the highly exploitative role he offers Tess. She, of course, opts instead for a love-based marriage with Matt, even telling Dunson that she will bear Dunson's son if he will stop his quest to kill Matt.

Thus, the resolution of the film is not only the resolution of the economic crisis as the cattle make it to the railroad but also the resolution of Dunson's initial rejection of femininity and heterosexual coupling with Fen: Matt and Tess incorporate the values of companionate marriage and the nuclear family into Dunson's capitalist empire. This resolution comes at the last minute and seems somehow unsatisfying, as if too simplified a solution to an irresolvable dilemma. After all, as much as the film emphasizes Dunson's regret at leaving Fen behind, the film is also a two-hour, spectacular celebration of the great masculine accomplishments Dunson and his workers achieve precisely because he at first rejected the nuclear family and pursued a world without women. The film is a celebration of imperialist and capitalist achievements of men working together. While the desire to engage with femininity and the emerging masculinities tied to the nuclear family remain a structuring principle of the narrative, the rejection of that desire is necessary if both Dunson and the audience are to take pleasure in the spectacle of a capitalist, homosocial environment. Dunson's rejection of Fen and heterosexual coupling is narratively structured as a mistake, but it is a convenient one that makes the spectacular pleasures of the film possible. As Carl Freedman notes, "The film contains subtle hints that he [Dunson] may be leading a life of sexual self-denial out of remorse for having left Fen to be raped and killed by the Indians. But the fundamental reason that Dunson must remain single is that only by refusing to stoop to entanglement with the feminine can he maintain the supremely confident and self-sufficient masculinity that he exemplifies throughout the movie" (Freedman, "Post-Heterosexuality," 22).

This extreme adherence to the primacy of male bonding and homosocial spheres of professionalism led Freedman to suggest that Wayne represents a model of what he calls "post-heterosexuality," a "mythic ideal not wholly original with, nor unique to, John Wayne, but — at least within modern American culture — one that is brought to its most compelling expression in Wayne's films" ("Post-Heterosexuality," 19). Freedman situates Wayne within a vision of "American macho" that is based on "an aversion to women, shading into a fear of feminine sexuality, and a concomitant emotional commitment to the 'male bonding' of masculine friendship" (18). This ambivalence toward women and embrace of male-male intimacy suggests a certain homoerotic element to Wayne's preference for the company of men, but Freedman claims instead that Wayne's characters and his star text indicate not homoeroticism so much as "post-heterosexuality": "The typical John Wayne character carries no significant suggestion of same-sex eroticism, but is not sexually involved with women either. He is a man with a heterosexual past, who has outgrown that phase of existence and so is free to glory in his unalloyed masculinity without being suspected of abnormality" (19). Of course, Freedman overstates the complete lack of homoerotic charge to Wayne's star persona; there is certainly a "significant suggestion of same-sex eroticism" in Wayne's aversion to women, which at times becomes misogyny while he seeks the company of men, particularly in *Red River*.[9]

Whether or not one accepts the homoerotic charge between Dunson and Matt or simply sees it as platonic love among men, the climactic struggle to express the intimacy between Dunson and Matt shows that the real interpersonal dynamics dramatized in *Red River* are not those between men and women but between men and other men. At heart, the film focuses on the tensions and antics of a diverse group of men rallying together for a common cause. More specifically, the emphasis on male camaraderie within a professional setting displays the processes of creating a kind of male-male intimacy within the public sphere of global capitalism. After all, at the end of Dunson and Matt's street fight, Dunson can communicate his love and respect for Matt only within the terms of capitalism and commodification, adding the initial *M* to his Red River *D* brand, essentially making Matt a public partner in his enterprise. This slippage between the personal and the professional within the all-male spheres of capitalism suggests that the film attempts to articulate the processes by which intimacy between men can be established, particularly within the homosocial professional world created by global capitalism, a world where women are relegated to the domestic labor of the private sphere and men's labor is increasingly associated with a mobile public sphere.

As numerous analyses of *Red River* have pointed out, the film shows the construction of a domestic family unit made up of men, particularly through the character of Groot, who takes on a more "feminine" role within this homosocial world by cooking and caregiving (see, for example, Sanderson, "*Red River*"). (Walter Brennan did the same again a decade later in *Rio Bravo*.) As the cook on the drive, Groot prepares all the meals for the men, and it is Groot who tends to Dunson's wounds after a skirmish with potential deserters midway through the drive. In the absence of women, the men form a homosocial nuclear family: Dunson as the hard, disciplinarian patriarch, Groot as the self-sacrificing mother, and Matt and the rest of the cowboys as the potentially unruly children. Within the homosocial structures of the capitalist public sphere, the film etches out the possibilities of emotional and familial fulfillment among men engaged in the dangerous mobility of capitalism and labor.[10]

The film that launched Wayne to international superstardom in the years after World War II dramatizes the emergence of a new economic regime and the subsequent renegotiation and reconstruction of gender relations, particularly the shifting patterns of masculinity within global capitalism and a particular rejection of femininity, domesticity, and the nuclear family, even as those values became part of a modern conception of identity. Thus, Wayne in *Red River* articulates an ambivalent, even objectionable form of tyrannical masculinity whose celebration of male camaraderie and all-male endeavors is nevertheless pleasurable. The film's vision of men working hard on a massive and dangerous project while forming bonds with one another (even when things go bad) offers a sense of accomplishment, the pleasures of work well done. Moreover, the images of Wayne's body (and Clift's younger body) at work and engaged in violence offer other kinds of voyeuristic and often homoerotic pleasures in their construction of male intimacy and hard, efficient violence. Such pleasures help manage the ideological tensions of Wayne's repugnant tyranny and rejection of femininity.

HETEROSEXUAL ANXIETIES BEYOND *RED RIVER*

In the roles Wayne took on in the decade after *Red River*, the ambivalence about femininity, women, and heterosexual coupling continued to be a key component to his star persona and his global appeal. Throughout the decade, Wayne's most prominent roles put him at odds with heterosexual coupling and the nuclear family as he pursued the masculine endeavors of capitalism and empire building, often while paired with younger men who act as surrogate sons. In *Fort Apache* (1948) and *She Wore a Yellow Ribbon* (1949), Wayne plays U.S. cavalrymen who either show no interest in women and coupling (*Fort Apache*) or are widowed (*Yellow Ribbon*); in each case, his character helps facilitate the coupling of the younger generation. In *The Searchers* (1956), he plays a man who falls in love with his brother's wife and so chooses to wander nomadically rather than embrace a settled domestic life, joined by a half-Cherokee young man whom he "found" as a baby years ago on his travels. In *The Wings of Eagles* (1957), he plays a navy pilot turned screenwriter who continually pushes his wife and daughters out of his life in order to remain in the all-male worlds of the military and Hollywood. And in *The Man Who Shot Liberty Valance* (1962), he plays a formidable rancher who gives up his love interest to an optimistic and ambitious lawyer played by Jimmy Stewart so that she can have the opportunities of education and travel in the modern world.

In fact, Wayne further established himself as a superstar the year after *Red River* with *Sands of Iwo Jima*, taking on a role that brought him his first Oscar nomination and mirrored almost exactly the gendered dynamics of *Red River*. In Wayne's portrayal of a drill sergeant whose dedication to the marines causes his wife and son to abandon him, the film celebrates Wayne's commitment to all-male spheres as his harsh, tyrannical leadership helps win the war in the Pacific. And yet Wayne's masculinity is problematized and critiqued, especially in the contrast between his and John Agar's character, a young marine who at first despises Wayne's character but eventually sees the merits of his harsh masculinity. In back-to-back roles that propelled Wayne to superstardom and defined the boundaries of his star text, Wayne portrayed characters who tragically and yet conveniently reject nuclear-family commitments in order to pursue the grand adventures of male-male professionalism.

John Wayne in this period displays a vision of masculinity in which heterosexual coupling and the nuclear family are always denied as the primary means of creating a modern social identity, even as they lurk in the background, a structuring absence for the kind of masculinity Wayne represents. Instead, his films posit the centrality of homosociality and professionalism to their construction of masculinity, but do so in a way that troubles the darkness and hardness of their all-male worlds. Thus, at a historical moment when the international definitions of masculinity increasingly incorporated modern notions of romantic love and the domesticity of the nuclear family, Wayne provided an ambivalent masculinity with a tense relationship to these emerging gender patterns. Wayne's masculinity was, instead, based in the gendered division of labor of global capitalism, which celebrates the increasingly mobile, all-male world of professionalism and camaraderie while simultaneously acknowledging the dangers and ambivalence of a harsh, violent masculinity.

CHAPTER TWO

Exile, Community, and Wandering

INTERNATIONAL MIGRATION AND THE SPATIAL DYNAMICS OF MODERNITY IN JOHN FORD'S CAVALRY TRILOGY

*I*N HER REVISIONIST AND CRITICAL HISTORY OF THE American West, Patricia Limerick notes that Hollywood's construction of the western frontier glosses over one of the central concerns of the history of the West: parceling, buying, and selling land. Limerick writes: "If Hollywood wanted to capture the emotional center of western history, its movies would be about real estate. John Wayne would have been neither a gunfighter nor a sheriff, but a surveyor, speculator, or claims lawyer. The showdowns would appear in the land office or the courtroom; weapons would be deeds and lawsuits, not six guns" (*Legacy of Conquest*, 55). For Limerick, Hollywood's vision of the historical frontier contributes to the violent mythology of the American West but clearly misses out on the historical realities and importance of real estate, speculation, land claims, and legal disputes over land as property. But Limerick's observation about the western genre and John Wayne is only partly true. Yes, as far as depictions of history go, Hollywood's West gets a lot wrong, offering a melodramatic mythology of masculine heroism instead of the complex realities and inequalities (no less melodramatic) of the actual, historical west. And yet Limerick is somewhat off the mark when she claims that John Wayne's sheriffs or gunfighters (or cattle ranchers or cavalry officers, for that matter) fail to portray the "emotional center" of land and real estate. Wayne's roles in the western frontier almost always center on issues of land and the construction of space: the occupation and settling of land subject to competing claims, the policing of open space to allow the movement of people and goods into the frontier, the transformation of the landscape and social relations as new communities are formed by migration. While rarely an explicit examination of real estate and property, John Wayne's West nevertheless dramatizes how space and the landscape were transformed by capitalism and competition over land.

Limerick is making an insightful point about the obscured history of the American West and is not necessarily commenting on the Hollywood western, but by repeating the common assumption that the Hollywood western can be reduced simply to the melodrama of masculine violence, her comment suggests the need for a more nuanced understanding of the genre and, in particular, issues of space and the social relations of space. Although the western genre explores the complexities of space on the frontier—evidenced by the commonplace spatial dualities that critics use to describe the genre: civilization versus the wilderness, the garden versus the desert, the distant outpost versus the hostile surrounding open spaces—questions of time and history have always been privileged in the critical understanding of the western.[1] Scholars and critics most often reduce the complex spatial relations in westerns to metaphors for the inevitable progress and triumph of modernity and "civilization," even if the genre is ambivalent about the modernization of the old frontier. For example, as Thomas Schatz explains it in his foundational analysis of the classic Hollywood western, a U.S. culture coping with the ambivalence of modernity and empire—the Great Depression, the atom bomb, the Korean War—nostalgically looked back at a historical moment when modernization was incomplete and yet inevitable, a moment when the dangerous yet utopian wilderness of the past could be eulogized and mythologized. The spaces of the West, full of vast landscapes peppered with communities connected only tenuously to the institutions of modernity (the railroad, the telegraph, the military), become, in Schatz's and most other analyses, merely dramatic representations of the progression of history (*Hollywood Genres*, 46).[2]

This vision of Hollywood's West rightly foregrounds the importance of the jagged and incomplete process of modernization for the genre's narratives and iconography, but by emphasizing time and progress it ignores the sensational appeal of the genre's representation of space and the spatial social relations of the transforming frontier. While questions of progress were sometimes important in the genre's classic period, particularly in films that dramatize the passing of the frontier or the time of gunfighters, such as *The Man Who Shot Liberty Valance* (1962) or *Forty Guns* (1957), at the core of the genre's appeal are the pleasures and drama of space, of individuals traversing rough terrain on horseback, of communities struggling to form in the midst of open spaces. Films such as *Gunfight at the OK Corral* (1957) or *The Naked Spur* (1953) offer no sense of the temporality of modernization, reveling instead in a tense and violent world of masculine mobility as men ride from place to place or traverse dynamic landscapes in narratives that explore the tensions of wandering. Rather than history and temporality, the western offers a complex vision of space and of the landscape as it was being transformed unevenly by modernity.

Spectacles of space are foundational to the appeal of both the western genre and the John Wayne star persona, providing the grounds on which the genre's dramatic action unfolds and the space within which Wayne's masculinity thrives. Or, to be more accurate, the spectacular narratives and iconography of the western genre, along with Wayne's complicated masculine identity as the prototypical western individual, actively produce the dramatic unevenness of the spaces of the western frontier, constructing an ambivalent fantasy of space that has yielded arguably the most resonant and popular set of images and character types in the history of cinema around the world. In the John Wayne western, the dynamics of space, more so than of time, provide the pleasures and complex resonance of the films.

It is difficult to imagine the idea of a John Wayne western without John Ford, who not only helped shape the basic contours of the Wayne persona in works such as *Stagecoach, 3 Godfathers* (1948), and the Cavalry Trilogy (1948–1950) but also directed Wayne in some of his most iconic and popular roles in *The Searchers* and *The Man Who Shot Liberty Valance*. And, indeed, it is in Ford's collaborations with Wayne, and in Ford's distinctive vision of the western, that we see some of the most complicated representations of space, mobility, and social relations on the western frontier. As has often been discussed in the ample criticism on Ford's work, his westerns gravitated toward issues of community and family, especially communities and families created through exile, migration, and settlement. The Fordian western hero is almost always a wanderer through open space, exploring his tense relationship with the settled community through movement and drifting; for example, the mobile Wyatt Earp pausing his cattle drive to seek his brother's killer in *My Darling Clementine* (1946), the good-hearted outlaws finding redemption in a deadly trek across the desert with a newborn in tow in *3 Godfathers*, or the ceaseless drifting of Ethan Edwards in *The Searchers*, which makes literal Ethan's distance from the community through self-imposed exile. Such spatial and social dynamics are central to the western genre as a whole, but they seem to find their most nuanced and persistent manifestation in the westerns of Ford.

Ford's construction of community, individualism, and the space of the frontier is almost always analyzed in nationalist terms, as part of the mythology of American identity, the immigrant experience, and the pioneer spirit. But I want to explore a broader context for Ford's contribution to the John Wayne western, given the international appeal of not only John Wayne but also the western genre in general in the 1950s. Focusing on Ford's Cavalry Trilogy with John Wayne—*Fort Apache* (1948), *She Wore a Yellow Ribbon* (1949), and *Rio Grande* (1950)—I suggest that Ford's westerns construct the spaces of the frontier in ways that dramatize and reflect the broad transformations of space and social relations occurring internationally in the years after World War II through international migrations and the migrations of urbanization. As modernization and the globalization of capitalism in the postwar years after yielded an increasingly mobile world population—migrations to rapidly expanding urban centers, across national borders in search of economic opportunities, to former imperial metropolises—the internationally popular John Ford westerns provided the narratives and iconography of mobility: of migratory individuals forming new communities while retaining their old identities, of communities in seemingly "distant" spaces maintaining their connections with nationalism or modernity and seeing themselves as culturally important, of men and women negotiating the gendered spatial dynamics of migration and geographic mobility.

This is not to say that Ford saw himself as giving voice to the cultural and social implications of international transformations in population mobility (clearly, Ford saw his own work as reflecting American nationalism), but simply to point out that his explorations of community, individualism, and mobility reflected a set of cultural assumptions about modernity and migration that, while important throughout the twentieth century, intensified in the postwar years and transformed everyday life for populations around the world (including those in the United States). Ford, as a first-generation Irish American, often examined issues of immigration and assimilation in his films, issues that are relevant to U.S. culture but hardly exclusive to it. It shouldn't be surprising, then, that Ford's Cavalry Trilogy empathetically explores the social and communal implications of mobility and migration, enshrining "distant" and diverse communities on the geographic margin as the true emotional and cultural centers of modern life, even while examining the ambivalence and danger of mobility in the competitive spaces of the cinematic frontier. Other scholars have detailed the complex nuances of Ford's films in relation to these themes, but I offer here a much broader set of historical contexts within which to understand the dynamics of Ford's films as internationally popular texts.

What is new in my analysis of Ford concerns issues of space and the cinematic production of space. Informed by the theories of space put forth by theorists such as Henri Lefebvre and geographers such as Neil Smith and Doreen Massey—who see space not as a kind of empty container within which history and social actions take place but rather as a set of spatial relations that are produced by society and structures of power—I analyze the dynamic ideas about space, geographic social relations, and mobility produced through the narratives and imagery of the John Wayne–John Ford western.[3] It has long been understood that the spaces of Ford's cinematic frontier—whether the imposing landscapes of Monument Valley or the rustic but comfortable spaces of the forts and small towns—offer highly meaningful visual expressions of Ford's thematic concerns regarding community values and individual mobility. But more than simply using the landscape and sets as symbolic indicators of key themes, the Cavalry Trilogy actively produces a set of ideas, values, and visceral sensations that organize and structure a particular configuration of space within the modern world. Mirroring the kinds of spatial reorganizations transforming economic, political, and social relations in the years after World War II through the globalization of capitalism and the concurrent increase in population mobility, the Cavalry Trilogy reproduces the spatial relations of new and diverse communities built out of migration and within spaces of uneven development, spatial relations that required new negotiations of gender and racial values. Within that emerging spatial order, of course, John Wayne proved the ideal masculine subject, able to navigate the complex cultural negotiations of modern space.[4]

THE MARGIN AS CENTER: MIGRATION AND MODERN COMMUNITIES IN FORD'S FRONTIER

Frank Nugent, the film critic turned screenwriter who would go on to write eleven screenplays for Ford, once recalled what Ford had said about the inspiration for the Cavalry trilogy: "In all Westerns, the Cavalry rides in to the rescue of the beleaguered wagon train or whatever, and then it rides off again. I've been thinking about it—what it was like at a Cavalry post, remote, people with their own personal problems, over everything the threat of Indians, of death" (quoted in McBride and Wilmington, *John Ford*, 99).[5] The cavalry in the traditional western has always been a kind of nebulous and transient presence within the genre, at times materializing out of the frontier to save the day, at times not materializing at all. But as Ford suggests, his cavalry films explored the spatial dynamics of the idea of the cavalry more complexly, seeing in the cavalry a diverse community brought to a remote place threatened by other seminomads. By focusing on the community of the cavalry outpost, the films take up the construction of space in the frontier, examining the settled yet migratory military family of the fort that supports the mobile patrolling and policing of open space.

The films of the Cavalry Trilogy don't constitute a true narrative trilogy, with each building off the next, but rather are variations on similar themes and story lines centering on a cavalry outpost, its leadership, and the general community of the fort. While using John Wayne's characters to examine different stages in the lives the forts' leaders—he is a young, unmarried officer in *Fort Apache*; an old, widowed commander on the verge of retirement in *She Wore a Yellow Ribbon*; and a middle-aged fort commander attempting to reconcile with his family in *Rio Grande*—the three films offer similar narratives about refined women from the East entering the world of the fort and upsetting the balance within the community during a violent Native uprising.

Fort Apache tells the story of a fort's new, glory-seeking commanding officer, Lieutenant Colonel Owen Thursday (Henry Fonda), who has been assigned to the outpost after some unspecified career mishap. Thursday's teenage daughter, Philadelphia (Shirley Temple), quickly falls in love with Lieutenant O'Rourke (John Agar), a cadet fresh from West Point who happens to be the son of the fort's Irish American sergeant major (Ward Bond), a match that Thursday sees as beneath her. Meanwhile, Thursday attempts to engage the increasingly hostile Apache in an epic battle that will make him famous and get him reassigned, much to the dismay of his second in command, Kirby York (John Wayne), whose relaxed leadership with the men and encouragement of the romance between Philadelphia and O'Rourke make him Thursday's foil.

Released two years later, *She Wore a Yellow Ribbon* tells the story of Captain Nathan Brittles (Wayne), an aging cavalry officer on his last patrol before retirement (just as in *Red River*, Wayne was aged with makeup for the role). As Brittles attempts to secure the desert from violent Cheyenne and Arapaho raids in the weeks after Custer's defeat, two of his lieutenants vie for the affections of the visiting Olivia Dandridge (Joanne Dru), the niece of the fort's major. Lieutenant Cohill (John Agar) is a career cavalry officer whose affection for Ms. Dandridge is tempered by his disdain for her condescension of army life on the frontier, while Lieutenant Pennell (Harry Carey, Jr.) is a spoiled and rich young man who plans on resigning and taking Ms. Dandridge back to New York.

In *Rio Grande*, Wayne plays Kirby Yorke (the *e* signifying that it is not the same Kirby York as in *Fort Apache*, although some critics have interpreted them as being the same character at different stages of life). Yorke is a U.S. cavalry colonel on the western frontier along the Mexico border. He has been estranged from his wife and son for fifteen years, ever since he was ordered to burn down her family's Southern plantation during the Civil War. When his son fails mathematics at West Point, enlists in the cavalry, and is subsequently assigned to Yorke's command, Yorke's wife, Kathleen (Maureen O'Hara), shows up at Yorke's fort to try to buy their son out of the cavalry, all while tensions with the Apache mount. Throughout the narrative, Yorke's son tries to prove himself to his father in combat with the Apache (despite Kathleen's insistence that Yorke keep him out of harm's way), and Yorke and Kathleen begin to reconcile and heal old wounds.

In typical John Ford fashion, all three films infuse larger story lines with the comical antics of the fort's soldiers, particularly the fort's hard-drinking, hard-fighting Irish sergeant (played by Victor McLaughlin in all three films), while *Yellow Ribbon* and *Rio Grande* celebrate the masculine heroics and down-to-earth wisdom of a southern trooper named Tyree (Ben Johnson), who still refers to his comrades as "Yankees" (it is ambiguous whether it is supposed to be the same character in both films). Additionally, all three films focus on the rituals of everyday life on the military outposts: morning roll call, the comical initiations of new troopers, the systems of support the wives offer to one another, even an elaborately choreographed dance that is supposed to dramatize the integrated cohesion of the officers, enlisted men, and their families in *Fort Apache* (a dance that ultimately dramatizes only the tensions between Thursday and his men). Relying heavily on Ford's often-used "family" of actors in all three films, the exploration of domestic life in the fort balances out the emphasis on violence and heroics. Each film provides a loving and often sentimental view of community and familial bonds on the frontier.

And yet the Cavalry Trilogy does not simply celebrate a generic ideal of family and community. The families and communities at the core of Ford's frontier are almost always multiethnic groups brought together by geographic and social migrations. Rough but lovable Irish American enlisted men, former Confederate soldiers, Texans on the run from the law, and the poor "dogface" troopers who make up the rank and file—the forts in the Cavalry Trilogy are populated by individuals and families from diverse and usually marginalized backgrounds: "mavericks, underdogs, outsiders" who are usually highly suspicious of authority (Kitses, *Horizons West*, 32). Ford's "frontier communities are filled with ethnics, in the more general sense that Ella Shohat speaks of ethnicity, namely as a means of describing a wide range of disenfranchised outsiders" (Berg, "Margin as Center," 75). As a first-generation Irish American who grew up at a time when anti-Irish discrimination was rampant, Ford unsurprisingly valorized outsiders, and as Berg argues, Ford's personal background led to a deep suspicion of assimilation and a celebration of his ethnic characters, particularly the Irish, Ford's "Ur-ethnics" (76). While Native Americans in Ford's films usually (but not always) occupy a highly stereotypical position, the Cavalry Trilogy celebrates the coming together of multiethnic communities and expression of ethnic identity.

Examine, for example, the burial of trooper "John Smith," mortally wounded during an Arapaho attack in *She Wore a Yellow Ribbon*. Brittles acknowledges at Smith's funeral that the elderly trooper is actually a former Confederate brigadier general named Rome Clay, who joined the cavalry under a false name after the Civil War in order to continue serving in the military, even if only as a lowly trooper. Brittles allowed Clay's fellow southerner Sergeant Tyree to act as the troop's captain during the general's final, dying moments (perhaps indicating Tyree's rank in the Confederate army), and Brittles then gives the old general a heartfelt burial with a makeshift Confederate flag provided by the fort commander's wife. The problematic romanticism of the Old South aside, the openness with which Brittles allows his sergeant to pretend to be an officer, and his willingness to give the old soldier a burial fitting his rank in an army that fought against the United States, suggests that the world of frontier cultural identity is being valorized over the official regulations of the U.S. military, even as individuals are incorporated into the fold of the cavalry community. Southerners such as Tyree are not expected to assimilate into a homogenous sense of U.S. national identity (indeed, Tyree continues to refer to himself as an outsider in the "Yankee" army), but instead are celebrated for maintaining their cultural identity and ethnic difference. Moreover, the scene idealizes the military as a community and not simply as a nationalist entity; for trooper "John Smith," military service did not seem to be tied to a sense of U.S. national duty (especially since he still essentially defined himself as a Confederate general), but rather offered a communal ideal, a social space where southerners could participate alongside the Irish and other ethnics without losing their cultural identity. He gave up his name but not his southern identity.

These dynamics within Ford's military communities are spatial as well as ethnic and cultural. The formations of Ford's frontier communities are explicitly based on mobility and migration. In them, a diverse set of outsiders seeks refuge in the open spaces of the frontier, "refugees from constricting societies," evading the "hypocrisies of civilization" manifest in towns or in the films' abstract sense of the East Coast (McBride and Wilmington, *John Ford*, 21, 17). Central to the dynamics of Ford's West is "the tension between ethnics, who have been exiled to the social and geographic Margin, and the elite WASP mainstream who drove them there" (Berg, "Margin as Center," 76). These tensions are explicitly at the core of *Fort Apache* in the form of Thursday's disdain for his remote assignment, and such tensions inform Kathleen's reluctance to embrace fort life in *Rio Grande*. But more broadly, all three cavalry films construct a world in which social and ethnic outsiders find solace in the structures, rituals, and support of cavalry life deep in the frontier. Berg goes so far as to argue that the cultural and geographic mobility of Ford's ethnic outsiders constructs a dynamic and flexible view of ethnicity that draws from "multiple affiliations"; as the film's outsiders wander through the complex cultural spaces of the frontier, they created "fluid, evolving, and organic" ethnic identities (76). Pedro Armendariz's Sergeant Beaufort, a Spanish-speaking former Confederate officer who identifies Mexico as his homeland and crosses the Mexican border with Wayne's Kirby York in *Fort Apache* to meet with the Apache, exemplifies Ford's emphasis on fluid identity and characters able to move freely between cultures. (And as I develop more in Chapter 4, Wayne's characters, despite the common association of Wayne with an intractable, domineering white masculinity, also often move freely between cultures and explore the fluidity of identity.)[6]

Ford's exploration of ethnic identity and the diverse communities created though migration and mobility arguably has its roots in his experiences as the child of Irish immigrants. As Kitses argues, "Ford's central subject became the experience of being uprooted and searching for roots, of leaving home and coming home, of exile and return" (*Horizons West*, 42). But while Kitses and other critics see these themes as characteristic of the American experience, the thematic concerns of exile and wandering reflect also the increasing impact of migration on the construction of community and locality for populations around the world after World War II. In the postwar years, mobility and migration became more and more a part of everyday life for international populations, dramatically transforming the spatial relations and social relations of modern life. One example of such mobility was the new or continued urbanization process in which populations moved from rural areas to the cities to seek new economic opportunities or flee rural poverty. This was true not only of large U.S. metropolises but also of European cities such as London, Paris, and Berlin, and of the former colonial cities around the world. According to Joel Kotkin, "Cities such as Bombay, Calcutta, Dehli, Lahore, Lagos, Cairo, and Manila swelled to many times their size under colonial rule" in the postwar years and at the start of decolonization in the 1950s (*The City*, 131). Rapid urbanization, of course, was not an incidental phenomenon but rather an inherent aspect of the globalization and modernization of the world economy. The industrialization of the developing world, as promoted by agencies of development such as the World Bank, along with the mobility of developed-world capital across national borders, was (and is) predicated upon the infrastructures of urban environments and their reorganization of social and communal values.

The wave of urbanization was tied also to increasing levels of international migration. The postwar imperatives for economic recovery resulted in liberal immigration and emigration policies in many nations and regions in order to facilitate the movement of labor and thereby boost the economy and help impoverished populations seek out economic opportunities, primarily in urban centers (Solimano and Watts, *International Migration*, 25). For example, European labor shortages in the 1950s and 1960s led to an expansion of "guest worker" programs, which opened the gates for immigrants from around the world. The process of decolonization that began in the 1940s and 1950s (starting with India and Pakistan in 1947, continuing in Libya in 1951, Morocco and Tunisia in 1956, and reaching its peak across Asia and Africa in the early 1960s) yielded an increase in immigration from former colonial territories to former imperial metropolises. Those migrations increased dramatically throughout the second half of the twentieth century, accelerating so much that mass migrations of people have become a fundamental component of most accounts of globalization in the contemporary world (see, for example, Salt, "International Trends"). As a result, individual mobility and heterogeneous urban populations became an important historical reality for many people around the world in this period (for both those who migrated and those whose communities were transformed by immigrants), complicating the relationship between place, culture, and identity as migratory individuals created new and diverse communities while maintaining cultural ties to distant places.[7]

Reflecting these international cultural transformations, the Cavalry Trilogy explores the geographic relations of rural versus urban life but also uses the idea of the distant frontier to dramatize the construction of locality in the context of vast geographic migrations, urbanization, the nation-state, capitalism, and modernity in general. The films offer images and narratives of diverse and heterogeneous migrant-founded communities that are not simply "distant" or rural compared with the urban East; instead, the films use the cinematic construction of the frontier to suggest a sense of locality that forms in relation to structures such as the military or the nation, a construction of the local that can exist only in the larger contexts of population mobility necessitated by a globalizing capitalism. In other words, Ford's communities are not constituted merely of cultural outsiders planted in the wilderness, but of ethnic migrants seeking to maintain the connections between their new communities, their geographic roots, and the larger structures of modern life through communication media (newspapers, the telegraph), transportation (the stagecoach, the railroad), or the structures of national institutions (the military). Thus, Ford's Cavalry Trilogy provides an internationally resonant set of images and stories that dramatize the complex localism of communities in a way that might easily reflect heterogeneous urban neighborhoods in Chicago, Tokyo, or Rio de Janeiro. At stake in the films is not simply open space—the geographic distance between the outpost and the urban East—but rather spatial relations—how the migrations and mobility inherent in globalizing capitalism restructure the construction of locality and local communities.

The Cavalry Trilogy films often work to undermine the spatial biases of modernity that see distant outposts (distant, that is, from urban centers) and their marginalized communities as less developed, less modern, and therefore less important than the "central" spaces of the culture, represented in the films by the idea of the urban East. As each film explores the community of a distant fort, it undermines the biased logic that sees the local community as unimportant, emphasizing that the complex communities built out of migration are not the margin but the cultural center of the world of the film. In *Fort Apache*, for example, Thursday's character repeatedly puts his disdain for being assigned to the fort in spatial terms intended to explain how un-advanced and un-modern life on the frontier is with respect to the East Coast or Europe. In a stagecoach with Philadelphia on the way to the outpost, he lists all the small outposts that they pass through—from "mud hole to mud hole," as he puts it—on their way to the last stop, Fort Apache. He thinks that he has been "shunted aside" and sent out to the wilderness with no chance for advancement or glory. Likewise, he is taken aback that Lieutenant O'Rourke, the son of an enlisted soldier from Fort Apache, could have received an appointment to West Point, not expecting that the elder O'Rourke is a holder of the Medal of Honor (an honor allowing his son to attend the military academy).

In essence, Thursday embraces some of the problematic ideas about modernity central to the discourses of modernization theory that emerged in the years after World War II. In an effort to industrialize the developing world and institute the tenets of capitalism, rationality, bureaucracy, and other ideologies central to modern, Western life, developed-world proponents of modernization argued that modernity entails a totalizing and irrevocable break with outmoded and "backward" traditional cultures, enshrining the Euro-American West as the core against which the periphery of the developed world was measured, and naturalizing the cultural (and geographic) centrality of Western modernity. Thursday approaches his banishment to the distant frontier with the same assumptions about modernity and its logic of core and periphery, seeing the urban, modern East Coast as the core, the center of the nation against which all the supposedly distant (culturally and geographically) outposts on the periphery must measure themselves.[8]

Thursday is a bigoted and arrogant authoritarian whose foolhardy pursuit of personal glory gets himself and most of his soldiers killed, so his conception of space and culture is refuted by the film's critique of his character. Unable to see the Apache as anything but "illiterate" and "uncivilized savages" because of their remoteness from the modern core and other, more impressive Indian nations like the Sioux or the Comanche, Thursday does not recognize or respect their strength on the battlefield. After York warns Thursday about a trick the Apache commonly use to mask their location, Thursday dismisses the warning: "You'd have me think Cochise studied under Alexander the Great, or Bonaparte at least," condescendingly dismissing both the Apache as an adversary and York's local knowledge of them. He orders a devastating charge into a canyon crowded with Apache warriors, leading to the death of most of his command (excepting York and the younger O'Rourke). Unable to understand the situation beyond his own racism, he refuses to believe that any tribe existing at the periphery of a clearly Eurocentric definition of modernity and knowledge could be capable of such clever tactics. Thursday's detachment and self-importance is often read as vanity and vainglory, the narcissism of a selfish and racist officer who foolishly seeks laurels on the battlefield, but it indicates also the extent to which he cannot situate himself within the spatial dynamics of a world of migration and mobility. By seeing his spatial dislocation from the core to the periphery only as a justification for his superiority, he fails to recognize what the film sees as the truly modern configuration of social relations based on the migration of peoples through sometimes dangerous, borderless spaces. Much as he underestimates the Apache, he can't see the value of the fort's community and its perspective on the spaces of the frontier.

The film offers a kind of fantasy in which the politics of center and margin are tossed aside in favor of the utopian possibilities of migration, celebrating the kinds of communities formed by those "shunted aside" by various social and cultural events. And within this fantasy, Wayne's character, Kirby York, provides the model of a modern subject, someone attuned to the spatial dynamics of frontier communities and possessing an ability to see the complex spaces of the frontier as modern and vibrant. York moves freely between the class structures that Thursday works so hard to erect, a high-ranking officer who, as Thursday admits, will lead the fort one day, but who dines with the O'Rourkes and enjoys the comic escapades of the Irish sergeants. York's openness extends even to his relationship with the Apache. In direct contrast to Thursday's bigoted and willful inability to respect the Apache, York has cultivated a respectful relationship with the Apache and their leader, Cochise. It is through York's ability to demonstrate respect and build trust with Cochise that the Apache are convinced to return to the reservation. York promises them that the corrupt agent from the Indian Affairs Office will be replaced and that more sustainable policies will be in place concerning the Apache (of course, neither York nor Cochise know that all Thursday has in mind is an ill-advised frontal assault on the Apache). As in all the Cavalry Trilogy films, Wayne's character here demonstrates a kind of local knowledge and local competence, even when acting as the representative of a national institution such as the military, that facilitates not only his survival in the world of the frontier but makes him the "natural" leader of a modern community.

These same dynamics characterize the spatial politics of *She Wore a Yellow Ribbon*, a film that opens by highlighting the connection of distant outposts in the frontier to the modern world through various technologies and services. The film's narrative begins with word of Custer's defeat spreading throughout the frontier via telegraph, newspapers delivered by stagecoach, and the pony express, suggesting that emerging media technologies are making the distinction between center and periphery obsolete. Even a cavalry outpost such as Fort Starke, deep in the frontier, is connected in complex ways with modernity, since news media and communication technology keep the frontier community tied to the imagined national community, even as Native Americans threaten to cut off such connections.

Moreover, the film's contrast between the rival suitors Cohill and Pennell foregrounds the class basis of these spatial dynamics. Just as Thursday's disdain for the "mud hole" of Fort Apache is both spatial and classed—he sees himself as belonging to a higher class than the Irish American family his daughter wants to marry into—Pennell's initial resentment of cavalry life on the frontier stems from the fact that he is a spoiled rich kid from the East Coast who can resign his commission at any time because he doesn't need the army's pay. Echoing the visual distinction between Thursday and York, even on patrol Pennell wears a crisp blue uniform with an official cap, while the more practical Cohill appears dustier, wearing a floppy and worn cavalry Stetson. Thus, Pennell's eventual embrace of the cavalry repudiates the class divisions within Fort Starke's community while affirming the importance of the cavalry community and its mission in the frontier. Pennell decides to reenlist only after he secretly witnesses the fort's unscrupulous sutler (provisioner) and Indian agent attempting to illegally sell guns to the Arapaho, who are ready to start a war in the wake of news of Custer's defeat. Accompanying Brittles, Pennell witnesses the Arapaho turning on the sutler, unceremoniously shooting him with an arrow and then dumping the body of one of his companions on an open fire. The scene illustrates the education and maturation of Pennell as Brittles reveals to him the dangerous violence of an unpoliced frontier, prompting Pennell to commit fully to the mission of the cavalry. Interestingly, it is also this moment that seemingly solidifies Pennell's surrender of his romantic ambitions regarding Ms. Dandridge, ambitions that revolved around the hypothetical urban life of luxury they would enjoy together in New York. So both Pennell and Dandridge give up on any dreams of urban sophistication on the East Coast in order to participate in the community of the fort, Pennell as a cavalry officer in the midst of a war and Dandridge as the hardworking wife of Lieutenant Cohill, a practical soldier. In the film, the class pretentions of the urban East function as a foil to the hard work and seeming importance of the cavalry as a community and a military force, despite its geographic remoteness.

Similarly, in *Rio Grande*, Kathleen's conceptions of elitism and privilege are undermined by her emerging respect for her husband's sense of duty and the realization that her son's personal sense of masculinity is more important than his class position. When she arrives at the fort and requests that Jeff be bought out of his enlistment so he can be tutored in math and get his commission as an officer in another manner, she is rebuked by Yorke, who described her attitude as demanding "special privilege for special born." For Yorke, Jeff's commitment to the military and his ability to prove his masculinity to the soldiers of the fort is more important than the class standing and privileges that come with being a commissioned officer, even though being an enlisted man would irreparably limit Jeff's possibilities for advancement. Eventually, Kathleen comes around, not only accepting Jeff's decision but also becoming part of the fort's community and taking on the typical duties of an army wife (washing and ironing clothes, supporting the troops, and waiting tensely to see whether Jeff and Yorke make it back from battle unharmed).

The film's repudiation of class structures and their spatial politics, in fact, borders on the far-fetched. Are we really to believe that Jeff, raised in the privileged life of his mother in the South, would really embrace life as an ordinary trooper on the frontier in the cavalry? Would he commit to a life of such hardship without at least the benefits and privileges of being an officer, especially when Kathleen makes it clear that there are other avenues available to him to enter the army as an officer? According to the logic of the film, this sacrifice makes sense because it illustrates the rejection of class privilege (a privilege associated with the spaces of the East—in this case the upper classes of the Southeast) in favor of the lure of life in the distant frontier and participation in the vibrant community of the fort. As Peter Lehman has demonstrated, Ford's films consistently repress the explicit role of capitalism in the West in order to affirm the family or community ("How the West Wasn't Won," 133); thus, Jeff's wholesale rejection of his class privileges and class standing is one such act of repression, pushing to the margin a realistic consideration of class division in favor of a celebratory vision of the frontier margin as a cultural center.

By exploring the spatial and cultural dynamics of cavalry forts as distant localities nevertheless vitally connected to the larger structures of cultural life, the Cavalry Trilogy provides a particularly salient example of the spatialized social relations of modern life as described by Anthony Giddens. Challenging the widespread assumption that the institutionalization of modernity is essentially dehumanizing and eradicates older forms of meaningful interaction and community, Giddens sees modernization as more of a reorganization of interactions, identities, and personal relations. In particular, he points to the role that space plays within social relations within modernity. Recognizing that modernization means a restructuring of space as populations, media, labor, goods, services, and ideas move more rapidly and more often across national and cultural borders, Giddens argues that space informs social relations on two fronts: disembedding—"the 'lifting out' of social relations from local contexts of interaction and their restructuring across indefinite spans of time-space" (*Consequences of Modernity*, 21)—and reembedding—"the reappropriation or recasting of disembedded social relations so as to pin them down (however partially or transitorily) to local conditions of time and place" (79–80). Life within modernity functions along these two spatial planes: one's sense of identity and social interactions is stretched across long distances in relation to large institutions like nations or corporations, while at the same time new social relations and new communities are formed in the local spaces that emerge from such distanciation. Thus, modernity does not eradicate community and personal interaction, but rather reorganizes social relations as people create new ties, new relationships, and new identities within vastly transformed spatial structures such as migration, urbanization, or distanciated connections via communications technologies.[9]

Examine, then, the surprisingly large role that newspapers from big cities on the East Coast play in the events that unfold in *Fort Apache*. Colonel Thursday initially deems the Apache a race of "digger Indians," in contrast to the great Indian nations like the Sioux or the Comanche, because of the "well publicized" campaigns against the other tribes. And his esteem of the Apache changes only when clippings from Eastern newspapers confirm that the Apache chief Cochise is a well-known figure to those papers and their readers. Thus, the Eastern newspapers and Thursday's desire for publicity and glory prompt him to send two of his men illegally across the Mexican border to trick Cochise into returning to U.S. soil. Engaging the Apache in battle ultimately fulfills Thursday's desire for publicity through his own death, which transforms him into a national hero and brings reporters to the fort to cover the new campaign against the Apache. In the final, controversial scenes of the film, Thursday is falsely glorified by his second in command for the sake of the reporters from the East.

One of the central dynamics of the film is the restructuring of social relations in space and the construction of a locality that is both distant and yet structured in relation to modern institutions that are stretched across space. The spaces of the frontier are geographically remote and situated near a permeable national border across which Native peoples flow back and forth, but they are also spaces connected in complex ways to institutions of modernity, in this case newspapers and the bureaucracies of the military, which facilitated the migration of the fort's inhabitants to the frontier in the first place. Like the frequently broken telegraph wire that provides the fort with a tenuous connection to the outside world, or the bureaucratic regulations of the U.S. army, which are frequently bent or broken in the far reaches of the frontier, the presence of the Eastern newspapers dramatizes the complex ways that the open, heterogeneous, and somewhat borderless spaces of the frontier are unevenly structured in relation to modernity and the processes of modernization. The film displays the disconnection between the vision of the world proffered by the mass media and other modern institutions (Thursday's biased, "East Coast" views of the Apache, the false glory of Thursday's death) and the much more complex lived experiences of locals, all while still recognizing the necessity and power of such modern institutions. At stake in the film, therefore, are the ways that individuals construct modern social identities in relation to the spaces of the nation, locality, and the idea of modernity itself—how social relations are disembedded across geographic space and then subsequently reembedded in a complex construction of locality.

This emphasis on the spatial relations of Ford's West and the construction of a modern locality helps explain the troubling final scenes in *Fort Apache*. After Thursday's disastrous battle against the Apache (meant to evoke Custer's last stand), the film jumps forward a few years as York, now the fort's commander, stands in his office answering the questions of East Coast reporters about his new campaign against the Apache. The reporters ask about Thursday's death, referring to a famous celebratory painting of the event that hangs in Washington and that York saw there upon his last visit. In a response that evades the historical truth of Thursday's death, York says that the painting is "correct in every detail" and that "no man died more gallantly, nor won more honor for his regiment." Then, donning a hat like that used by Thursday (not York's typical slouchy western hat, which violated military regulations) and using one of Thursday's stock phrases ("Questions?"), York leads the reporters out of his office as he heads off to finish the war with the Apache that Thursday started. They meet Philadelphia, now Philadelphia O'Rourke, and her son, who has a variety of namesakes: Michael Thursday York O'Rourke. Like the ending of *The Man Who Shot Liberty Valance*, in which myths of the West take precedence over historical truth, York's words and deeds obscure the history of Thursday's vanity and ignorance for the sake of national mythologies and a celebration of the cavalry and its oppressive, colonialist mission.

The scene has challenged and perplexed critics for years because of how it seems to contradict not only York's character (he has internalized Thursday's attitude despite his clear disdain for Thursday's bigotry) but also the themes of the film itself, namely, by celebrating Thursday as a leader and embracing war with the Apache in spite of the film's clear sympathy for the plight of the frontier's Native inhabitants. Robin Wood has criticized the scene for doing "violence to the previous development of the Wayne character" ("Shall we Gather?," 28). Explanations for the scene have included the theory that Thursday, while arrogant, bigoted, and foolish, was at least a strong leader whose leadership qualities the previously laid-back York seeks to reproduce (Kitses, *Horizons West*, 64), and an appeal to Ford's ambivalence about "civilization": the tragedy of Thursday's transformation indicates "with Brechtian clarity" that reasonable, sane, and noble people perpetuate insane systems of violence and oppression (McBride and Wilmington, *John Ford*, 109).

But the seeming contradictions of the scene are resolved somewhat in the context of Ford's spatial politics and the construction of locality. The films of the Cavalry Trilogy do not, after all, straightforwardly celebrate locality in opposition to structures of nationalism of imperialism, but rather explore new forms of locality that exist in relation to larger systems of modernity such as the military. The films do not celebrate remoteness from the perceived urban center in and of itself, but rather the new dynamics of population mobility and modernization that decentered space and made possible the vibrant, mobile, and somewhat diverse communities of the frontier. York's local knowledge and local competence must function within institutions, such as the cavalry, that stretch across geographic space, linking the remote fort to the structures and bureaucracies of nationalism of which Thursday was a part. Thus, York's donning of Thursday's demeanor and his perpetuation of the mythology of Thursday's death affirm the distanciated social relations that make the community of the fort possible. York is clearly playing a role in the spatial drama of the film, performing as the fort's commander rather than as the local hero, someone who functions as the intermediary between the local community and the structures of nationalism. Note that York in his new role had recently returned from Washington, D.C., thereby reinforcing the fort's connections to the urban East through his own mobility.

What is more, by mythologizing Thursday, York ultimately helps enshrine the cultural centrality of the spaces of the frontier and the fort's community. It is the misperception of Thursday's death that brings cultural attention to the fort, thus the presence of the reporters. So while Thursday, through his own death, finally gets the attention and glory he sought, by obscuring the truth of Thursday's last stand, York is able channel that attention to the fort and its inhabitants. His interview with the reporters celebrates not just Thursday but also the other men who died. When the reporters get Collingwood's name wrong (one of the officers killed in the final battle), York is fast to correct them, noting that those who died will never truly die because they live on in the spirit of the fort: "They're living, right out there. Collingwood and the rest. And they'll keep on living, as long as the regiment lives. The pay is thirteen dollars a month, their diet beans and hay—they'll eat horsemeat before this campaign is over—fight over cards or rotgut whisky, but share the last drop in their canteens." While dramatically performing the role of the fort commander for the sake of the reporters, York shifts attention to members of the community, their sacrifices and camaraderie as well as the community's status as the cultural center of the new, modern world. So when Thursday's name along with York's is incorporated into the name of Philadelphia and Lieutenant O'Rourke's little boy, the act is less a tribute to Thursday than a sign that, in death, Thursday has become yet another migrant integrated into the fabric of the community, despite his resistance to the community in life.

But as the image of cavalry soldiers marching off to battle the Apache at the end of the film suggests, the Native peoples provide a clear limit to inclusion in the diverse ethnic community celebrated in Ford's films. Ford explores the possibilities of community for cultural outsiders in the geographically remote spaces of the frontier, but those outsiders cannot be racially different. As Berg puts it, "Native Americans in Ford's films serve to fix the cultural limits for Margin ethnics. If the Mainstream represents Ford's fear of what the Margin ethnics will likely become via assimilation, the Native American is what they *can't* become—another race" ("Margin as Center," 80–81). Ford's ethnic communities negotiate a middle ground between the urban, WASP mainstream represented by characters such as Thursday and the racial threat of the Native peoples on the frontier. Ford's films thus examine the cross-cultural dynamics of migration and new communities while retaining the racial tensions that often result from population mobility. They envision a modern world that offers the seemingly utopian pleasures of mobility and multiethnic communities while acknowledging the kinds of racialized competition over space and resources facilitated by migration and urbanization.

GENDER RELATIONS ON THE FRONTIER: THE BURDENS AND FREEDOMS OF MIGRATION

In one sequence in *Fort Apache*, Lieutenant O'Rourke expresses his affection for the newly arrived Philadelphia by taking her horseback riding outside the confines of the fort's walls. Their explorations of Monument Valley are captured by the same expansive cinematography as the wandering of the cavalry. The two figures crisscross the open space as spectacular rock formations loom in the distance, offering the sensations of freedom and a youthful sense of adventure. For Philadelphia, who has been raised in urban settings on the East Coast, the ride seems exhilarating and suits her effervescent and spunky personality. But as they ride, they come across the grisly remains of several cavalrymen who had been overrun by hostile Apache. Sickened and distraught by the horrific discovery, Philadelphia is whisked back to the fort, where O'Rourke is berated by Thursday for putting his daughter at risk out in the open and dangerous spaces of the frontier. In a matter of minutes, the landscape of the frontier is transformed from a utopian space of freedom to a hostile territory where violence lurks. Earlier in the film, Philadelphia had experienced the pleasures of the frontier and her own mobility as she used her hatbox mirror to surreptitiously gaze at the handsome O'Rourke riding on horseback behind her, daringly enjoying her desire for the young man as they traversed open space in a scene expressing the sense of optimism and youthful joy that the frontier had to offer. But with the discovery of the dead troopers, Philadelphia sees too much in the frontier, her earlier wonder replaced by the realities of death and war in the contested spaces of the West.

Philadelphia's foray into the open spaces of Ford's Monument Valley indicates, not surprisingly, that the spatial relations of the frontier were experienced in vastly different ways by women and men. For O'Rourke and the other soldiers, the open and dangerous spaces of the frontier provide a context for roaming, exploration, and violent heroics, while for the women of the fort, the open spaces of the frontier inevitably become a threat to their lives (and, it is often implied, their sexuality). While all the members of Ford's frontier communities are migrants of one kind or another, once they are settled in the new social structures of fort life, gender roles assume specialized spatial functions. Men navigate the complex spaces of the frontier, wandering on patrols or scouting ventures that test their masculinity and then returning home to the fort and the comforts of domesticity. But women become synonymous with the community itself, creating a settled, domestic world that stands in opposition to the nomadic tendencies of the masculine sphere.

Ford's depiction of women on the frontier relies heavily on the standard stereotypes of women in the western genre, focusing on women solely as wives, mothers, or romantic partners who help articulate masculine individualism by providing its antithesis in the structures of the family and community. That is how the gender relations of the western genre often function: men seek refuge from the domestic world of femininity in order to explore the dynamics of masculine violence and mobility (see, for example, Tompkins, *West of Everything*; Mitchell, *Westerns*). But as Gaylyn Studlar points out, Ford's westerns, while still stereotypical, focus on the dynamic interactions between masculinity and femininity and go further than other westerns in exploring the essential humanity of women and their fundamental importance to the functioning of society ("Sacred Duties"). Compare the Cavalry Trilogy with Hawks's *Red River* (discussed in the previous chapter). While the specter of heterosexual coupling and domesticity lingers in the background of the narrative, *Red River* actively keeps femininity at the margins in order to explore the all-male personal interactions of the highly mobile cattle drive. The Cavalry Trilogy, on the other hand, develops strong and interesting female characters such as Philadelphia Thursday or Kathleen Yorke, and the films offer a more careful consideration of how to reconcile masculine mobility with feminine domesticity, most explicitly in *Rio Grande*'s narrative of reconciliation between Kirby and Kathleen. While the spaces and roles offered to women are quite limited in Ford's West, women nevertheless occupy an important space in the gendered dynamics of his films, much more so than in the westerns of Hawks, Anthony Mann, John Sturges, or others, in which the active mobility of men across the frontier dominates the imagery and narrative.

Indeed, in *Red River*, Wayne's Tom Dunson denies the importance of women's migration for the creation of frontier communities, seeing mobility as an exclusively masculine characteristic, separate from the domestic and settled world of women, despite the fact that he left his fiancée in a cross-country wagon traversing the spaces of the frontier. The Cavalry Trilogy recognizes more fully the presence of women in narratives of migration, even as the films perpetuate the split between masculine mobility and a settled feminine domesticity. In each of the films, the intrusion of a woman who has migrated from the East Coast establishes the domestic narrative conflicts of the films, but rather than constructing the intrusion as an unwelcome foray into the dangerous world of male violence on the frontier, the woman's integration into the fort's community becomes a necessary and welcome affirmation of the community's values. Ford often embraces the notion that "within a landscape inhospitable to human enterprise, masculinity and femininity share in—and are equalized by—the pioneer experience" (Studlar, "Sacred Duties," 48). His westerns frequently dramatize women as migrants and pioneers, as in Mrs. Jorgensen's "Texican" soliloquy defending the pioneer life of suffering and desperation in *The Searchers*, or in Clementine Carter's integration into the community of Tombstone in ways that Doc Holliday cannot in *My Darling Clementine*. Ford's films, including the Cavalry Trilogy, routinely explore the centrality of women's migration to the maintenance of frontier communities.

Compared to portrayals in other westerns, Ford's depiction of women and migration offers a more historically accurate picture of the history of the American West (despite the cultural mythology of the enterprising male pioneer and frontiersman, the presence and labor of women was foundational to the occupation and settling of the U.S. frontier; see Armitage and Jameson, *Women's West*), and it also reflects the historical realities of the international migrations, discussed above, that transformed social relations in the years after World War II. The cultural conception of migration and immigration usually presents the international migrant as a "young, economically motivated male" (Pedraza, "Women and Migration," 303), but women in the second half of the twentieth century constituted a large, almost equal share of international migrants. In the United States, for example, women outnumbered men in the annual flow of immigrants as early as 1930, a trend that persists to this day (304). Those demographics were similar internationally. Although a 2002 UN study of international migration found that in the 1960s women were 47 percent of all international migrants, it is plausible that a similar, significantly high number of women were international migrants in the preceding decade and a half (United Nations, *Migration Report*). In the second half of the twentieth century, women as well as men participated in the accelerating movement of peoples across national borders that has transformed social relations and locality in the modern world.

Ford's Cavalry Trilogy provides a dramatic representation of the importance and, at times, hard consequences of women's migration, offering audiences around the world images and narratives of women as migrants (albeit migrants who must defer to masculine mobility and embrace domestic responsibilities). The price that women paid for migrating to the frontier was the acceptance of suffering and hardship as part of their feminine duties. At the end of *Rio Grande*, for example, Kathleen demonstrates her integration into the fort community by performing her own feminine suffering for the benefit of her husband and the entire fort. Waiting anxiously for Jeff and Kirby to return from battle, she at first rushes to Jeff's side, but upon seeing Kirby lying wounded on a stretcher, she walks solemnly alongside her husband, holding his hand. The long processional is like a somber parade, with all the fort's women watching to see whether their husbands will make it back or not. Kathleen's act is not simply a private gesture for her husband, but also a public acknowledgment that she will embrace the role of the suffering wife and give up her privileged life in the Southeast. We might point similarly to the appearance of Philadelphia at the end of *Fort Apache*. In contrast to her previous youthful vigor, she appears haggard and worn down, wearing work clothes suited to the domestic labor of the fort, in contrast to the sophisticated costumes she wore throughout the film, as she watches her husband and the other soldiers march off to war. For each of the women, migration to the frontier offers the seeming pleasures of a diverse and supportive modern community, but such a community is built upon women accepting their own suffering, reflecting Ford's tendency to "present melancholy portraits of women's economic, emotional, physical, and sexual vulnerability in the West" (Studlar, "Sacred Duties," 66).

Indeed, suffering and sacrifice are central to Ford's vision of the West as he explores the personal burdens and hardships of both women and men in the frontier. Wayne's Nathan Brittles is a lonely old man who visits the graves of his wife and daughters every night. The dates on the graves indicate they were killed at the same time, perhaps during an attack on the fort. Brittles reports every night to his family, telling them about his upcoming retirement and his inability to imagine a life outside the structures of the cavalry. Similarly, Kirby Yorke's devotion to duty both in the Civil War (burning down his wife's ancestral home) and on the frontier keeps him estranged from his family, longing for their presence but unable to put his military duties aside to reconcile their differences. According to Studlar, what Ford expresses through Wayne here is the necessity of sacrifice: "Westerners — male and female — must submit themselves to the Christian sacrifice necessary to secure their communal (and national) identity. That sacrifice entails the burdens of isolation and loneliness, the submission to physical hardship, and the unpredictable loss of friends and family to nature or to human inflicted violence" ("Sacred Duties," 47). Thus, the new social possibilities of communities formed from migration yield gendered patterns of suffering and hardship that are both somber and yet celebrated in the logic of the films.

For the men in Ford's West, their suffering results from their duty to mobility and spatial exploration, duties that temper their personal sacrifices with the utopian sensations of mobility and an imperative to keep space open. All three films dramatize the spatial dynamics of the frontier as the cavalry police and protect space, facilitating the flow of people and information into the frontier via the stagecoach or telegraph. In *Fort Apache*, for example, the men of the cavalry are often out repairing telegraph lines cut by hostile Apache, even though the broken lines don't seem to matter much to the functioning of the fort, since they maintain, at best, a loose connection to the East and army regulations. The men in all the films are tasked with maintaining and protecting open space, keeping the spaces free for the movement of people.

Moreover, all three films focus on border spaces as central to the spatial dynamics of the landscape. Situated close to the U.S.-Mexico border deep in the Southwest desert, the spaces of the Cavalry Trilogy explore the structures and sensations of borderlands, a space made more complex by the presence of Native Americans who move freely back and forth across the border to avoid the jurisdiction of the cavalry. In response to such freedom of movement, two of the films feature illicit but officially sanctioned forays across the border. In *Fort Apache*, Thursday sends York on a long, dangerous trek across the border to speak to Cochise and convince him to return to the United States, while Yorke takes a small troop illegally across the border in *Rio Grande* to rescue the fort's children. In both instances, national borders are constructed as a nuisance, arbitrary distinctions that keep the cavalry from protecting the open spaces of the frontier and maintaining its own mobility. In the films' visions of open space, mobility is valorized more than the spatial structures of the nation, just as the pleasures of men performing heroic and violent actions across space take precedence over structures that confine space.

In the Cavalry Trilogy's celebration of masculine mobility, perhaps more important than these narrative elements is the iconography of open space, the visceral pleasures of men on horseback exploring rocky crags within the spectacle of Monument Valley. Ford, after all, privileged the cinematic spectacle of the landscape over the realities of geography: the crags of Monument Valley are nowhere near the U.S.-Mexico border. The pleasures of all three films are rooted in the visual spectacle of riders on horseback gallantly maneuvering through the open landscape in a masculinist vision of mobility and freedom. The spaces of Monument Valley, with its open expanses broken up by massive and dramatic crags, provide an almost utopian playground for the heroic movement of the men in the film, offering an optimistic vision of the possibilities of borderlessness and migration. Through sprawling, extreme long shots capturing the intricate spaces of Monument Valley or a vast and open horizon, the Cavalry Trilogy celebrates masculinity that moves freely and adeptly navigates those spaces; the films construct skilled mobility as part of modern subjectivity. More than simply signifying a set of meanings about open space and mobility, the Cavalry Trilogy offers a visceral, embodied sense of what a modern, mobile masculinity might feel like. In expressing and investigating the physical pleasures of men working together and exploring space, the films offer a compelling fantasy of borderlessness and nomadism tied to the increasingly mobile world of international migration.

Thus, the typical duality of the western frontier on film—it is both paradise, an escape from "civilization," and yet also a barren and dangerous wasteland— reflects a general ambivalence about the spatial relations of a world of migration and mobility, particularly for men. The open spaces of the frontier promise adventure and freedom of movement, the possibility that marginalized outsiders can create new and socially important communities. And yet the frontier is simultaneously a space of great danger, a harsh terrain that promises death or devastation, and the personal sacrifices on the part of the cavalry that are necessary to maintain the openness of this space consistently yield lonely old men weary from the grief of the past. The spatial and social relations produced in the films reflect the ambivalence and hardships of migration as much as they explore the vibrant dynamics of new communities.

More often than not, Native peoples in all three films are treated as just another part of the dangerous landscape, a natural threat symbolizing the hardships and hazards of the frontier. In fact, Native peoples in the films are often visually constructed as claustrophobic hindrances to the openness of space. In contrast to the open horizons behind shots of the cavalry or long shots of a lone soldier against the rocky crags of Monument Valley, Native peoples in the films often close down the open horizon. In *Fort Apache*, for example, the Apache are frequently filmed in spaces with vertical depth, occupying many levels of the depth as they surround the cavalry. When Wayne as York enters Cochise's camp, he is shot from above, revealing layers of Apache on the hillsides. And when the cavalry makes its disastrous charge at the end of the film, a similar angle is used to show the vertical depth of the Apache as they crowd the space. In both shots, the horizon is lost; there is a claustrophobic closing of open space as the Apache enclose and threaten the once utopian spaces of the frontier. In *She Wore a Yellow Ribbon*, tribes on the warpath in the wake of Custer's defeat are constantly popping up over a ridge on the horizon, transforming an open horizon into a closed and violent space.

Particularly in *Fort Apache*, the Native peoples (like the cavalry) are simply another band of seminomads with a claim to the land who want the freedom to move about in peace. Indeed, the claustrophobic treatment of space in scenes with the Apache might be interpreted as a dramatization of their struggle with the U.S. government, a visual depiction of their enclosure on reservations or the necessity of their hiding out across the border in Mexico, alienated from the kinds of mobility that the cavalry now enjoys, an interpretation supported by York's sympathetic description of the Apache's treatment by the government

FIGURE 2.1. *The depth of the Apache as they close off the open spaces of the frontier in* Fort Apache *(Argosy/RKO, 1948).*

and corrupt Indian agents. Across the three films, the threat posed by Native peoples constructs a vision of space marked by competing claims and the simultaneous pleasures and dangers of borderlessness.

Ultimately, the Apache play a larger role in the intersection of race and gender ideologies in the films. Even in *Fort Apache*, which, more than the other films, attempts a sympathetic examination of white relations with the Native peoples, the Apache function as a scapegoat that maintains the performance of masculine and feminine values in the fort's community. The narratives of all three films, which are based on women who migrate across vast landscapes to help create new communities, associate women with movement through space, normally a masculine attribute. But once the migration to the fort is complete, the films justify the settlement of the women in the fort's domestic sphere because of the persistent threat of Native violence outside the walls of the fort. Indeed, whenever women wander away from the domestic sphere of the fort, Native violence quickly ensues. The correspondence is seen in Philadelphia's foray discussed above, in the failed attempt to evacuate Ms. Dandridge and the major's wife in *Yellow Ribbon* (the women's presence keeps the cavalry from getting to the stagecoach station before it is attacked and burned), and in the attempt to evacuate the fort's women and children in *Rio Grande* (the women and children are kidnapped by the Apache). At the same time, although the films explore the possibility that men can embrace domestic life in the fort, the men are duty bound to protect the women from the Natives, which keeps them separate from the domestic sphere. In both cases, the violent threat of the Apache ensures that the gendered worlds of men and women in the fort stay separate: men stay tied to mobility and women remain spatially tied to the fort.

These gendered spatial dynamics suggest the process of suburbanization that was rapidly transforming the spatial structures of urban life in the fifties. The ideology of the suburb as a modern social space is rooted in a gendered and raced segregation — specifically, the relocation of women and domesticity from the metropolitan center. Making the public-private division geographic, suburbs create a feminized space of domestic duties and consumption, and a masculine space of work and the accumulation of capital, spaces that the man can move freely between through his mobility. Moreover, suburbanization responds to the migrations of people to urban centers and the resulting heterogeneity of cities by segregating women from a "dangerous" (that is, racialized) urban life (for a detailed discussion of the racial and gender logic of the suburb, see Hayden, *Redesigning the American Dream*). That motivation was particularly salient in the postwar years as more and more people from around the world migrated to urban centers. The suburb emerged as a respite from those flows of people and the chaotic urban life that they created; for example, European suburbs expanded as people from the Middle East and other regions were brought in to fill labor shortages. In addition to the well-documented postwar growth of U.S. suburbs, cities such as Buenos Aires, Melbourne, Sydney, London, Madrid, Dusseldorf, Hamburg, Rotterdam, Amsterdam, Paris, Osaka, and Tokyo saw massive suburban growth throughout the twentieth century, but especially just after World War II (Kotkin, *The City*, 122–125).[10]

In their negotiation of masculinity, femininity, and the raced spaces of the frontier, the Cavalry Trilogy affirms the spatial ideologies of suburbanization, using the racialized threat of the Native peoples on the frontier to rationalize the segregation of the domestic sphere from the public mobility of men and violence. While the diverse communities of the films' forts reflect the social dynamics of migration and heterogeneous communities, the formation of such communities relies on the Native American as an Other that obscures ethnic (but not racial) differences. The threat of Native violence not only allows Irishmen and former Confederate officers to be united in a superficial vision of diversity, but also endangers the women and children of the fort and thus legitimizes the violent exploits of the cavalry. Thus, the communities rely on a construction of the frontier as a dangerous and racialized space in the same ways that suburban planning considered racially diverse urban centers to be hazardous spaces of crime and filth that require violence to protect women and children. Neil Smith has noted how the rhetoric of the frontier — in which the city is seen as an untamed wildness explicitly comparable to the cinematic frontier — has dominated discussions of urban life (*Urban Frontier*). (Reinforcing that connection, *Fort Apache* was remade in the 1980s as *Fort Apache: The Bronx*, a gritty urban cop drama.)

Within these gendered and raced spatial structures, John Wayne offers an ideal form of masculine leadership for the cavalry outposts in the films. In *Fort Apache* and *She Wore a Yellow Ribbon*, Wayne's characters facilitate the kinds of heterosexual coupling that symbolizes the formation of frontier communities, helping integrate women from the East into the cultural values of the frontier. Yet Wayne's characters themselves remain distant from domestic responsibilities and prove adept at navigating the open spaces of the frontier. In *Fort Apache*, romance is not considered a possibility for Kirby York, despite his youth and charm in the film, but he helps bring together the cross-class couple of O'Rourke and Philadelphia. In *Yellow Ribbon*, although he is a lonely old man whose family has long since died, he playfully aids in the union of Cohill and Dandridge. In both instances, since Wayne is freed from family life and the feminine values of domesticity, he can wallow in the pleasures of mobility and masculine heroics within the dramatic open landscapes of Monument Valley while domesticity is safely displaced onto younger characters. Reinforcing the key characteristics of the John Wayne persona established in *Red River*, Wayne's masculinity in the films acknowledges the importance of marriage and family but is conveniently (though tragically) distant from feminine values, so he can pursue the homosocial world of violence and professional duty unencumbered. In Ford's Cavalry Trilogy, Wayne is an ideal star to negotiate the importance of women and community while insisting on the necessity of masculine mobility and distance from the domestic sphere.

In Ford's films, the balance between family and masculine heroics within the Wayne persona is more nuanced and tragic than in other Wayne films. In Wayne's collaborations with Howard Hawks, for example, romance explicitly takes a back seat to male bonding. As discussed in Chapter 7, a film such as *Rio Bravo* wallows in the pleasures of men hanging around with one another on the job, and Wayne's character's romantic relationship with the only substantive female character (Feathers, the gambler) revolves around her becoming one of the boys. But in Ford's films, we see Wayne as much more vulnerable and longing for familial attachments, if only to suggest the depth of his sacrifices as he remains committed to his professional duties. The image of Wayne as Nathan Brittles casually talking to his wife's grave offers a sentimental example of this dynamic — Wayne is constructed as a loving and attentive husband and father with a deep longing for his wife and daughter's presence, and yet their absence from the film is somewhat necessary for Brittles's commitment to his professional duty and mobility. Of all three films, *Yellow Ribbon* is the most ambivalent about masculine heroics and violence, perhaps because of its sentimental emphasis on personal sacrifice. At the end of the film, Brittles avoids war with the hotheaded young Apache leaders, stealing their horses and ushering them back to the reservation without casualties. Providing one last lesson for the young officers who will replace him, Brittles finds a nonviolent course of action. Remembering and honoring the sacrifices necessary to the masculine heroics of the cavalry are central to the film's vision: even as Brittles passes the torch to the next generation, his troopers provide him with a watch engraved with "Lest we forget," a reminder of past sacrifices. The memento tempers the celebration of violent and nomadic masculinity that comes in the final minutes of the film as Brittles is spared from retirement by being promoted to lieutenant colonel and chief of scouts for the fort and the cavalry rides through the landscape of the frontier on its colonialist mission.

Wayne's vulnerability and familial attachments are on display in *Rio Grande* when he meets his son for the first time in fifteen years. Calling the young trooper Yorke into his tent upon Jeff's arrival at the fort, Wayne's Kirby Yorke gives him a stern and official speech about duties and responsibilities, assuring him that he will get no preferential treatment and dispelling any myths about the romanticism of life on the frontier. In a similar tone, Jeff barks back that he expects no such treatment and came to the fort only as a trooper, not as Kirby's son. It is an exchange full of masculine posturing as each fulfills his expected tough and unemotional role as a soldier. Once Jeff is dismissed from the tent, however, Kirby, after making sure that Jeff is out of sight and then marking the spot on the tent where Jeff's head touched the canvas, stands where Jeff stood to see whether Jeff is as tall as he is. While the moment might suggest masculine competition—Kirby making sure that he is still taller than Jeff—the scene suggests instead a sense of fatherly pride and connection, of wanting to share some similarity with Jeff in spite of the fact that, face-to-face, Kirby is unable to relate to him outside the structures of professionalism and duty.

As this scene suggests, the final installment of the trilogy actively takes up the negotiation between family and the professional duties of the cavalry. With a narrative that resembles a kind of male melodrama more than a western (a point acknowledged by Kitses), Wayne's Kirby Yorke attempts to reconcile a dedication to masculine professionalism and the nomadic mobility of the cavalry with the settled world of domesticity and romanticism. A stubborn and professional soldier whose devotion to duty led him to destroy his wife's ancestral home in the Civil War, years later Yorke is a lonely and weary leader, yearning for the comforts of domesticity that he forfeited because of his sense of military duty and sentimentally carrying with him a music box that plays the tune "I'll Take You Home Again, Kathleen." While Yorke's relationship with his estranged son provides the narrative impetus for Kathleen's arrival at the fort, the real negotiations in the film surround his relationship with Kathleen and his tenuous attempts to put professionalism aside in order to integrate romance and family life into his world.

As described in more detail in the previous chapter, a central component of Wayne's persona in this period was the marginalization of the spheres of domesticity and femininity in favor of contexts of homosocial bonding. In his films, a superficial desire for the structures of the nuclear family can be conveniently pushed aside in order to pursue the grand exploits of male adventure; in that way, the cinematic construction of John Wayne's masculinity manages the increasingly and globally pervasive split between feminized domestic and masculine public spheres. But in *Rio Grande,* the pull of masculine mobility and the desire to flee from femininity are presented much more ambivalently than in most Wayne films, and the comforts of romance and domestic life are much more appealing. The difficult and violent life on the frontier that Yorke has grown accustomed to is one of hardship and personal sacrifice, even though it provides opportunities for male bonding and physical heroics. In fact, the pleasures of masculine heroics are experienced most by the young troopers in the film, echoing the sentiments in *She Wore a Yellow Ribbon* that with maturity comes a desire for the comforts of domesticity or, in the cases of Nathan Brittles, nostalgia for its loss. In *Rio Grande's* narrative of reconciliation, the dynamic tensions of the balance between masculine adventurism and a settled domestic existence are much more pronounced, even allowing Yorke to bend military regulations and give Jeff the supposedly safe assignment of escorting the women and children from the fort.

But it is not that conciliatory gesture that reconciles Yorke and Kathleen in the end. When Jeff's supposedly safe assignment becomes a target for the Apache, who kidnap the fort's children, Jeff and the other new recruits help the cavalry undertake a dangerous rescue mission across the Mexican border, in the midst of which Kirby is wounded. It is after that battle that Kathleen takes her husband's side as a suffering soldier's wife, presumably recognizing that Yorke's military duty serves a greater purpose: protecting the open spaces of the frontier from the threat of the Native peoples. As Deborah Thomas notes in her analysis of the film, the threat of the Apache throughout much of the film symbolizes the hostility and tensions between Yorke and Kathleen, only to become the scapegoat for their reunion, a common threat that can at least superficially reconcile their irreconcilable differences ("John Wayne's Body"). For Thomas, *Rio Grande* never quite resolves the gendered spatial tensions that run through all three films: the film fails to produce a reasonable sense of "home," a space acceptable for Yorke as a professional soldier and Kathleen as a privileged southern woman to inhabit together happily. Indeed, compared with the domestic spaces of *Fort Apache*, which are too dilapidated for Thursday's taste and yet suggest the cozy comforts of domestic life, there aren't really any domestic spaces in *Rio Grande*—Kirby's tent is makeshift and temporary, lacking any sense of settled space that he and Kathleen can inhabit together. The easy stereotyping of the violent and brutal Apache produces too easy a solution to fundamentally different gendered spatial structures in the face of this lack of "home."

It is within the careful balance of these gendered and raced spatial tensions that the resonance and appeal of the Cavalry Trilogy can be found. At a historical moment when increasing levels of migration and population mobility around the world were transforming the patterns of everyday life, and when social relations were stretched across space and yet also localized in new and diverse communities, Ford's narratives of migratory men and women, communities of cultural outsiders, nomadic masculine wandering, and an open, dramatic landscape marked by intense, interracial competition over land and resources captured the complex cultural transformations of space in the postwar world. Dramatically producing a set of spatial relations that celebrate migration and community formation while insisting on the tense hardships and personal sacrifices of individual and communal mobility, Ford's films explore the anxieties and pleasures of migration and mobility within an uneven modernization, creating the spatial structures within which a masculinity such as Wayne's can thrive. In fact, even as Ford's films actively produce a set of spatial relations prevalent in the modern world, they actively produce the idea of John Wayne, fundamentally intertwining Wayne's projection of a modern masculinity with the delicate balance between mobility and settlement that has come to define modern life.

UNEVEN MODERNIZATION AND THE APPEAL OF THE WESTERN FRONTIER

The creative presence of Ford as director is only one of many influences that connect the Cavalry Trilogy to issues of migration, mobility, and open space. After all, Ford is working within the confines of an internationally popular genre whose complex images of the western frontier had long dramatized issues of contested space and power for movie audiences around the world. Throughout most of the twentieth century, the imagery and narrative structures of the western genre were used internationally to express and explore the construction of space and modernity. Within U.S. culture, we tend to think of the western in the same ways we think of John Wayne: a quintessentially American form to be celebrated as the American Shakespeare or else condemned for its promotion of imperial domination. And yet, as anyone can attest who has seen chic western-wear children's clothing sold in Paris boutiques or has seen the recent Thai western parody *Tears of the Black Tiger*, the iconography of the western genre resonates around the world in complex ways. Internationally, the images of the western often signify much more than a form of U.S. culture, offering instead a pop-culture style expressive of consumerist modernity.

Westerns have always been popular beyond the cultural and geographic borders of the United States. George Fenin and William Everson, for example, point out that "English youth retains more loyalty to the Western than does American" and that the German, Italian, and French markets show "major interest in American westerns," as do markets in Indonesia, although officials there regard the genre as "potentially dangerous propaganda for their own minority groups" (*The Western*, 320–321). Fenin and Everson point out that with the U.S. juvenile market split after World War II because of television, the single largest market for film westerns was African Americans in major urban centers such as New York and Chicago and throughout the South (320); JoEllen Shively discusses the popularity of the western and John Wayne among many Native Americans ("Cowboys and Indians"). Studies by both Burns and Ambler have documented the intense popularity of the western in Central Africa in the 1940s and 1950s and the subsequent efforts of nervous British officials to understand and regulate the tastes of African filmgoers. As Burns puts it, "American westerns (referred to locally as 'cowboy' movies) became the most popular films and were so widely shown that, by the end of the Second World War, for many African moviegoers the 'cowboy' and the cinema had become synonymous" ("Wayne on the Zambezi," 103). Furthermore, Bloom notes that "American westerns were an international sensation" in France and French colonies in North Africa between the world wars, arguing that the western trope of the "good badman" was "interpreted against the grain of civil authority by audiences in French North Africa" ("Beyond the Western Frontier," 199, 205).[11]

Given its immense international appeal and the incorporation of its narratives and imagery into different national cinemas, the western as a generic form is clearly about more than narratives of U.S. national identity. The appeal of the genre to such diverse groups—booming mining cities in Northern Rhodesia, youth in the UK, black urban audiences in the United States—suggests that at stake in the spectacles of the western frontier is far more than the limited concerns of white Americans celebrating their past. Instead, the western genre provides a vibrant and sensational depiction of violence and mobility amid the open spaces of a frontier whose pleasures resonate powerfully to diverse international audiences.

The global appeal of John Wayne in the John Ford western is intertwined with the genre's depiction of a dynamic and complex space being transformed by modernity. Just as international migration in the 1950s was only one part of a larger process of modernization and global capitalism (it was facilitated by new technologies of transportation and the international flexibility of capital accumulation), the frontier community at the heart of Ford's films is only one of many examples of modernity that unevenly structure the spaces of the cinematic frontier. The communities in Cavalry Trilogy explore the new social possibilities allowed by movement, mobility, and the masculine violence necessary to make accessible the spaces of the frontier, but those social possibilities are intertwined with the uneven impact of modernity on the landscape of the frontier, exemplified by the railroad, the stagecoach, the telegraph, and the presence of the military, with its regulations and nationalist mission. As the language of wilderness versus civilization in much of the criticism of the western suggests, the frontier spaces within which Ford's modern communities develop are marked by a fundamental give-and-take between the open spaces of the landscape and the arrival of modern technology and social structures. The heterogeneous communities envisioned in Ford's films are both a result of this give-and-take—the creation of new social and spatial relations away from the biases of the East Coast—and also another element of civilization encroaching on the frontier.[12]

Thus the much-analyzed landscape of the western does not simply provide a spatial metaphor for the progression of modernity across the landscape but also produces the spaces and sensations (both pleasurable and fraught with tension) of an uneven modernization, a landscape defined by the spatial dynamics of modernity. Examine, for example, the role of the western in the Rhodesian mining cities, as analyzed by Charles Ambler. Ambler discusses the pervasiveness of the U.S. western in the Copperbelt region of Rhodesia, specifically the residential compounds built by the mining companies to house workers who had migrated from rural regions in search of work. For those audiences, the westerns presented cinematic experiences that were essential for adapting to modern, urban existence. "To the young women and men who flocked to film shows on the Copperbelt, the often disjointed and exotic images of the 'Wild West' that Hollywood films conveyed comprised a crucial repertoire of images through which to engage notions of modernity—a vital concern for residents of this industrial frontier" ("Popular Films," 136). The images, iconography, and characters of Hollywood westerns were accepted as components of modernity and urban existence, providing a style that "could be drawn on to define and navigate modern, urban life" (146).

Thus, as audience members we are not waiting for the intriguing spatial dynamics of an uneven modernity to disappear into a thoroughly modernized present. We do not look to the western, as Tompkins claims, for "escape from the conditions of life in modern industrial society: from a mechanized existence, economic dead ends, social entanglements, unhappy personal relations, political injustice" (*West of Everything*, 4). Instead, the images and narratives of the genre are compelling because they dramatize the same kinds of unevenness and spatial transformations that make up so much of modern life: the dynamics of mobility and the creation of communities out of people from diverse backgrounds, the sensations of mobility and traversing space (whether crossing borders or navigating the urban landscape), integrating oneself into the structures of organizations, communities, or professions that stretch across geographic space. In essence, the western provides the sensations of what it means to be modern within the spatial relations of a modernity that is always experienced as uneven, jagged, and incomplete.

It should be no surprise, then, that John Wayne functions as the exemplary western hero. Wayne's persona, not only in the Cavalry Trilogy but also across his career in the fifties, explored what it means to be a mobile man within dynamic, competitive spaces being transformed by modernity. I explore these issues in more detail in Chapter 4, but in Wayne's navigations of both space and the social relations of the cinematic frontier, his masculinity became intertwined with the spatial structures of Hollywood's vision of the West as it explored masculine individualism and the labor of one's body while negotiating one's relationship with the new communities and professional duties of mobility and migration. In a world in which the transformation of space produces new and utopian possibilities along with harsh economic and cultural realities, John Ford helped construct, through Wayne, a model of modern masculine subjectivity able to navigate the pleasures and tensions of a modern, spatially complex world.

CHAPTER THREE

John Wayne's Cold War

MASS TOURISM AND THE
ANTICOMMUNIST CRUSADE

T HE SOVIET PREMIER JOSEPH STALIN, IN THE FINAL, unstable years of his life, decreed that John Wayne had to die. According to the film historian and celebrity biographer Michael Munn, John Wayne was so associated with anticommunism that several attempts on Wayne's life were undertaken by different communist organizations, including one supposedly orchestrated by Stalin himself (*John Wayne*, 125–128). By serving as president of the Motion Picture Alliance for the Preservation of American Ideals from 1949 through 1953 and participating actively in the House Un-American Activities Committee (HUAC) investigation into communists in Hollywood, Wayne was the public face of Hollywood's anticommunism in the most intensive years of the Red Scare of the early 1950s. So in 1951, acting on Stalin's orders, two Soviet hit men posing as FBI agents showed up at his office in Hollywood, seeking access to Wayne, but the real FBI, having already learned of the assassination attempt, arrested the men. Luckily for Wayne, Stalin's successor, Nikita Khrushchev, was a huge fan of the actor's and rescinded the order to have Wayne killed. In 1955 (according to Wayne himself, as reported to Munn) a group of Burbank communists began organizing a plot to kill John Wayne, but were run out of town by stuntmen friends of Wayne's. According to Wayne's own accounts, his anticommunism made him a target of a vast, organized communist conspiracy to end his efforts to rid Hollywood of communists.[1]

While it is easy to associate Wayne with strident McCarthyism because of his role in Hollywood's communist witch hunts, both of his anticommunist projects of the 1950s explore a much more complex set of justifications for fighting communism, melodramatically using the threat of domestic infiltration while simultaneously invoking the kinds of international capitalism and consumerism that modernization, development, and international trade hoped to produce. Because of Wayne's political activism in the early 1950s, he made several propagandistic anticommunist films that crusaded against supposedly despicable and treacherous communists, be they hidden communist cells in the United States or Soviet military agents seeking tactical knowledge of the U.S. military: *Big Jim McLain* (1952) and *Jet Pilot* (shot between 1949 and 1953 but not released until 1957). But rather than functioning as straightforward mouthpieces for McCarthyism (although both do just that at times), the films attempt to balance a heightened and defensive sense of U.S. national identity and jingoism with the emerging internationalism of the period. Although pet projects of Wayne's, both films were the products of a Hollywood studio system highly invested not just in U.S. global power but also in the creation and maintenance of international, capitalist markets for their products.

Echoing the common anticommunist conspiracy theories of the day, both films concern themselves with the idea of infiltration and of the United States being under attack from within (the key rhetorical claim that helped McCarthy rise to power over other anticommunist politicians). Each film constructs communism as an evil threat to the inherent goodness of the United States, valorizing the heroism and sacrifice of members of the U.S. military while railing against a perceived, vast communist conspiracy against freedom and America. Both films thus conformed to the dominant American anticommunist ideology of the period. As Bonnie Jefferson outlines it, in the 1950s several themes characterized American ideas about communism:

- Communism was monolithic.
- Communism sought world domination.
- Communists were barbaric.
- Communists sought to destroy the family, the church, and all personal freedoms.
- Communism was a direct threat to the United States and its democratic institutions and would target these institutions from the inside; carefully placed spies would destroy important institutions of freedom before we could realize what had happened. ("Wayne: American Icon," 32)

Marked by a simplified good-evil logic and a fear of "outsiders" contaminating national values and institutions, the beliefs permeate Wayne's anticommunist films of the early 1950s. Often relying on lengthy anticommunist sermons built into the dialogue, the films create a vision of the world in which the United States not only is under siege by communism but also has already been secretly invaded by communists and communist sympathizers.

While *Big Jim McLain* and *Jet Pilot* explore nationalist fears of infiltration indicative of McCarthyism, the films' anticommunism cannot be reduced to a sense of domestic anxiety. Both films negotiate a position in between the international isolationism of conservatives in the United States and the liberal anticommunism of U.S. foreign-policy makers, who saw international modernization and development, international trade, and U.S. military intervention abroad as the key weapons against the spread of communism. As part of the economically liberal anticommunism pervading U.S. foreign policy in the years after World War II, the United States helped create the United Nations, the International Monetary Fund, and the World Bank, liberal institutions designed to promote the globalization of capitalism and consumerism in the international battle against communism. The implementation of that foreign policy set the stage for McCarthy, who advocated instead for isolationism; he accused Truman's State Department (along with a host of other U.S. institutions, such as Hollywood) of being riddled with communists who were assisting a vast international conspiracy against the United States. From that perspective, the kinds of international interdependence facilitated by the UN, along with a vision of global capitalism, weakened the United States in it stand against infiltration by domestic communists. Those competing discourses defined U.S. anticommunism throughout the 1950s, with many anticommunist positions embracing elements of each perspective.

Attempting to balance the divergent anticommunist perspectives, both films position the pleasures and experiences of tourism as essential to the anticommunist effort: Wayne hunts for communist agents amid the resorts of Hawaii in *Big Jim McLain*, and attempts to win over and woo a female communist agent poolside in Palm Springs in *Jet Pilot*. Each film explores in detail the sights, sounds, and experiences of a modern, capitalist vacation, suggesting that the kinds of mobility and consumption at the heart of mass tourism is a key battleground in the world's fight against communism. Both films dramatize the massive increase in international tourism that began in the 1950s and was a key component of globalization and the spread of global capitalism. In the postwar decades, the numbers of international tourists grew exponentially. In 1948 there were 14 million international tourists; by 1955 that number had grown to 46 million; and by 1965 there were 144 million (Shaw and Williams, *Issues in Tourism*, 30). Sparked by the postwar economic boom, the reorganization of labor and leisure due to development policies around the world, and the increase in business tourism as capitalism globalized intensively in the 1950s, the number of people seeking out the kinds of mass tourism experiences and activities on display in films like *Big Jim McLain* and *Jet Pilot* skyrocketed.

The growth in tourism was tied to the globalization of the world economy that liberal anticommunists promoted. The globalization of the world economy and political relations made the growth in international tourism possible. Specific factors included advances in transportation technology such as air travel (which developed largely thanks to technological advances in World War II), political policies that made border crossings easier (for people, money, and goods), and the increased amount of leisure and consumption time structured into work schedules. As Shaw and Williams put it, tourism "is one of the most powerful exemplars of globalization" (27). Yet tourism itself is a powerful force in the globalization of the economy, encouraging the flow of people, goods, and money across national borders and spreading the beliefs and ideologies of capitalist consumption: "Tourism involves more than just the flows of people, or even economic transfers; it also implies transfers of consumption patterns, values, and lifestyles across international boundaries" (29). The spread of mass tourism was both a result of and an important impetus for the globalization of Western capitalism.

Wayne's anticommunist films attempt to cinematically re-create and promote the pleasures and experiences of tourism as Wayne's body inhabits different modern, tourist spaces: beachfront resorts, modern hotel rooms, sunny pools. According to the films, tourism and the kinds of consumption it encourages are powerful weapons in the rhetorical battle against communism, as well as practices that need to be protected. There is thus a tension in the films' logic between the intensely nationalist rhetoric of the U.S. anticommunist crusade and the celebratory emphasis on international mobility within tourism. On a discursive, didactic level, both films conform to the dominant argument within the United States against communism by focusing on national borders and the threat of infiltration—ideologies that were often associated with Wayne's anticommunist beliefs—but in the images and ideas invoked on a more visceral and experiential level, the films promote the mobility and consumption of modern, global capitalism. Wayne's cinematic Cold War, in other words, offers an international and cosmopolitan argument against the dangers of communism by celebrating the modern, consumerist, and romantic pleasures of tourism and travel.

BIG JIM MCLAIN

Produced by Wayne's production company with his partner Robert Fellows, *Big Jim McLain* is a good example of the economic benefits earned by Wayne as he cultivated his image as an anticommunist leader. A highly propagandistic film, *Big Jim McLain* would likely not have been financed and produced if not for the industry's desire to publicly demonstrate its disdain for communism, a desire that was at times ideological but also reflected the economic necessity of supporting popular anticommunist sentiments (Jefferson,

"Wayne: American Icon"). Wayne plays Jim McLain, an investigator for HUAC who tracks and prosecutes communists in the United States. Although frustrated by communists hiding behind the Fifth Amendment when called before the committee, McLain continues his work with his partner, Mal Baxter (James Arness), a Korean War veteran who hates "commies" with a passion. Sent to Hawaii to look into a suspected communist cell, the HUAC officers work with a veritable roll call of good, hardworking Americans helping with the cause, from the Chinese American Honolulu police chief to formerly communist labor bosses who work to ferret out communists and communist sympathizers within their ranks. As his investigation leads him to an underground cell seeking to close off shipping to and from Hawaii, thereby instigating a communist revolution, McLain meets and falls in love with a young war widow who joins him in his hatred for communists and accompanies him in his investigation. As they get closer to the communists, Mal is eventually captured and killed by the communists, but McLain wiretaps an important meeting and arrests the cell's leadership. The communists are eventually called before HUAC, but go free because they invoke their Fifth Amendment rights (apparently, in the legal world of the film, "taking the Fifth" allows anyone to avoid prosecution for any and all crimes, no matter how strong the evidence).

To say that the film's anticommunism is hyperbolic is an understatement. In the world of the film, communism is not a political belief but a vast, centralized conspiracy bent on world domination that answers directly to Moscow. All communists are "Kremlin agents" seeking to undermine the American way of life in any way possible. What is more, any communists who have been exposed by the press are mere "window dressing," whereas the real leaders and important members are underground; one never really knows who could be a "commie" (indeed, one of the up-and-coming anticommunist union leaders ends up being a communist himself). The sinister nature of the party is reported on by former communists who have left the party, describing it as a "vast conspiracy to enslave the common man." In fact, one former communist agent feels so guilty about her participation in communism's "crimes against humanity" that she exiles herself as a nurse at the leper colony on Molokai.

The communists portrayed in the film are a series of ridiculous, fearmongering stereotypes. Sturak (Alan Napier), the high-ranking Communist Party official visiting the Hawaiian cell, is thin and slightly effeminate, an elitist intellectual who treats the local cell condescendingly (and has a sinister-looking mustache to boot). The local communists, on the other hand, are "pudgy and have a slovenly appearance" (Jefferson, "Wayne: American Icon," 34), their corrupt morals tied to a body type that is constructed as unhealthy and dirty. Loyalty means nothing to the communists: when members express doubt or guilt over their actions (as many inevitably do, given the horrendous deeds they commit), they are dealt with harshly by the party leadership. One cell member, Namaka, feels excessively guilty after he sabotages a ship and inadvertently kills a childhood friend, so Sturak orders an underling to have Namaka committed to a mental institution, where he is administered a fatal dose of drugs before he can give McLain any information. Moreover, McLain's love interest, Nancy (Nancy Olson), who has been unknowingly working for a suspected communist agent, describes her boss as having "a neuter as a personality," a kind of sociopath who has no emotion and is incapable of inspiring any emotion in others. Invoking a host of typical and superficial stereotypes about communism during the McCarthy years, the film constructs communism and communists as pure evil, a kind of cult capable of infecting people with villainous beliefs.

The film goes out of its way to invoke hyperpatriotic images of national identity and national security in its indictment of communism, not so subtly constructing communism as a threat to the very existence of the United States and the inherently good values that the nation represents. The film opens, in fact, by retelling the opening of Steven Vincent Benét's short story "The Devil and Daniel Webster," which claims that if you call out to Daniel Webster (the nationalist American politician who worked to bolster the authority of the federal government in the 1830s through the 1850s) at his grave on a stormy night, Webster will call back to you, "Neighbor, how stands the union?" The image of the windswept tree looking over Webster's grave then dissolves to an image of the Capitol in Washington, D.C., where a HUAC hearing is taking place. The national mythology of Daniel Webster as an icon of U.S. solidarity is blended into the McCarthy-era investigations, linking anticommunism with the maintenance and existence of the United States as a nation. Not surprisingly, then, the film includes other heavy-handed nationalist imagery, including a scene in which McLain and his partner visit the memorial at the site of the sunken USS *Arizona* in Pearl Harbor. While a military band plays a somber march in the background, McLain, in voice-over, delivers a eulogy for the fallen sailors and their sacrifice. *Big Jim McLain* even ends with newly trained marines hopping on ships as their names are called out, celebrating the soldiers and their sacrifice in a scene that invokes many World War II propaganda films.

Although the film's opening and closing use excessively nationalist spaces and images — Webster's New England grave, the Capitol dome, a congressional hearing, a navy ship with men marching onboard — the bulk of film takes place in and constructs a very different set of spaces — swanky Hawaiian beachfront hotels, restaurants, nightclubs, and other tourist and leisure spaces. Indeed, given the film's excessive concern with national identity, national security, and national pride, setting the investigation in Hawaii — at the time, a U.S. territory and not a state — at first seems a strange choice. But the film's use of Hawaii as a space and an idea makes perfect sense within *Big Jim McLain*'s appeal to the importance of tourism and consumerism in the ideological battle against communism. While the film explicitly uses a rhetoric of nationalism and possible contamination from abroad to frame the threat of communism, the visual spectacles of Hawaii and Hawaiian tourism implicitly promote an ideology of cosmopolitan travel, leisure, and consumption as the real spaces that need to be saved from the taint of communism.

Hawaii, after all, is a rather complex cultural space marked by a racially and ethnically heterogeneous population and a long history of U.S. and European imperialism. Shortly after the Europeans arrived at the island chain and began establishing ports, immigrants started arriving in Hawaii, including not only white Europeans and Americans but also large numbers of Japanese, Filipinos, and Chinese. Although the history of Hawaii's government since the 1890s, when the native government was overthrown and the United States annexed the islands as a territory, has most often reflected the interests of white American settlers, by the 1900s the islands were predominantly inhabited by Asian Americans, as they are today. At the time *Big Jim McLain* was filmed there, the political power of white plantation owners was beginning to crumble as the population of Asian descent grew. The complexities of Hawaii's history and culture are often occluded by its tourist economy and the construction of the islands as exotic spaces of relaxation and adventure.[2]

Big Jim McLain participates in the erasure of this history in favor of exotic and sexualized images of an island paradise, but the film attempts to incorporate a broader view of Hawaii. The film makes several references to the large Japanese population of the islands, including scenes filmed at a Shinto temple and the inclusion of a racially diverse Honolulu police force. In fact, Dan Liu, Chinese American chief of the Honolulu police department, played himself in a large role in the film. The use of Hawaii in the film can be seen as serving a double purpose: as the site of U.S. military operations, the islands can function as a space of national pride and heroism, but as a diverse, occupied territory, Hawaii might act as a metaphor for developing-world spaces that need to be protected from the supposed global expansion of communism as conceived by U.S. foreign policy in this period.

Nevertheless, much of the film feels like an advertisement produced by the Hawaiian tourism board. The film wallows in the spectacle of pristine beaches, elaborate resorts, and fine dining, with the native inhabitants reduced to roles as exotic decorations or entertainers performing in grass skirts. From the time McLain and his partner walk off the airplane and are given leis by a sexualized, grass-skirted welcoming ensemble (one of whom is happily kissed on the mouth by McLain's partner), the film makes clear the pleasures of visiting Hawaii and enjoying its beaches and resorts. Especially as McLain woos Nancy and eventually proposes to her, his time in Hawaii is constructed as one stunning ad-

FIGURE 3.1. *Jim McLain (John Wayne) and Nancy (Nancy Olson) enjoying the pleasures of Hawaiian tourism in* Big Jim McLain *(Wayne-Fellows Productions, 1952).*

venture after another on the island. They go sailing, ride the surf in canoes, go hiking up to spectacular vistas, and dance into the night at local nightclubs.

Moreover, the film showcases the resort spaces of the islands, including the cushy hotel room McLain occupies, with its tall ceilings and book-lined walls, and outdoor restaurants with live entertainment provided by the locals. Those scenes showcase the modern architecture and design of the resorts—even scenes in which Wayne confronts the communists at their secret meeting makes a spectacle of the sleek, modern beachfront home where the meeting takes place.

Tourism, then, is constructed in *Big Jim McLain* as vital to the anticommunist project. The overlapping of HUAC investigations and consumer-driven tourism in the film illustrates the centrality of mobility and a capitalist vision of recreation to anticommunist rhetoric. Despite the film's highly nationalist moralizing rhetoric, the film is less about the importance of U.S. strength in the face of a nefarious threat and more about keeping open and free the routes of global capitalism that allow the privileged and mobile classes to enjoy "exotic" spaces such as Hawaii. So while, on a superficial, narrative level, the film focuses on protecting national borders and national identity, the kinds of spectacles and experiences in the visual pleasure of the film emphasize protecting tourism as a form of global capitalism from the taint of communism. In short, as the film seems to argue, the triumph of communism would mean the end of people enjoying the surf on Hawaiian beaches.

JET PILOT

While *Big Jim McLain* addresses the supposed threat of communist infiltrators, *Jet Pilot* tackles U.S.-Russian military relations and the arms race, specifically aviation technologies. Produced by Howard Hughes as an attempt to showcase advanced American jet technologies, the film was shot in between 1949 and 1953, in the early years of Wayne's superstardom, but Hughes insisted on tweaking and perfecting the film for years, delaying its release until 1957. By that time, jet technology was no longer a new spectacle for U.S. audiences, and like *Big Jim McLain*, the film was a commercial and critical flop.

Jet Pilot focuses on an international espionage and romance narrative. Wayne plays Colonel Shannon, a top U.S. Air Force pilot stationed in Alaska (like Hawaii, one of the last two territories to become a state, suggesting the imperial reach of the U.S. military). One day, radar picks up a rogue Soviet plane entering U.S. airspace. The air force escorts the plane to its base, only to find that it is piloted by a sexy Russian officer, Anna (Janet Leigh). Anna claims that she is fleeing the USSR to avoid being shot for disobeying an order, so the air force orders Shannon to spend time with her, take her flying, and try to learn anything he can about the Soviet air force. After weeks of flying and vacationing in Palm Springs, Shannon falls in love with Anna and elopes with her, only to find out that she is actually a Russian spy named Olga who has been attempting to send information back to the Soviets. Sickened but still in love, Shannon tricks Anna/Olga into thinking that he would like to escape to the USSR with her, but in reality he is now spying on the Soviets for the United States. Eventually, Anna/Olga realizes her love not only for Shannon but also for the pleasures of life in the United States, where the two return and live happily ever after.

Rather than emphasizing the strict good-evil logic at the heart of *Big Jim McLain*'s anticommunist crusade, *Jet Pilot* instead argues that communism cannot compete with the material, consumerist pleasures of capitalism. The film dramatizes the appeal of consumerism to Anna during her time in the United States, making a highly gendered appeal to her desire for fancy clothes and nights out at swanky restaurants in Palm Springs. In one scene, Shannon and Anna discuss their political revulsion and simultaneous sexual desire for each other, all while shopping for new clothes in a posh Palm Springs women's clothing store. As they flirt with each other while calling each other's politics "revolting," they weave in between mannequins dressed in elaborate and colorful outfits while Anna wears a stylish and modern swimsuit.

As the scene implies, their eventual surrender to their physical desires despite their political differences foreshadows Anna's eventual surrender to the material and consumerist pleasures of capitalism, which she admits has certain "dangerous advantages" over communism. Indicating how capitalism and patriarchy are completely intertwined, the scene showcases both the presumed pleasures of women in shopping for clothing that will make them alluring and the sexual pleasures of men looking at women in fashionable and revealing clothing. As the film's logic suggests, how can communism compete with a beautiful woman in a modern and colorful swimsuit? And why would a woman not want to make a spectacle of herself for the sexual gaze of a man like John Wayne?

Interestingly, it is not the sexual pleasure of Anna's body that becomes the focal point of capitalism's triumph in the film. Instead, the final scene of the film makes it clear that the consumerist pleasures central to Anna's conversion are the appeal of John Wayne's body and a good steak. After Anna and Shannon fight off Soviet fighters and make it back safely to the United States, the scene dissolves to the couple sitting in a Palm Springs hotel, digging into a juicy steak, and exchanging romantic kisses. The romantic and sexual appeal of Wayne's body, along with the visceral delight of a sizzling, American steak (both of which were objects of international trade in the 1950s), brought Anna to embrace and consume (literally) the benefits of capitalism.

The importance of the steak was foreshadowed earlier in the film when they first enjoy a meal in Palm Springs. As the couple is about to share a passionate kiss on a moonlit balcony, Anna stops herself and is pulled away by the smell of steak on a skillet (again, romance and eating steak are strangely linked). Thinking that the whole restaurant would share the one steak, Anna is shocked to see that everyone gets his or her own, immediately declaring that the Cold War is hopeless for the Soviets, for no one could compete with the savory sensations of a good steak on every plate. Just as with Anna in a swimsuit, the appeal of capitalism is structured as visceral and embodied rather than merely ideological and theoretical: consumerism promises sexual allure and gastronomical delights.

That Wayne's character is so explicitly linked to a delicious steak illustrates that Wayne's body is the real object of desire in the film, the body that is able to convert the communists to democracy through its rugged appeal. Given Wayne's status as a global star whose body was, in fact, consumed by audiences around the world, the film links the pleasures of capitalism to the pleasures of watching Wayne. That Anna chooses capitalism partly because of the appeal of Wayne's body might playfully suggest that international audiences will choose capitalism over communism because of the spectacle of Wayne in action on the big screen, a product of global capitalism and international trade. In short, one of the promises of capitalism both for Anna and for global audiences is the pleasure of seeing Wayne's body performing feats of action and heroism.

Through the film's emphasis on eating steaks at good restaurants, shopping at swanky stores, and staying at hotels with swimming pools, *Jet Pilot* reveals the centrality of tourism to the film's anticommunist rhetoric. While Hughes may have conceived the film as a showcase for U.S. aviation, the real spectacles of the film are the colors, textures, and sensations of a vacation in Palm Springs with John Wayne. In its attempts to showcase the pleasure and abundance of everyday life within capitalism, the film focuses almost entirely on the pleasures of tourism and leisure, from sunny scenes alongside a swimming pool to an assortment of liquor options as the couple dances into the night. Within the film's propagandistic vision of the U.S. standard of living, life is a never-ending vacation in the sun.

Life in the United States, of course, seems even more spectacular compared with the stereotypical construction of life in the USSR as witnessed by Shannon. When he goes back to Russia with Anna as a double agent, the spaces of the "communist paradise" are constructed as run-down, dirty, utilitarian, and often archaic. All the buildings are square wooden structures in shades of grey, brown, or olive green. The roads are muddy, and it always seems to be overcast. Shannon's quarters are much the same, with sparse wood walls, little space, and no comfort. In short, the space is constructed to convey a simplified set of assumptions about life within communism: it is uncomfortable and dreary.

But rather than contrasting Soviet spaces with the spaces of everyday life in the United States—for example, a suburban home or a corporate office—*Jet Pilot* uses instead the spaces of tourism. In fact, the space of a posh Palm Springs hotel room is directly compared with the living spaces under communism as Anna marvels at the size and design of the hotel room (although, while nice, she finds the use of space wasteful and invites two other couples to share the room with her and Shannon). The hotel room is a textbook example of modern design and style from the early 1950s, including its split-level layout and its green and blue décor. Sleek and roomy, it offers all the modern amenities, from a fireplace to multiple bedrooms.

Just as with the visceral appeal of a delicious steak, the film relies on the experiential appeal of capitalism through the hotel room, a stylish and modern sensation created through the construction of space. The design of the room, after all, invokes a sense of modern design and architecture that became quickly globalized in the 1950s as the standard look of modern housing and leisure around the world (King, *Spaces of Global Cultures*). The room represents a kind of modern, global style used around the world to signify wealth, comfort, and good taste, not only in rapidly globalizing hotel chains such as Hilton but also

FIGURE 3.2. *The sleek, modern hotel room of Colonel Shannon (John Wayne) and Anna (Janet Leigh) in Palm Springs in* Jet Pilot *(RKO, 1957).*

in the design and décor of new homes. The space of the hotel room inspires the sensations of modernity and affluence, mirroring the ways that space was constructed in different parts of the world and building the association between its sleek design and the feeling of modern subjectivity.

So while *Big Jim McLain* structures communism as a threat to the kinds of pleasures and experiences of tourism, *Jet Pilot* instead posits tourism and modern leisure as the antidote to communism, offering the pleasures of shopping and tourism as the alternative to the drab world of Soviet life.

ROMANCE, TOURISM, AND POLITICAL IDENTITY

As the appeal of Wayne's body as a romantic spectacle suggests, romance is central in both films to the articulation of the pleasures of tourism and the fight against communism, despite the fact that Wayne's star persona in the period was most often distant from structures of romance and family. As discussed in Chapter 1, Wayne's most popular and resonant roles in the 1950s put his character at odds with women and family as he set aside his romantic and familial duties in order to pursue grand masculine adventures. And yet in both of these films, romance is not only compatible with Wayne's goals but also foundational to them. In *Big Jim McLain*, Nancy almost becomes McLain's assistant during his investigation, going over clues and leads in the hotel room and even accompanying McLain to the bust of the communist ring. And in *Jet Pilot,* converting Anna to capitalism and wooing her are essentially the same project, linking the development of a healthy relationship with the fight against communism. So why is it that when Wayne is winning World War II or establishing a vast cattle empire or making the western frontier safe for settlers, most often women are only hindrances to such masculine labor, but when the world needs to be made safe from communism, women and romance are so important?

In part, the centrality of romance to Wayne's anticommunist masculinity stems from the increasing importance of the married couple as the ideal tourist demographic in the period, particularly in the ways that tourism and the honeymoon became intertwined in the postwar years. As Bulcroff and his coauthors point out in their history of the modern honeymoon, the 1950s was an important moment in the rise in a travel-based honeymoon vacation. In part because of economic prosperity in the United States and elsewhere, and in part because of increasing social pressures in the United States to marry and start a family at a younger age, the 1950s saw a popularization of the honeymoon as a social ritual and a source of tourist revenue. Tourist destinations such as Niagara Falls, the Poconos, and Hawaii began to construct themselves more heavily as ideal honeymoon locations and businesses began offering crafted honeymoon packages (Bulcroff et al., "North American Honeymoon," 470, 476, 478). The newly married couple became an important economic factor in tourism in the period as well as a resonant symbol of the tourism industry, suggesting that the pleasures of tourism as the antidote to communism were increasingly linked to the pleasures of heterosexual romance and the family.

Wayne's somewhat cosmopolitan tourist masculinity in his anticommunist films finds a way to bridge the dichotomy of romantic settling versus adventurous wandering by integrating domesticity into his mobile adventures. Wayne's on-screen persona so often eschews the entanglements of women and romance because domesticity and family life, while culturally important, are at odds with the homosocial spheres of action that his films celebrate as integral to national security and empire building. But a tourist masculinity can live out the exciting adventurism of mobility and exploration while also maintaining domestic connections by bringing his wife along and staying in international hotel chains that offer a consumerist vision of "home." Thus in *Big Jim McLain* and *Jet Pilot*, Wayne's love interests are successfully integrated into his masculine adventures, either by aiding McLain's investigations or jetting around to U.S. tourist spots such as Palm Springs or Yuma, Arizona. Importantly, neither film envisions any kind of domestic space for the couples to inhabit — presumably, Nancy will continue to travel around with McLain in his anticommunist investigations, while Anna and Shannon will fly together in a highly nomadic lifestyle. Just as in films such as *Rio Grande* or *Rio Bravo*, the couple's union can occur only if they avoid the problem of a domestic "home" and prefer instead to reproduce the spatial dynamics of tourism: masculine, mobile adventures blended with simulated domesticity.

The emphasis on romance in the films reflects also the centrality of marriage to ideologies of nationalism and imperialism. Issues of romance and the related issues of intimacy, sexuality, and marriage are commonly assumed to be private, based on the personal and emotional decisions of individuals, often in the supposedly private spheres of the home or bedroom. But these seemingly intensely private concerns are often very public and often form the foundation of cultural ideas about gender, race, and citizenship. Noting how the discourses of public and private obscure the connections between intimacy and the functioning of social institutions, Lauren Berlant argues that intimacy can be seen as "a public mode of identification and self-development" in which emotional and affective attachments between individuals become implicated in the ideological structures of social institutions, while feminist and other challenges to those dominant ideologies are constructed as challenges to the culturally accepted narratives about intimacy and pleasure ("Intimacy," 3, 7). Nancy Cott in *Public Vows*, her history of marriage and nationalism in the United States, points out that the institution of marriage, while based in modern societies on an ideal of romantic love, is an essential component in defining one's citizenship and affirming cultural definitions of gender, sexuality, and race.

Thus, the primacy of marriage in *Big Jim McLain* and *Jet Pilot* is connected to the films' concern with nationalism and political identity. In the context of the Cold War and the need to prove one's loyalty to the nation, the image and ideology of a "wholesome" marriage serves as a reminder of Wayne's nationalism. Plus, as Steven Cohan points out in *Masked Men*, preserving an image of a "normal" nuclear family in the 1950s was often a key way of signifying a "normal" (that is, American, capitalist) identity, so making sure that Wayne's characters embody the normative ideal was deeply tied to the anticommunist crusade.

The images of Wayne romancing young women in various tourist spaces in both films, therefore, suggests not only the centrality of romance to the promotion of international tourism but also the centrality of the married couple to constructions of U.S. national identity. The images and ideologies of the heterosexual couple in these films affirm the pleasures and sensations of tourism and tourist consumption, constructing both marriage and tourism as key sites under threat from the communist menace. So while the rejection of women in Wayne's typical films facilitates the mobile wandering of the male hero, sensationalizing the mobility of the male body within global capitalism, in Wayne's cinematic Cold War, embracing women and romance becomes an important means of affirming the inherent goodness of tourist mobility.

CHAPTER FOUR

John Wayne's Body

TECHNICOLOR AND 3-D ANXIETIES
IN HONDO AND THE SEARCHERS

*I*N THE MIDDLE OF *HONDO*, WAYNE'S CHARACTER EN-gages in a ritualized knife fight with an Apache warrior on a cliff overlooking the expanses of the southwestern desert. Exploiting the visual pleasures of the film's 3-D and Warnercolor technologies, the scene displays colorfully costumed bodies rhythmically confronting each other and rolling across the dusty precipice, as well as close-ups of knives thrusting straight toward the camera.[1] In this way, the scene clearly signifies a particular vision of the white male body: able, kinetic, efficient, and ultimately superior to the raced body of its Native American opponent. Using the new technologies of an increasingly global Hollywood to fetishize both the physical labor of the male body engaged in brutal yet graceful action and the open, competitive spaces of the western frontier that necessitates such violence, *Hondo* projects across national borders a vision of hardened, physical, and mobile masculinity. Exemplifying Wayne's star text in the fifties, the scene revels in the nimble agility of Wayne's large frame performing acts of raced violence while using color and 3-D technologies to construct a sense of borderlessness that is, like the cliff Wayne battles on, spectacular and rife with possibility, but also dangerous and precipitous.

The colorful, vibrant, and tense confrontation between the two bodies, therefore, offers a particular set of sensations about male bodies, movement, violence, and the open spaces of the frontier. The 3-D scene seeks to viscerally and bodily engage the audience of such spectacles, to make them jump and experience the textures and tensions of the world on the screen. The scene offers a sweaty and intense set of feelings and sensibilities about male bodies engaged in a kind of intimate violence, an immersion into the conflict itself as the bodies reach out toward the audience. Moreover, the sweaty display of Wayne's body hard at work in intense competition provides a sense of labor, toil, and mobility that mirrors the sensations of men's labor within capitalism. The scene not only

FIGURE 4.1. *Wayne defeating his Apache foe as Vittorio, the Apache chief, looks on in admiration in* Hondo *(Batjac/Warner Bros., 1953).*

evokes a sense of power and dominance through identification with Wayne's body, but also creates feelings of labor and exhaustion, the sensations of competition and exertion. At the same time, the images of bodies moving quickly on a cliff overlooking an expansive space offer a sense of mobility and freedom, even if such freedom means navigating violent confrontations. So at a historical moment when the spread of global capitalism and modernization were radically altering the scale and scope of labor and identity around the world, the spectacle of Wayne as evidenced in this scene provided not just an image but a set of sensational fantasies about how the male body survives and labors in a borderless and exploitative world.

The scene expresses and negotiates the dualities and contradictions of labor within global capitalism, reflecting the brutal physical competition of the global labor market while offering a fantasy of physicality for those whose labor was becoming increasingly white collar. *Hondo* exalts the mobility and movement of the white male body in space while expressing the dangerous and violent realities of mobility inherent in labor migrations. Wayne's vision of masculinity here explores the gendered tensions of a system of global capitalism of which the United States is only one part, indicating the centrality of John Wayne's body to the articulation of a modern masculinity in the midst of global capitalism.

This chapter explores the significance and resonance of John Wayne's body within the shifting constructions of a globalizing masculinity in the 1950s. Using Wayne's two mid-decade hits, *Hondo* (1953) and *The Searchers* (1956), I demonstrate here how Wayne's body dramatized and sensationalized the changing values of masculinity and labor, offering a powerful, embodied fantasy of a modern male identity within global capitalism. In particular, Wayne's body expressed the emerging importance of enduring wage labor and the centrality of mobility to constructions of masculinity around the world in this period.

Hondo and *The Searchers* prove significant in this respect. Both films explicitly dramatize a series of tensions surrounding labor, movement, gender, and race. *Hondo*, for example, tells the story of Hondo Lane, a freelance scout for the U.S. cavalry on the Southwest frontier, who wanders out of the wilderness one day into a homestead occupied by Angie Lowe (Geraldine Page) and her son Johnny (Lee Aaker). Mrs. Lowe tells Hondo that her husband is simply out for the day, but it is clear to Hondo that he has been gone for some time, leaving Mrs. Lowe in the rundown homestead amid an Apache uprising. After Hondo helps with the daily chores on the homestead and shares a few moments of sexual tension with Mrs. Lowe, he borrows a horse and continues on his way. After he checks back in at the nearest town, a bitter local drunk tries to ambush and rob him in the desert. Hondo is quicker on the draw, kills the man, only to discover that it is Mr. Lowe. Meanwhile, Mrs. Lowe and her son earn the respect of the Apache chief Vittorio, who makes Johnny a member of the tribe. When the Apache later capture Hondo, they mistake him for Mr. Lowe; instead of killing him, they take him back to Mrs. Lowe because Johnny needs a father to teach him to be a man. Hondo and Mrs. Lowe continue their romance, but guiltily on Hondo's part as he tries to decide whether he should tell Mrs. Lowe that he has killed her husband. All the while, the tensions between the Apache and the cavalry heighten, and in the end Hondo, Mrs. Lowe, Johnny, and Hondo's friend Buffalo (Ward Bond) decide to flee the frontier and move to Hondo's ranch in California.

Three years later, *The Searchers* offered another narrative centered on Wayne's violent skills and the dynamics between wandering and settling. In the film, Wayne plays Ethan Edwards, a former Confederate soldier from Texas who, in love with his brother's wife back home, has spent three years after the end of the Civil War wandering, quite possibly as a lawless gunslinger. Just one night after his return to the family home — an isolated ranch in the desert — the Comanche, led by the chief Scar (Henry Brandon), slaughter most of the family, taking two daughters captive. The Comanche rape and eventually kill one daughter, leaving her body behind for the rescue party to find. The other, Debbie (Natalie Wood), is kept by the Comanche and is eventually taken as a bride by Scar. The film follows Ethan's search, along with the help of Martin

Pawley (Debbie's part-Cherokee adoptive brother, played by Jeffrey Hunter), as he tracks the Comanche across the frontier for five years, trying to find Debbie. For an increasingly demented Ethan, the goal is not to save her but to kill her over the shame of her miscegenation. Meanwhile, Martin's potential engagement to the daughter of a neighbor is put on hold, threatened by his devotion to the nomadic search, or at least to keeping Ethan from murdering Debbie once she is found. In the end, they catch up with Scar and the Comanche. Although Debbie at first insists that she must stay with the Comanche because they are now her people, she eventually accepts being rescued. After a tense standoff, Ethan embraces Debbie rather than harming her, and Martin finally settles down. Ethan, however, seems fated to continue his wandering, unfit to join the settled lives that await Martin and Debbie.

Each film explores dark and tortured constructions of masculinity in relation to labor, mobility, and the violence of the western frontier, offering stories about men who must navigate (both literally and ideologically) their relationship to the community and their commitment to the hypercompetitive and violent world of wandering. What is more, both films rely on cinematic technologies to make a spectacle of Wayne's body, using Warnercolor 3-D for *Hondo* and Technicolor VistaVision wide-screen in *The Searchers* to create vibrant and engaging images of Wayne roaming the frontier. The films mark an important intersection between cinematic technologies and the construction of the spectacular male body in action.

Both cinematic spectacles, moreover, were massive international hits for Wayne in the mid-1950s, a fact showcased by Warner Bros., which produced *Hondo* with Wayne's production company, Batjac, and distributed *The Searchers*. According to a press release dated March 1, 1954, *Hondo* received "Unanimous critical acclaim" as "Warner Bros.' 3-D entry at the Brazilian Film Festival." On March 17, Warner Bros. announced that the film "started a fourth week yesterday . . . at the Warner Theater [in London], following three stanzas of smash business." And according to a Warner Bros.' press release from August 17, 1954: "In its initial playdates in Japan's eight largest cities 'Hondo,' John Wayne starrer for Warner releases, has grossed a fantastic 66,946,590 yen. After it tours the province it is expected to top Y100-million." Two years later, *The Searchers* proved even more popular in international markets. On August 30, 1956, Warner Bros. boasted that *The Searchers* is "proving itself as one of the company's top grossers in its foreign engagements." Explicitly comparing the international success of *The Searchers* to Wayne's previous success in *Hondo*, the studio stated: "'The Searchers' has outgrossed the previous film in Japan, at the Osaka, Kyoto and Kobe theaters, over two weeks, by 20 percent and at the end of its first week at the Fukuoka Theater in that country by 50 percent; its first week in Paris was 125 percent greater than 'Hondo' and in its first two weeks in London the picture out-drew 'Hondo' by 40 percent."[2] In short, both mid-decade hits helped establish the international drawing power of John Wayne and the John Wayne western.

Both films construct a vision of the western frontier that is much more tense and filled with anxiety than the typical John Wayne western of the period. *Red River* and the Cavalry Trilogy are largely optimistic about the utopian possi-bilities of community formation and the western hero's movement through-out the frontier—celebrating the kinds of heroism and community that can be built out of migration and the movement of goods across distances—but in *Hondo* and *The Searchers* those possibilities become more elusive, especially as manifested in the racial tensions of the films. Both films grapple with issues of miscegenation and a complex vision of race relations on the frontier, with *The Searchers* offering a particularly brutal representation of Wayne as someone gripped by racist rage, at times desecrating the dead bodies of Native Ameri-cans. Within those anxieties, John Wayne provides a dark and yet somehow compelling fantasy, a kind of masculinity that makes explicit the tensions and psychological trauma of wandering and working in the open spaces of the fron-tier, yet also a vision of hardworking individuality that explores the embodied pleasures of work and mobility.

ANALYZING JOHN WAYNE'S BODY

All movie stars are, in one way or another, defined by the mediated images of their bodies, but from the moment that John Wayne rose out of the empty frontier of Monument Valley in *Stagecoach* (1939) as the camera tracked toward him, rifle in one hand, saddle in the other, Wayne's stardom was inti-mately tied to the spectacle of his large yet graceful body in the open spaces of the frontier. While other top Hollywood male stars in the 1950s relied on a par-ticular cinematic construction of their bodies, none were so defined by their body as Wayne. The meanings of Wayne, after all, cannot be separated from the images of his body at work in contexts of masculine violence: Wayne as Tom Dunson effortlessly parting the herd in *Red River* en route to his showdown with Matthew Garth, Wayne's large body slowly emerging from the empty frontier in *Hondo* as he wanders into the Lowe homestead, Wayne's ambling walk, bordering on a catlike prowl, hands held ready at his waist, as he patrols the dusty streets in *Rio Bravo* (1959). While stars such as Cary Grant, William Holden, and Marlon Brando used particular images of their bodies to express the key meanings of their star texts, Wayne's body in the 1950s was the central vehicle through which all the meanings of John Wayne were conveyed. Thus, as Deborah Thomas notes, "John Wayne has been constructed more than most (or at least more than most white males) as a star whose meaning is profoundly corporeal" ("John Wayne's Body," 75).

The sensational pleasures of Wayne's body stem from his unique and compelling combination of both size and grace. On the one hand, as Thomas notes, Wayne's body is seen as "bearing the marks of the statuesque and monumental: tall, hard, unyielding and representative of various institutional codes" ("John Wayne's Body," 75). Wayne's body is constructed on film as large and immovable; most characters in his films comment on his size and stubbornness, and most of the public discourses surrounding Wayne mirror that obsession with his six-foot-four-inch frame. Imagine Wayne in *Rio Bravo* constantly towering over his companions in the dusty border town under siege. To appreciate Wayne is to celebrate his size, to celebrate the feelings of physical dominance evoked by images of Wayne towering over others or filling up a small doorframe.

On the other hand, Wayne's monumental size is coupled with an extraordinary grace of movement, a fluidity to his body, and an almost rhythmic sense of mobility that one doesn't expect in a man of his size. As one scholar notes, "For Wayne, each gesture is effortless. Each move comes purely, naturally, and intuitively, giving his performances a slow, fluid grace" (Belton, "John Wayne," 25). Think of Wayne as the Ringo Kid diving onto the team of horses on the out-of-control stagecoach, or Wayne as Hondo Lane adeptly gunning down the disgruntled rancher who tries to ambush him in the wilderness, (or even Wayne skilfully dancing the jitterbug in *The Fighting Seabees* (1944)).[3] As William Luhr notes of Wayne: "He often uses his body to project contradictory signals. While his height, bulk and breadth suggest dominance and physical power, he frequently postures himself in a relaxed, restful manner, as if comfortable in his physical power and reluctant to display or employ it" ("Wayne and *The Searchers*," 78). Images of Wayne in action explore the utopian sensations of an idealized masculinity: large and dominating, yet flexible, graceful, and often relaxed under pressure.[4]

Interestingly, these attributes remained central to the depiction of Wayne's body even as his body grew older throughout the 1950s. The lean and somewhat youthful Wayne from *Fort Apache* (he was forty at the time) aged throughout the decade into the thicker and more haggard-looking Wayne that we see in *The Man Who Shot Liberty Valance*. Even in the six years between *Hondo* and *Rio Bravo*, Wayne's body changed appreciably from the slender cavalry scout wrestling Apache to the skilled but somewhat lumbering sheriff keeping order in the town of Rio Bravo. After *The Searchers*, in fact, "bodily injury and debility would be increasingly important to Wayne's performances" as his age and public bouts with cancer changed the signification of his body (Luhr, "Wayne and *The Searchers*," 88). And yet his aging body only slightly shifted the meanings of his body in action, and in some ways accentuated the key characteristics of his star persona. The depiction of Wayne's violent skills shifted throughout the 1950s from an emphasis on his mobility on horseback and physical agility to an emphasis on his quick draw and skill with a rifle (although elements of both persisted throughout the decade). But his age only furthered his associations with size and painful endurance, offering later in the decade even more compelling images of his large frame and fatigued face persisting in the face of adversity and danger. In fact, being middle-aged or older was part of Wayne's emergence into stardom in the first place: in films such as *Red River* and *She Wore a Yellow Ribbon*, his hair was grayed and makeup was used to make him look like an old but tough character. Thus, the maturing of Wayne's body in the 1950s furthered his image as a wizened and world-weary cowboy, a figure whose toughness is rooted not in youthful vigor but in intense determination and violent skills perfected over time.

On a discursive-ideological level, the pleasures of watching Wayne's tough, skilled body cannot be separated from the highly oppressive bodily pleasures of colonial domination and patriarchy that were constructed by Hollywood for white men. From that perspective, Wayne's size becomes an indication of his moral righteousness and gendered racial superiority as he towers over women and people of color in his films. His immense size is also linked in his films with his ability to persevere in pain and endure the elements, signifying the kinds of bodily control that, as Dyer points out, are central to the construction of whiteness as dominant over racial Others with "out of control" bodies (*White*). Moreover, Wayne's ability to move freely and efficiently throughout space is part of Hollywood's gendered representational strategies that construct a three-dimensional space within which the male protagonist asserts his masculinity through active movement, conquering such space, while women become static, passive objects of a mobile male gaze. At the same time, Wayne's mobility through the open spaces of the western frontier naturalize his connection to the land and his authority over that land, affirming the natural authority of white males to occupy and possess territory. Wayne literally embodies the intersection of patriarchal and colonialist ideologies in the articulation of white male dominance.[5]

And yet, as many critics and scholars have noted in their own critiques of Wayne's politics, the pleasures of watching Wayne's body and the sensations evoked by Wayne often complicate their ideological interpretations. Jean-Luc Godard once famously noted that he hated "John Wayne upholding Goldwater [the conservative politician and presidential candidate] and [loved] him tenderly when he abruptly takes Natalie Wood into his arms in the next-to-last reel of *The Searchers*" (quoted in Edgerton, "Reappraisal of John Wayne," 284), finding in the image of Wayne's large body gracefully sweeping a young girl into an embrace an emotionally compelling fantasy more powerful than the ideological meaning of Wayne as a political symbol. Similarly, Gary Wills's critical biography of Wayne, *John Wayne's America* (1997), rejects and harshly critiques Wayne's conservative politics and yet simultaneously shows an immense fascination with Wayne's body, even comparing pictures of Wayne to Michelangelo's and Donatello's statues of David. In the sensations inspired by images of Wayne's body, Wills finds something so compelling that it often stalls his ideological project. These observations are not to deny the ideological resonance of Wayne and his films, but to suggest that compelling images of powerful male bodies function in more complex ways when one considers their real pleasures and sensations, a complexity inherent in both Godard's and Wills's contradictions.[6]

This complexity is especially true of Wayne's body when one considers the immense transnational popularity of Wayne. Audiences outside a Euro-American context clearly found something appealing about Wayne, and it would be reductive to assume such audiences simply internalized white male privilege as a kind of "false consciousness" rather than sought out films, stars, and images that pleasurably responded to their cultural experiences, needs, desires, and anxieties. Hortense Powdermaker, for example, suggests that audiences in contexts of colonization, decolonization, and territorial disputes would be drawn to the western genre as a masculinist fantasy of territorial control and mobility: "The hard-fighting cowboy, moving freely on his horse in wide-open spaces, surmounting all obstacles and always winning, is indeed an attractive hero for a people intensely fearful of losing some of their wide-open spaces to Europeans, who until recently held all the power" (quoted in Burns, "Wayne on the Zambezi," 109). As JoEllen Shively points out in her study of Wayne among Navajo and Anglo film viewers, many Native Americans identify with Wayne as a tough, capable figure close to nature and the land ("Cowboys and Indians"). Wayne's body offered a broadly appealing fantasy of strength, capability, and mobility that resonated with diverse audiences around the world.

This is not to suggest that the pleasures of Wayne's body somehow transcend history and politics in their management of Wayne's ideological tensions. Too often the pleasure and desire at the root of watching and appreciating bodies is seen as universal or biological, a kind of innate aesthetic or erotic gaze. To the contrary, I see the pleasures of watching Wayne as fundamentally ideological and historical, even as those pleasures obscure some of the more repugnant aspects of Wayne's politics. My goal here is to contextualize and historicize the pleasures of Wayne's body within the material history and ideologies of the 1950s.

In the following sections, I connect the pleasures of watching Wayne's body with the material history of capitalism and modernization, specifically the increasing commodification of the male body within the drudgery of wage labor and the importance of movement and mobility within globalizing capitalism. The international projection of Wayne's body as a site of fantasy and pleasure, I contend, is deeply tied to the sensations and fantasies of labor and mobility structured into global modernity and global capitalism. *Hondo* and *The Searchers* prove ideal for illustrating these connections and revealing the complex fantasy of a capitalist male body offered by Wayne, but I address also the general values and characteristics associated with Wayne's body throughout the 1950s.

WAGE LABOR AND THE COMMODIFICATION OF THE MALE BODY IN *HONDO*

Hondo provides a particularly useful starting point for examining the construction of Wayne's body and its relation to labor and capitalism, because the film explicitly asks: what kinds of labor are appropriate for men's bodies? The film's narrative reflects the tensions in John Wayne's star text between violent, homosocial professionalism and nuclear-family domesticity as appropriate forms of masculinity, but in *Hondo* the choice is expressed primarily through the labor that Wayne's body is suited for. Although the film celebrates the professional skills of Hondo Lane by offering the spectacle of his violence in the dangerous world of the frontier, Hondo nevertheless proves his appropriateness as a potential husband and father to the Lowes by doing chores around the homestead that Mr. Lowe has abandoned: shoeing horses, repairing structures, fixing tools, all of which he is adept at. He even demonstrates his fitness to be a father to young Johnny, although his vision of child rearing centers on preparing young men with the skills necessary to survive in the frontier rather than tending to their emotional needs. In one scene, Hondo learns that Johnny can't swim, so he hoists the boy off the ground and effortlessly tosses him into a nearby stream, watching Johnny struggle until he figures out how to reach the bank (and he threatens to do the same to Mrs. Lowe when she confesses that she can't swim either). The kinds of daily labor and the work of fatherhood that mark Hondo as an appropriate husband and father, however, are antithetical to the violent and seminomadic lifestyle that Hondo has chosen for himself as he wanders the frontier gathering information for the U.S. cavalry. The tension in the film between romance and masculine professionalism expresses itself in the kinds of labor that are constructed as appropriate for Wayne's body: shoeing horses or fighting Apache.[7]

As in many other Wayne films, *Hondo* cultivates a sense of toil and exhaustion, emphasizing the sometimes-dull routines of labor. The film lingers on daily chores such as mending fences and shoeing horses, along with the more

exciting labor of evading Apache on the frontier. In many ways, the film supports Tompkins's study of the western genre, which asserts that one of the primary characteristics of the genre is its insistent emphasis on the male body
hard at work, the visceral, sweaty affect created by the western hero (*West of
Everything*). The pleasures of Wayne's body in the film are the pleasures (and
tensions) of work, the sensations and satisfactions of a task accomplished effectively, which are rooted in a bourgeois sensibility about labor, the work ethic,
and individuality.

Within this insistent emphasis on employment and the routines of labor,
Wayne offers a fantasy of ease and mastery of one's body through violence and
movement. Like his other films, *Hondo* celebrates and makes a spectacle of
Wayne's body and its violent efficiency. Hondo is fast and accurate with his
guns, a fact we are reminded of not only in his killing of Mr. Lowe and his
battles with the Apache, but also through his rifle, which was awarded to him
in a shooting contest. Hondo is the consummate western hero: his sweaty labor
represents the core of the genre, and his near-superhuman speed and agility
legitimate his violent acts.

Wayne's speed and skill are almost always an aspect of his star persona. In
nearly all his films of this period, Wayne's characters show almost superhuman
skill and fluidity in action, as well as a reliance on brute force. In *Red River* he
almost effortlessly spins, draws, and kills the gunslinger Cherry Valance on his
determined march to face down Matt Garth; in *Sands of Iwo Jima* he adeptly
maneuvers into position to take out a Japanese bunker after all other marines
fail; in *The Searchers* he outshoots and outwits all threats amid the open space
of the frontier, be they Comanche or unethical white profiteers; in *Rio Bravo*
he maintains order against a horde of hired guns through his skill with a rifle.
So while the fantasy offered by Wayne's body creates the sensations of difficult
but routine labor, it somewhat contradictorily engenders feelings of mastery
and power.

The emphasis on labor and skill, of course, should not be surprising, since
the narrative contexts for Wayne's labor on-screen are often contexts of capitalist employment. Because Wayne is often working on-screen, his actions, more
than those of most western heroes, reflect professionalism. *Red River*, for example, explores issues of managing employees on a massive cattle drive; and in
his war films and cavalry films—such as *Fort Apache, She Wore a Yellow Ribbon,
Rio Grande, Sands of Iwo Jima, Flying Leathernecks* (1951), and *The Horse Soldiers*
(1959)—a commitment to the military is seen in the commodified terms of
doing one's job. The most prominent example of this professionalism, however,
occurs in *Rio Bravo*, in which Wayne as the sheriff of a small town besieged by
hired gunmen rejects the help of amateurs, choosing to deputize only those
with the appropriate qualifications (even if they are drunks). Throughout the

film, he uses a discourse of professionalism in describing his duty to his position. Although his violent actions serve broader goals such as justice and community, it is clear in the film that Wayne's efficient violence is a commodity that he wields because it is his job.

In *Hondo*, Wayne's violent skills are marked as individual commodities that he will contract out to organizations like the cavalry. A freelance scout for the government rather than a member of the cavalry himself, Hondo provides not the disciplined violence of the military but rather a marketable skill to be deployed in contexts of his choosing. He is an entrepreneur, a kind of mercenary whose commitment is based on the sale of his skills, which keep him distanced from the community his labor protects (he is clearly not part of the community of ranchers that must be evacuated, even though he does aid them). This is not to say that Hondo (or any other professional gunman that Wayne played) is interested only, or crudely, in profit. In *Hondo*, and most notably in his trilogy of westerns with Howard Hawks (*Rio Bravo*, *El Dorado*, and *Rio Lobo*), Wayne's characters provide a kind of responsible capitalism; he sells his labor and is the consummate professional, but he won't exchange his loyalty for money and is skeptical of greed run amok. Hondo Lane is an entrepreneur who sells his skill and labor, but he never does so in situations that are marked as greedy and unethical in the melodramatic world of the western (a potentially resonant fantasy within a capitalist system where wage laborers around the world had much less control over when and how they sold their labor).

The representations of capitalist labor, bodily mastery, and day-to-day labor in the Wayne western are not an escapist fantasy so much as a reflection and reproduction of the sensations and drudgery of wage labor within a globalizing economy. As R. W. Connell notes of the globalizing processes throughout the second half of the twentieth century: "One of the most important dynamics in the creation of a global market society is the transformation of growing numbers of men around the world into wage labourers" (*Men and Boys*, 63–64). As the spread of global capitalism transformed labor relations around the world, it resulted in a gendered division of labor between female domestic workers and male wage workers, which subsequently transformed patterns of masculinity by insisting that some men (particularly those in developing regions) define their masculinity through their body's labor: "The unskilled labourer has essentially one commodity to put on the market: his bodily capacity to labour. Under the imperative of profit, wage labour consumes the body through cumulative fatigue, industrial illness and injury, etc. In a common pattern in working class life, the physical capacity to endure these efforts becomes a test of manliness" (64). In contrast with the kinds of physical labor that men at the lower end of the class hierarchy had been relegated to for ages, the new regime of labor being exported internationally through modernization became less dependent on brute strength and more dependent on endurance over time and the ability to work robotically. For increasing numbers of men around the world who found themselves drawn into the global market economy and wage labor starting in the 1950s, a pattern of masculinity emerged in which their manhood was defined around their body's willingness and ability to endure pain and suffering while continuing to labor. Their bodies, in other words, became commodities consumed by global capitalism.

At the same time, ironically, the emerging international division of labor that intensified in the fifties necessitated the decline of production-based wage labor in the developed world in favor of bureaucratic and service-related occupations, producing a kind of nostalgic yearning for masculinities tied to the exertion of the body. As Steven Cohan points out, the emergence of bureaucratic, corporate labor became essential to hegemonic masculinities in the fifties in the United States (and, I would suggest, throughout developed- and developing-world elites), defining masculinity around domestic consumption rather than production and bodily labor (*Masked Men*, xii). Those gendered shifts produced mass-produced fantasies of hard-bodied homosocial masculinities such as Wayne's, which expressed middle-class male fantasies of masculinity tied to the kinds of bodily strength and movement divorced from white-collar labor.[8]

The sensations evoked by Wayne's labor on-screen offer not just a model of how masculinity within capitalism should be constructed but also a sense of what capitalist masculinity should feel like. Offering a somewhat contradictory experience of work—the visceral sense of difficulty and toil and yet a nearly omnipotent sensation of mastery and efficiency—the fantasy of Wayne's body explores the ambivalence of wage labor: the sweat, the toil, and the bodily pain, but also the empowering sensations of mastery and endurance that, as Connell notes, quickly became a standard way of expressing working-class masculinity. At the same time, as white-collar labor expanded during this period, the sensations of Wayne's body provided a compelling fantasy of embodied masculinity that corporate capitalism denies office workers, the sensations of sweat, movement, and even painful toil as an embodied pleasure.

Pleasure in the painful sensations of labor is central to another important characteristic of Wayne's laboring body: his shouldering of responsibilities, expressed through bodily suffering and endurance. As Thomas points out, "His toughness is not a matter of hard muscularity (as one expects from an action hero) but of endurance, of taking punishment and of going on" ("John Wayne's Body," 79). His films "emphasize the nature of his toughness not as the action hero's strength and speed but as a considered shouldering of responsibilities, even when he is shown to be wrong and stubbornness slides into obsession" (79). His size signifies more than a perceived moral or racial superiority; his

FIGURE 4.2. *Wayne's body enduring the elements on his long trek in* The Searchers *(C. V. Whitney/Warner Bros., 1956).*

height and big shoulders become markers of the ability to endure pain and bear responsibility in the execution of one's work.[9]

Examine, for example, Wayne's role as Ethan Edwards in *The Searchers*. As the film's narrative progresses, Edwards's obsessive search for his kidnapped niece becomes an extended display of the suffering and endurance of Wayne's body as it trudges on through the dangers of the frontier and the elements. The film's wide-screen Technicolor makes a spectacle out of not only the expanses of Monument Valley but also the superhuman resilience of Wayne's body as it steadily wanders throughout the southwestern desert for years.

Hondo subjects Wayne's body to brutal punishments as part of his professional existence. Not only does Hondo have to subsist without complaint in the dry, harsh wilderness of the frontier, but his seminomadic information gathering often puts him in painful situations with the Apache. After Hondo is captured by the Apache in the film, Vittorio tortures him and highlights the ability of Hondo's/Wayne's body to endure pain in a scene designed to showcase the spectacle of the suffering male body. Strapping Hondo to the ground in a Christlike position, the Apache force burning embers into the palm of his hand in a test of bravery to see whether Hondo will cry out in pain. Close-ups of Wayne's determined, pain-gripped face holding back screams offer the sadistic pleasures that critics like Steve Neale see as fundamental to the representation of the male body in Hollywood—the film punishes the fetishized display of the male body—while also expressing the anxieties of a grueling wage labor that defines masculinity within modern capitalism. So while the body and its labor

FIGURE 4.3. *Hondo being tortured but not crying out, emphasizing his ability to withstand pain in* Hondo.

offer a potential source of capitalist self-determination, *Hondo* reveals as well the dark and painful realities of that construction of masculinity.

There is nothing new in pointing out either the centrality of bodily suffering to an articulation of masculinity or the masochistic pleasure of watching men's bodies in classic Hollywood. But understanding the sensations and bodily fantasies produced by those images helps connect the images to the desires, anxieties, and lived experiences of audiences in transnational contexts. The sensations of painful endurance evoked by Wayne are not simply masochistic pleasures but also masochistic pleasures mirrored in the emotional and physical experiences of labor within global capitalism. Amid massive shifts in the definitions of masculinity, Wayne offered an ambivalent fantasy: a commodified body whose strength lay in his ability to market his skillful and efficient physical labor, but also a body that had to express its masculinity through punishment and the painful endurance of labor. While international transformations of labor and masculinity privileged a Fordist vision of labor as endurance, Wayne offered a body that was dynamic and effortless in its physicality and yet had to shoulder the burdens and pain of the new economic system.

The relationship between Wayne's body and the global cultural context of the 1950s is echoed in Simon During's analysis of muscled white bodies within 1980s and 1990s global culture. During emphasizes that the appeal of globally circulated media "is . . . to be read in terms of the limited capacities of particular media to provide for individuals' needs and desires, especially male needs and desires, across the various territories that constitute the world image market" ("Popular Culture," 815). Arnold Schwarzenegger proved to be an important example because of the ways his muscled body, with its technological contexts and connotations, suggested the kinds of bodily discipline and bodily labor inherent in the world economy, on the part of both those whose bodies labor and those who use and deploy such bodies alongside technology to manage production. Noting that the workouts necessary to maintain a body like Schwarzenegger's "mime and personalize labor, especially the kind of (Fordist) labor that is exported in the global economy" (818) and that Schwarzenegger's body was constantly situated within narratives and contexts that emphasize the "body-as-resource," During suggests that the global appeal of Schwarzenegger can be understood in the ways that it provides a sensational fantasy of male bodies that directly responds to and mirrors the experiences of bodies within the global economy (833).

Like Schwarzenegger's importance in the 1980s and 1990s, John Wayne's role within the 1950s global culture was deeply tied to the spectacle of his body and its capacity to express a particular set of male "needs and desires" stemming from the transformations of global capitalism and labor during that period. Wayne's fantasy of a tough "body-as-resource"—a body that can be fantastically skillful and yet endure pain and shoulder responsibility, that can move freely throughout space and yet dramatize the dangers and anxieties of doing so—mirrored the everyday sensations of modern masculinity and labor for men around the world.[10]

We should heed Charles Acland's warning that cultural critics should not interpret images of powerful bodies simply as reflective of feelings of power. He suggests that images of powerful male bodies within globally popular media might indicate widespread concerns with weakness and frailty: "Such figures can be a way to compensate for the overall vulnerability people feel in a global system, hence, paradoxically, they refer to people's sense of inconsequentiality and puniness" (*Screen Traffic*, 38). The international popularity of Wayne in the 1950s, then, might speak powerfully to the bodily vulnerability and powerlessness experienced by men and the culture at large; the sensations of enduring pain and toil, so central to the experience of watching Wayne, may indicate that the fantasies of physical mastery and skill Wayne offers resonate only because they offset the experiences of drudgery and suffering inherent in capitalism. Or perhaps it is more accurate to say that bodily mastery and physical suffering function as a dialectical pair in capitalism's vision of the body and labor; thus, the sensations of labor, work, and movement evoked by Wayne's body manage these contradictions through the sensations of a unified male body that can be both burdened and graceful.

THE PLEASURES AND ANXIETIES
OF MOBILITY IN *THE SEARCHERS*

Coupled with Wayne's ability to labor and endure pain is the centrality of mobility and exploration to the fantasy of his body, a fantasy that is just as conflicted as Wayne's body's skillful yet painful labor. Examine, for example, the iconic image of John Wayne as Ethan Edwards standing in the doorway of the Jorgensen ranch at the end of *The Searchers*. Often considered a prototypical image of the genre that encapsulates the western's key themes, the image juxtaposes the wide-open spaces of Monument Valley with the dark and enclosed spaces of the homestead, dramatizing at once Ethan's desire for nomadic freedom of movement and his rejection of the stability and security of settled, domestic life. Although the image is literally about space and movement, most of the genre criticism of the western sees the juxtaposition of the two spaces as merely allegorical for the seemingly more important element of time, particularly the supposedly temporal progression from "wilderness" to "civilization," from "lawlessness" to a "modern" social order. From that perspective, Ethan — a liminal figure of lawlessness who is nevertheless aligned with and necessary to the creation of order — becomes a catalyst for temporal progress, a figure whose ceaseless wandering through space is narrowly considered the last movements of an older order giving way to the new. His wildness provides the violence upon which the civilization of the homestead is built, a violence that is then repressed as being out of date in the modern world. Privileging time in that way collapses the representation of space in the western into abstract values that support a supposedly neutral, natural, and necessarily temporal modernization.

But the image of Wayne standing in the dark doorway, the vast openness of the desert looming behind him, clearly dramatizes a set of values and conflicts about space and one's relationship to different and sometimes competing spatial orders: the borderless nomadism of Ethan and the Comanche versus the stratifying settlements of ranchers and homesteaders like the Jorgensens. Rather than the transition from the new to the old, the spatial confrontation in the film conveys the anxieties resulting from competing modes of situating oneself within and across space. Rather than displaying the violent processes of an irrevocable and totalizing temporal modernization, *The Searchers*, like other classic westerns of the 1950s, offers the spatial conflicts of individuals navigating the uneven and incomplete sprawl of modernity across the landscape.

At the core of the film's narrative are the dynamics of movement and stasis, the pleasures of movement compared with the desire to settle down (pleasures that are central to the film's iconographic treatment of Monument Valley). As Jim Kitses explains of *The Searchers* (and in relation to the western in general):

FIGURE 4.4. *Wayne as Ethan Edwards in* The Searchers.

> At the root of the journey film, and fundamental to its appeal, are the
> dialectics of stasis and movement, constancy and change, settling and
> wandering, inside and out, home and away. . . . By definition Westerners
> are travelers, immigrants, pioneers. In terms of the structure of oppo-
> sitions that make up the Western's spine, it is the classic pairs of the
> wilderness and civilization, of the settled versus the nomadic, that define
> the cultural field within which Americans exist. (*Horizons West,* 93)

Arguing that the experience of movement and then settlement is a fundamental
component of the U.S. immigrant experience and therefore a central aspect of
U.S. national identity, Kitses claims that *The Searchers* taps into that experience,
asking culturally important questions about the value and heroism of movement versus settlement. Ethan represents the ambivalence of nomadism, the
constant mobility that provides the heroic spectacles of the film, but because he
is demented, he jeopardizes the community it purports to protect; he is "root-
less, homeless": "Like the Indian corpse whose eyes he shoots out, 'he travels
between the winds'" (94).

The film exemplifies one of the key components of Wayne's body in this
period: his capacity to wander and explore space in ways that are heroic, pleasurable, yet also dangerous and potentially destructive of the community. The
sensations of Wayne's body are those of spatial mobility, particularly as evoked
by images of Wayne on horseback, negotiating the spaces of the frontier (often
those of Monument Valley, where John Ford often placed Wayne). The sensations are most apparent in films such as those in John Ford's Cavalry Trilogy,

in which the spectacle of men riding through the open frontier is foundational to the films' pleasure, but are also central to films such as *3 Godfathers, Hondo*, Wayne's disastrous attempt to play Genghis Kahn in *The Conqueror, Legend of the Lost, The Horse Soldiers*, and *The Searchers*. Perhaps because he started his career by crisscrossing the frontier on horseback in a slew of B westerns, it is difficult to separate the pleasures of Wayne from the pleasures of the lone horseman, scaling rocky cliffs or careening through the open frontier with his trusty steed. Part of the spectacle of John Wayne's body is its mobility and freedom to explore space and cross borders too dangerous or inaccessible to others, creating the sensations of mobility in an increasingly borderless world.

Such mobility, moreover, is almost always connected to contexts of capitalism. The nomadic wandering of the prototypical western hero often occurs in the context of migratory labor, of moving from place to place to offer gunfighting services or of being required to explore the territory because of a job like leading a cattle drive or pursuing an outlaw as a sheriff or a U.S. marshal. The need to wander, which Kitses sees as an archetypal component of human existence, is almost always tied in the western to the restructuring of space created by capitalism, to the need to migrate from town to town to find employment, to bring one's goods to distant markets, or to keep the flow of people open via the railroad or the stagecoach. At stake in the (necessarily masculine) freedom of movement so central to the western genre are not simply the universal pleasures of movement through space but also the ways that the movements necessitated by global capitalism in the 1950s (and today) are often constructed as pleasurable in the genre.

In the case of *The Searchers*, Kitses's connection between the sensations of mobility and the U.S. immigrant experience tells only part of the story. The experience of vast transnational and cross-cultural movement with the aim of reconstructing a new sense of home is not unique to U.S. culture and can be said to characterize the cultural dynamics of the migrations and transformations of space around the world in the 1950s. Likewise, the cinematic western frontier is not simply a space for mythologizing U.S. national identity, but rather a complex symbolic space dramatizing issues of intense social competition, community, and modernization. This duality perhaps explains why the genre was so popular around the world in periods of uneven modernization (see Chapter 2 for a more detailed discussion of 1950s mobility and the western's construction of space).

The Searchers exemplifies these spatial dynamics, offering a sense of space and mobility that reflects the changing spatial structures of modernization. The settlement of the Edwards family farm seems an appropriate example of people who have traveled west and are loosely connected to the East via "tentacles of progress" like the railroad and the stagecoach (Schatz, *Hollywood Genres*,

49), people who are attempting to construct a sense of familiarity and intimacy after having uprooted themselves and migrated to a new space. Ethan, however, is always removed from contexts of community formation, first by the Civil War, then by his lawless wandering, and next by his grand, self-destructive rescue mission. He constructs a kind of distanciated network of affiliations as he travels with Martin from outpost to outpost in search of the Comanche, always at work—a network represented partly by the film's semi-epistolary narrative. Much of the protagonists' quest is narrated via letters from Martin to his love interest, Laurie, who is waiting somewhat impatiently for Martin's wandering to end and his settled life in a nuclear family to begin. The sense of space produced by *The Searchers* mirrored the experience of migration and mobility for much of its global audience, including those who were attempting to construct a familiar and stable sense of space and home amid the migrations of people and the deterritorialization of culture as well as those who had to construct a sense of connection while being constantly on the move, seeking employment or spreading global capitalism.

The Searchers reflects the changes in space and the importance of mobility within modernization and the globalization of capitalism. The experience of space and the ways that bodies occupy space, after all, were being transformed dramatically in the second half of the twentieth century. Several historical phenomena emerging around the world in the 1950s helped transform space and social relations, resulting in the compression of space and its simultaneous distanciation.[11] Information and transportation technology became faster in the developed world and started to spread throughout the developing world because of modernization. At the same time, decolonization meant the reclamation of colonial space for privileged national elites throughout the era and marked the start of a wave of migration from the developing world to the developed. Those migrations, of course, were also tied to the spread of global capitalism as more and more people sought out emerging economic opportunities abroad. Meanwhile developing-world elites sought to bring the products (and later the factories) of U.S. and European capitalism to other parts of the world, while newer transportation technologies, such as air travel, helped construct a mobile business elite that traveled the globe.[12] Urbanization and suburbanization transformed the daily living conditions and economic opportunities for many populations around the world. And media, particularly the increasingly global Hollywood film industry and U.S. television, connected viewers in a global network of consumption. Because of these phenomena, culture became increasingly divorced from a specific local space (starting what some scholars have referred to as the deterritorialization of culture), while mobility and the movement of people and goods across borders became a part of modern life.

As a result of these shifting constructions of space and mobility, Zygmunt

Bauman sees the value of mobility as one of the most important factors of social inequality to emerge in the second half of the twentieth century. He contends that the processes of globalization should be seen as a "space war" in which elites seek to disconnect their power from local spaces and contexts, transforming their ability to move freely—and to move capital and production freely across insignificant national and cultural borders—into a means of social stratification. Mobility, the capability to flee from the responsibilities of the local, becomes a means of distancing elites from those unable to exercise or control mobility, making mobility "the most powerful and most coveted stratifying factor; the stuff of which the new, increasingly world-wide, social, political, and economic hierarchies are daily built and rebuilt" (*Globalization*, 9). Class, power, and the lived experiences of mobility, in other words, have become inextricably tied through modernization and globalization.

Bauman suggests, therefore, that two worlds have emerged: one for mobile elites, in which space can be mastered through an effortless and pleasurable mobility, and one for those on the bottom of the class hierarchy, in which space is oppressive, either through a stifling inability to seek economic mobility (which is almost exclusively a literal spatial mobility in the modern world) or through a chaotic mobility that they are virtually powerless to control (the migrations to cities to flee rural poverty, the migrations to the developed world to seek economic opportunities, and the spatially disconnected cultures and communities that result). He refers to these worlds as those of the "travelers" and the "vagabonds." Thus, mobility affects everyone: tourists participate in mobility and consumerism, while the vagabonds can only envy the control that the tourists exert over their mobility, an envy spurred on by the virtual mobility provided by the global media. Wealthy businessmen travel to Manila for work, while poor women from the Philippines become nannies for families in the developed world. Middle- and upper-class U.S. college students spend spring break relaxing in Cancun, while thousands of desperate Mexicans cross the border into the United States to seek out often-exploitative agricultural work. All these groups participate in the mobility of the modern world, but there is often a disconnection between those who control mobility and those controlled by it.

Bauman's discussion of the "space wars" refers to periods of intensive globalization from the 1980s to the present, but the transformations of space that paved the way for Bauman's analysis have their roots in the modernization and expansion of global capitalism in the 1950s, especially the transformations in mobility and migrations mentioned in Chapter 2. Moreover, as with the impact of modernity on the male body, the transformation of space is not just political and economic; it is a transformation of the bodily sensations of both modernity and space, in the ways that individuals and populations experience and feel the textures, rhythms, and sensations of modern, everyday life.

In this period, John Wayne provided a spectacle of the male body not just in motion but also in migration, traversing and exploring space, creating the sensations of mobility mirrored in the everyday experience of modernization and capitalism. For the growing number of tourist elites, Wayne's spectacle of borderless movement and nomadism heroically dramatized a masculine mobile ideal, providing a model of masculinity rooted in movement. For the vagabonds, Wayne's borderless wandering was at once a model of tourist mobility to envy and aspire to and at the same time a reflection of the growing importance to labor of migration and movement. As in Powdermaker's argument discussed above regarding the appeal of the free and mobile cowboy to the newly decolonized, Wayne's image can be read as a fantasy of empowering mobility for those whose lives were controlled by either a lack of mobility or the desperate mobility of migration. The sense of mobility and borderlessness created by images of Wayne's body provided a sensational fantasy of power and control in a world where borders were becoming increasingly porous to people and capital.[13]

The visceral impact of imagery in *The Searchers* supports this fantasy, offering a two-hour spectacle of the landscape of Monument Valley and the movement of men through that landscape. Using wide-screen and color technology, the film lingers on spectacular extralong shots of massive stone formations towering over people navigating the landscape, showcasing the pleasures of movement through borderless space. Moreover, the visual spectacle of the landscape is coupled with the spectacle of violent action based in movement as Ethan and Martin pursue and battle the Comanche. The landscape is fantastic and almost surreal in its Technicolor vibrancy, heightening the fantasy of movement through its crags and valleys.

The sensations of mobility provided by Wayne's body explore as well some of the chaotic ambivalence of borderless movement and the globalizing economy in the 1950s. The open spaces of the frontier in the western are not utopian and celebratory spaces but rather are characterized by a deep divide regarding their possibility. One the one hand, they offer all the pleasures and spectacle of borderlessness: the fantasy of dominating and exploring open and dramatic spaces (at least for the men in the genre). But on the other hand, the frontier of the western is a space of danger, a space filled with risk and violent competition, whether it comes from Native Americans, gunslingers, or nature. The inherent mobility of Wayne's body in his films explores these contradictions regarding space and movement, offering the pleasurable fantasy of complete mobility as celebrated by advocates of global capitalism, but also revealing the threats and risks of a vision of mobile professionalism: for example, the constant threat of the Apache in the Cavalry Trilogy, the torture of Hondo's body at the hands of the Apache, the crushing hopelessness of his quest in *The Searchers*. Thus, for both tourists and vagabonds, Wayne's body and its freedom to explore the spaces of the cinematic frontier doesn't simply celebrate mobility. Rather, Wayne's body acknowledges the centrality and pleasure of mobility to the sensational experiences of modern masculinity while recognizing that such a fantasy also teeters on the edge of pain and disaster.

The spectacle of masculine heroism based on mobility in *The Searchers* is questioned for its brutality and racism. While *Fort Apache* is a celebration of the masculine heroics of mobility that made possible the formation of a heterogeneous community, *The Searchers* reveals a questioning of the optimistic celebration of mobility, representing it instead as potentially brutal and cruel, although still necessary to protect the freedom of movement and migration that makes possible the re-creation of community among the homesteaders. Ethan's wandering is clearly at odds with the values of homesteaders like his brother and the Jorgensens. It is implied that Ethan's time after the war has been spent lawlessly and that there is perhaps a warrant for his arrest. Ethan's obsessive pursuit to find or kill Debbie, moreover, is presented as an increasingly demented quest as the years of wandering stretch out, the fanatical mission of an unbalanced racist bent on revenge. As numerous commentators on the film have pointed out, the film structures Ethan as the mirror image of the Comanche chief Scar; both are domineering figures of brutality and vengeance who are aligned with nomadism, with an unrelenting mobility that is unable to settle into the closed space of a community or homestead.[14] This dominance and restlessness find their expression in Ethan's character. As Arthur Eckstein has shown, Ethan's character was systematically made darker and more repugnant throughout the process of adapting the novel to the screen, culminating in Wayne's stunning and complex performance of Ethan's tortured bigotry and rage ("Darkening Ethan").[15]

In one scene, the film explicitly develops the connections between Ethan's heroic yet destructive mobility and the harsh effects of constant nomadism on the Comanche. Near the end of the protagonists' five-year quest, the two men cross the border into Mexico and arrange a meeting under false pretenses with Scar. As they ride into camp, it is made clear that the past five years of wandering and constant migration have taken their toll on the Comanche as much as they have on their ragged-looking white pursuers. As Ethan and Martin rest momentarily on a sandy clearing amid the rocky landscape, the wind whips sand between the teepees as a group of women and children look on at the men entering the encampment.

The Searchers has been widely analyzed for its ambivalent examination of racism and Wayne's troubling masculinity in the film, but this scene suggests that the ambivalence is rooted in the film's general questioning of the possibilities of mobility and community formation through migration. At the moment when the pursuer and the pursued finally converge in a space that is both monumentally dramatic and simultaneously desolate, the harsh consequences of their concurrent migrations become painfully clear. In a film such as *Fort Apache*, the scapegoating of Native Americans acts to catalyze the optimistic formation of modern white communities, but in *The Searchers* the Comanche in some ways provide a reflection of the brutal realities of the kinds of migration and violence upon which white settlement is built.

The pleasures and sensations of Wayne's active and mobile body as it explores the spaces of the frontier therefore function as a contradictory fantasy. Wayne's large body on horseback moving through space presents the utopian sensations of freedom, movement, and exploration in a world where borders are meaningless and space is open. Yet at the same time, that empowering fantasy teeters on the verge of self-destruction and threatens the stability of the community. In short, images of Wayne's mobile body offered audiences around the world a reflection of both the sensational possibilities and dangerous injustices of a world increasingly centered on mobility.

RACIAL TENSIONS IN THE FRONTIER

If Wayne's body provides a tenser, more anxious set of pleasures at mid-decade than was offered in films such as the Cavalry Trilogy, then those tensions cannot be separated from the racial discourses in *Hondo* and *The Searchers*. The construction of Wayne's body in both films centers on questions of race and miscegenation. In *Hondo*, Hondo Lane's suitability as a match for Mrs. Lowe is at first offset by his own miscegenation—he had been previously married to an Apache woman, thus his unusual knowledge of Apache culture and traditions.[16] But Hondo's racial transgressions can be overlooked not only because of his heroic skill and mobility (skills that ironically link him to the Apache and simultaneously allow him to fight for the white settlers) but also because of an even greater threat to white womanhood later in the film. After the chief Vittorio befriends Mrs. Lowe and makes Johnny a member of the tribe, he decides that Mrs. Lowe needs a husband so that Johnny can have a father to teach him to become a man. To that end, be brings a parade of his best warriors to the Lowe ranch to perform feats of strength and horsemanship so that Mrs. Lowe can choose the best for her husband. Visibly repulsed by the thought of taking on an Apache husband, Mrs. Lowe tries to explain that she is already married (not yet knowing that her husband is dead). The horror of white femininity threatened by nonwhite men can overshadow the cross-racial indiscretions of a white man within the film's gendered and raced ideologies.

Similarly in *The Searchers*, Ethan's racist obsession with Debbie's miscegenation with Scar is coupled with Ethan's intimate connections with and knowledge of Comanche culture. His ability to track Scar and his band for so long is due only to his expertise in their traditions and way of life. Wayne's Ethan Edwards, in fact, is so familiar with the Comanche that the film might suggest that a past and a repressed history with Native Americans is at the root of his xenophobia; as several scholars ask, why did Ethan "find" a half-Cherokee–half-white infant (Martin Pawley) on the frontier, which he brought to his brother and sister-in-law to raise? How did he recognize the scalp of Martin's mother in Scar's camp unless he knew her or the circumstances of her death?[17] Far from offering a straightforward portrait of white racism and miscegenation fears, *The Searchers* exploits fears of white femininity contaminated by nonwhite Others while hinting at the racial transgressions of the male hero.

The racial dynamics of both films should not be surprising, given the history of Hollywood westerns in the period. Both are part of a trend in 1950s Hollywood to address the presence of Native Americans on the cinematic frontier in a more nuanced and at times sympathetic way. While still relying on racist stereotypes and still affirming the inherent right of white settlers to inhabit the land, many Hollywood films attempted to explore issues of race with more complexity, exemplified by Delmer Davies's *Broken Arrow* (1950), which tells the story of a former U.S. soldier who tries to negotiate peace between the United States and the Apache after gaining a newfound respect for Native Americans. A number of scholars have addressed this tendency in the genre, with most arguing that the more nuanced representation of Native Americans allegorizes other major U.S. cultural issues. John Lenihan, for example, argues that Native Americans in the fifties were a "safe" outlet by which films could explore the tensions produced by the civil rights movement and the tensions between black and white America in the 1950s (*Showdown*, 55–89) while also exploring the possibility that the cycle of the "pro-Indian western" reflected Cold War tensions, giving voice to "yearnings for peaceful coexistence by emphasizing the desirability of negotiating with, instead of militarily destroying, enemy forces" (24–25).[18]

The racial tensions and the anxieties of cross-racial intimacy seem also to reflect the tensions of mobility within modernity and global capitalism. The presence of Native Americans in John Wayne's West, after all, creates a space in which multiple groups of people lay claim to a particular territory and attempt to negotiate peace and stability, or at least stasis, within that territory (although it is clear that one group is structurally privileged to inherit the territory in the films). That particular spatial situation does resonate with U.S. race relations in the 1950s, or with the international competition between the United States and the Soviet Union in the Cold War, but it is equally relevant to the colonial and postcolonial disputes between European empires and multiple emerging nationalisms, or to the competing populations arriving in cities worldwide and attempting to construct a sense of place and locality among other communities. By dramatizing the fears and possibilities of miscegenation, internationally popular westerns such as *Hondo* and *The Searchers* explore the implications of an increasingly mobile world in which encounters with other races and ethnicities are a part of global modernity. As I note in Chapter 2, films such as the Cavalry Trilogy envision a multiethnic community that remains distinct from the raced Native population, but *Hondo* and *The Searchers* express the latent cultural anxieties resulting from the possibility that such a racial distinction might be blurring.

John Wayne's body acts as a complex signifier of a kind of cosmopolitanism. Rather than simply forcing international audiences to identify with white masculinity as powerful and skillful (although that was partly the case), Wayne offered a broad, masculine fantasy of action, mobility, and a capability to engage with other cultures encountered in travel. Throughout his westerns in this period, he repeatedly plays characters with intimate knowledge of and close relationships with Native Americans, even when they are his military adversaries. In *Fort Apache,* Wayne's character, Kirby York, is not only knowledgeable about the Apache but also personally tied to them and regretful for the ways they have been mistreated by the U.S. government. York is able to cross into Mexico to speak with the Apache (with the help of a Spanish interpreter), revealing his knowledge of their culture and his personal ties to them: they accept him at his word because of his dealings with them in the past and his respect for them. In *Hondo,* even as he supports the actions of the cavalry, Hondo notes at the end of the film that Apache culture "was quite a way to live"; he adds, "I'm sorry to see it go," simultaneously offering his respect and rationalizing the culture's disappearance. In many of Wayne's most prominent roles, his nomadic mobility often meant a special connection with and knowledge of native cultures, even when the sexual nature of such knowledge might need to be repressed or when his character is structurally aligned with colonial dominance. There is a basic recognition within the film that an appropriate model of mobile masculinity in the world of global capitalism must be flexible enough to adapt to and learn about different cultural contexts, even if such knowledge is used only to further the Eurocentric goals of capitalism as a system rather than to foster an ethical evaluation of one's own culture.

Thus in *Hondo* the relationship between Hondo Lane and the Apache chief Vittorio reveals a kind of cross-racial masculine code of ethics; in a heterogeneous world based on mobility and violent skill, both the Apache and the white settlers privilege a particular kind of masculinity. For example, in a scene in which Hondo and Mrs. Lowe share an intimate moonlit discussion on the Lowe ranch, Vittorio emerges from the darkness to talk to the two. After Hondo impresses Vittorio with his keen observations about the location of Vittorio's warriors hidden in the darkness, Vittorio asks Hondo to lie to the cavalry the next day about the whereabouts of the Apache. Hondo, of course, insists that he cannot. Vittorio then tells Mrs. Lowe that she has a good man (still thinking that Hondo is her husband) and leaves as mysteriously as he arrived. According to the logic of the film, the values that Vittorio judges Hondo by are a kind of masculine ethics that transcends culture, thus allowing for their mutual respect, but part of this ethic as expressed in the film is a respectful understanding of other cultures and their practices (even in the context of a race war for terri-torial dominance). Hondo's status as a "good man," after all, is based not only on his honesty and loyalty but also on the knowledge and skills of survival that he shares with the Apache. *Hondo*, therefore, affirms the emergence of a broad, cross-racial pattern of masculinity exemplified by a seminomadic, skillful, and cross-culturally knowledgeable John Wayne.[19]

John Wayne's body offers a complex fantasy of what the male body could and should be within an increasingly mobile and capitalist world. As the demands of a globalizing capitalism, the increasing necessity of mobility and movement, and the racial and ethnic tensions resulting from such mobility altered the pat-terns and privileges of masculinity around the world, the sensational pleasures of John Wayne's body on the big screen displayed a spectacular model of male subjectivity that was at once powerful, active, mobile, and cosmopolitan while also revealing the dark and tortured possibilities of the modernizing and global-izing world.

CHAPTER FIVE

John Wayne's Africa

EUROPEAN COLONIALISM VERSUS U.S. GLOBAL LEADERSHIP IN *LEGEND OF THE LOST*

A S WAYNE'S CHARACTER IN *LEGEND OF THE LOST*, JOE January, leads Paul Bonnard (Rossano Brazzi) and a prostitute named Dita (Sophia Loren) through the vast Sahara, the burgeoning love triangle between the three characters produces tensions not only between the travelers but also between the different ways that the two men relate to Dita and the idea of Africa in general. In one scene, the three take a much-needed break along the banks of an oasis after getting caught in a brutal desert sandstorm. Exploiting the internationally popular sex appeal of the young Loren at the time, Dita bathes in the nude in plain view of the two men, with only a conveniently placed donkey blocking the camera's view of Loren's naked body. Bonnard, an idealistic and religious European, looks on with embarrassment at the sexualized display, awkwardly breaking his gaze by looking at the ground before looking back up at Dita, or by attempting to distract himself and January by drawing a map of their route in the sand. But for the rough and practical American, January, there is no embarrassment or awkwardness, only a sustained and appreciative gaze at Dita's body, followed up by a suggestive offer to help her bathe, which Dita at first scoffs at in offense. But when January compares the sight of her to a mirage, she sneaks a small and grateful smile at his attention.

Within the film's highly sexist and problematic logic, the two men's relationship with Dita suggests a broader allegory of European versus U.S. visions of Africa and the developing world. Bonnard's relationship with Dita is marked by a deep sense of piety and humanitarian obligation, even as he is drawn to her sexually. He idealistically wants to save Dita, to uplift her soul and rescue her from the life of depravity that she lived before the journey, even if such lofty goals are rooted in an erotic desire. But for January there is no missionary zeal or moral obligation to hinder his attraction to Dita and her body. January's practical and honest embrace of life's base pleasures—be they alcohol or sex— eschews the paternalism and repression of Bonnard's perspective, openly and unashamedly enjoying Dita's naked body. Bonnard's European perspective is at once idealistic and condescending, offering optimistic humanitarian values but a strong sense of superiority, while January's American perspective is crude and masculinist but also libertarian, seeking pleasure and profit in Africa and expecting the locals to do the same. Since the scene is constructed to elicit the audience's gaze at Loren's sexualized body, it is clear that January's perspective is privileged here, affirming the patriarchal and imperialistic pleasures of the American male abroad.

That the film explores European and American models of relating to Africa should not be surprising, given its background. A U.S.-Italian coproduction, the film was produced partly by Wayne's own company, Batjac, and partly by Dear Films Productions, the Italian production company of Robert Haggiag, a Libyan-born American film producer who operated out of Rome and specialized in U.S.-Italian coproductions that qualified for Italian state film subsidies, such as *The Barefoot Contessa* (1954). Shot partly at the massive Italian studio Cinecittà and partly on location in Libya, *Legend of the Lost* is a prime example of Hollywood's internationalization in this period, in which it sought out international coproductions, exploited foreign subsidies, and used international shooting locations. Sophia Loren at the time was a rising international star with immense popularity in several markets around the world, and Rossano Brazzi, an established Italian star, was one of Europe's most popular leading men in the 1950s. Clearly a vehicle to exploit the international star power of Wayne, Loren, and Brazzi, the film situates the biggest American star in the world and a leading European star in the open and highly contested spaces of Africa as they battle for the affection and worldview of a local woman (played across ethnicity by Loren). A film explicitly designed for international audiences thus dramatizes the conflicts between Europe and the United States concerning the ideological terrain of Africa.

The film tells the story of Paul Bonnard, a wealthy Frenchman who arrives in Timbuktu in search of a local guide to lead him into the desert. A corrupt local official introduces him to Joe January, an American guide, but not before Bonnard becomes entangled with Dita, a local thief and possibly a prostitute. Although Dita at first picks Bonnard's pocket, they later form a close bond as he shares his optimistic and faith-based views on the world with her. So when Bonnard and January refuse to let Dita come along on their trek, she follows them into the desert anyway and eventually joins them on their journey. As they traverse the desert, Bonnard confides in January that they are seeking an ancient, lost holy city rumored to be filled with gold and jewels, a treasure that Bonnard's father supposedly discovered before disappearing into the desert. Bonnard plans to find the treasure and use it for humanitarian goals such as fighting hunger and creating peace, the dream of his father. January, of course, is highly skeptical of Bonnard's quest, but happily leads him, since he is getting paid, all the while developing an attraction to Dita, whom he had known in Timbuktu as an immoral companion for his own drunkenness and debauchery.

Just as it seems as though their quest will fail, the three stumble onto the ruins of an ancient city. But instead of the holy city Bonnard sought, they find the ruins of an old Roman city, along with the body of Bonnard's father and clues suggesting that he had planned to use the treasure to live lavishly in Paris with his illicit lover. Distraught over his loss of faith in his father, Bonnard goes slowly insane, finding the treasure and then attempting to kill January and Dita before stealing all the equipment and vanishing into the desert. January and Dita chase him down, but Bonnard stabs January in the back. Dita shoots and kills Bonnard. In the end, January and Dita are rescued by the nomadic Tuareg of the Sahara, but only after they forgive Bonnard's dead body, since his initial optimism and faith will now allow them to pursue a new and moral life together.

The film's tale of European and American conflict over Africa and the support of the locals was highly appropriate at the historical moment of the late 1950s. Before the massive waves of decolonization that occurred in the late 1950s and throughout the 1960s in Africa came years of debate and tensions concerning European colonialism and the role the United States would play in the decolonization process. In the postwar years, the United States became a powerful and outspoken proponent of decolonization, frustrating its European allies by emphasizing self-determination and independence for colonized populations (and for their entrance into global trade). Although very rapid decolonization would occur in a few short years, it wasn't at all clear in the mid-1950s when or how quickly that process would take place, or whether U.S. and European interests would fully align over how the decolonization process was to unfold. The French were in the middle of a bitter battle in Algeria to maintain colonial authority throughout the mid to late 1950s and into the 1960s; they were not clearly preparing to divest themselves of their imperial holdings.[1] In some regions, decolonization was not even an assured outcome in the mid-1950s, since European colonizers attempted to redefine and retool the colonial mission to include more local self-determination and autonomy (Cooper, *Africa since 1940*). Thus the international production of a film such as *Legend of the Lost* in 1956 and 1957, which explores the relationship between European and American visions of Africa (a film shot in Libya, a former Italian colony that had been recently run by the French and the British and had earned indepen-

dence in 1951) takes on special historical significance for the cultural representation of the tensions of African decolonization.

Moreover, this was not the first, nor would it be the last, time that John
Wayne took on a role in which he functioned as a representative of American
visions of global capitalism and economic development. Throughout the 1950s
and early 1960s, Wayne frequently played an American abroad, often one explicitly representing the United States or American interests. Not including
Wayne's numerous war films (in which he played another kind of American
representing U.S. interests abroad), he played an American boxer seeking out
his Irish roots in *The Quiet Man* (1952), a former U.S. sailor who helps ferry a
small Chinese village away from the brutal communists to Hong Kong in *Blood
Alley* (1955), the desert guide Joe January in *Legend of the Lost* (1957), the first
U.S. consul to Japan in *The Barbarian and the Geisha* (1958) — a film I discuss
in more detail in the next chapter — an American big-game trapper in Africa
in *Hatari!* (1962), and an American Wild West show producer who travels to
Europe in *Circus World* (1963). All those films except *Blood Alley* were shot overseas. And though most of the films (except *The Quiet Man*) were considered
commercial and artistic failures, there was nevertheless a continued assumption
that such roles were both part of Wayne's persona and a good way to exploit
international productions.

Given Wayne's tendency to represent the United States abroad, and given
the film's insistent comparisons between January's and Bonnard's styles of masculinity and attitudes toward Africa, I examine *Legend of the Lost* as a film that
explores the shifting policies and attitudes toward Africa at a tenuous historical moment just before the breakdown of Europe's rule over the continent. The
film offers a loose allegory of U.S. and European conceptions of decolonization,
dramatizing a set of ideas about how the West can relate to and intervene in
the space of Africa. This is not to say that the film is a straightforward affirmation of U.S. or European foreign policies in this period or an explicit comment
on the decolonization process. Rather, the film should be seen as one part of
a larger political and cultural discourse in which the shifting ideas and tensions concerning colonialism and global capitalism were managed. The film's
attitudes toward colonialism and the U.S. role in Africa are made legible only
through their interaction with the historical contexts and discourses surrounding Africa and global politics in the mid-1950s. Using the dynamics between
Wayne, Brazzi, and Loren to examine different models of international relations, the film dramatizes the tensions of colonialism's last hurrah, ultimately
valorizing the individualist and capitalist practicality of Wayne's Joe January
and celebrating U.S. global leadership while still maintaining a certain nostalgia
for the racist idealism of European colonial zeal.

THE IMPERIAL IMAGINARY: AFRICA AS
A SPACE FOR EURO-AMERICAN ADVENTURE

This is not to argue that the film's celebration of U.S. models of global capitalism, in contrast to European paternalism, is in any way anti-imperialist. On the contrary, from its initial scenes of vast desert landscapes and kitschy "exotic" local cultures, *Legend of the Lost* continually deploys the tired and clichéd tropes of the imperial adventure film. So while the film explores the nuanced differences between Joe January and Paul Bonnard as models of developed-world participation in the developing world, ultimately those differences reveal a shared sense of imperial responsibility and racial superiority.

The film reveals the sense of purpose in Africa shared by the United States and Africa's European colonizers in the 1950s, despite U.S. arguments in favor of decolonization. For the United States, Africa was a major front in the Cold War and the international battle against communism. U.S. foreign policy recognized that underdevelopment, poverty, and colonial exploitation in Africa made African populations susceptible to the kinds of discontent and class warfare that could benefit advocates of communism and socialism. U.S. policies advocated strongly for decolonization, self-government, modernization, and entrance into systems of global trade, hoping that economic prosperity and the consumption of goods from overseas would stave off the threat of communism and generally function as a way to support its international efforts to promote democracy. But this general support of decolonization did not necessarily mean that U.S. and European interests were at always odds. Recognizing that hasty decolonization could destabilize Africa and breed the kind of intense political and social turmoil that could benefit communist agitators (and recognizing as well that the European powers had immense economic investments in their colonies, which they wished to maintain even after a transition to local control), the United States often supported either continued European involvement in Africa or a very slow decolonization process that didn't result in full independence until the mid to late 1970s (Kent, "Decolonization of Black Africa").

Indeed, as John Kent indicates in his study of the United States and decolonization in black Africa, the assumptions and arguments of U.S. policy makers in the 1950s relied on the same racist beliefs about black African "tribalism" and lack of development as did the European colonizers. As the United States attempted to balance a push toward decolonization and self-government with friendly relations with its European allies (who were necessary for waging the Cold War), U.S. foreign-policy makers at times made arguments similar to those of their European counterparts about the inability of "backward" and "primitive" African populations to effectively govern themselves and create viable governments and economies (Kent, "Decolonization of Black Africa," 170–171). Participating in the same condescending and Eurocentric view of Africa that had sustained the colonial system for so long, U.S. officials in the mid-1950s worried that the African people needed to modernize and educate themselves before they would be truly ready for independence. But the political pressure to support self-government and advocate for democracy began to override such worries as the United States continued to support decolonization (172–176).

Produced and distributed in the midst of these tensions over African decolonization, *Legend of the Lost* participates in racist attitudes concerning Africa and puts responsibility for the continent on either the United States or Europe. Showing the same anxiety about native African leadership, the film uses the space of Africa to showcase the contrast between U.S. and European worldviews while occluding the possibilities of native autonomy. Indeed, the bulk of the film captures in wide-screen the vast and open landscape of the Sahara as the three travelers cross the desert, constructing it as a "virginal" and exotic land, meaningful only in that it provides a space for Euro-American, masculinist adventurism or philanthropy. And typically for an imperial adventure film, Wayne's Joe January proves to be more knowledgeable about the Sahara than even the locals, legitimating his dominance of the landscape and naturalizing his leadership despite his status as an outsider. The prefect of Timbuktu describes January as the most experienced guide in the region, and it is January's tough survival skills that keep the trio alive throughout the film, displaying Wayne's familiar skill, knowledge, and ability to endure the elements. In one scene, in fact, January tells Bonnard that because of his close connection to the harsh land, the Sahara is his: "It's all I have." January is constructed as a natural guardian of and guide for the territory.

Legend of the Lost's iconography at times resembles that of the western genre and its construction of the U.S. frontier, linking the film to that genre's much-discussed colonial assumptions. Focusing on the heroic exploration of treacherous, open space by a rugged white adventurer on horseback (actually, donkey-back), *Legend of the Lost* often makes reference to the genre that Wayne was so associated with. Even the nomadic Tuareg are shot as Native Americans are in the western, that is, as dangerous and primitive wanders who suddenly and mysteriously appear on the horizon, threatening the freedom of movement of the hero. In the same way that the western naturalizes the occupation of "unused" land on the U.S. frontier, *Legend of the Lost* celebrates the adventures of Euro-American wanderers mastering space in the service of "civilization," in contrast to the "primitive" nomadism of the native inhabitants.

Moreover, in contrast to the open spaces of the Sahara, Timbuktu is represented as a clichéd Orientalist city characterized by bizarre rituals, thievery, and dangerous sexuality. Clearly shot on a set at Cinecittà, the scenes in Timbuktu construct Africa as stereotypically primitive and dangerous, a flat and typical colonial setting seen commonly in mainstream cinema's imperialist construction of Africa and the Middle East. The film opens with a funeral procession down the streets of Timbuktu overseen by the local prefect. It features dancers flailing wildly, loud drumming, and a harem of mourners veiled in black: an overwrought and almost campy representation of the exotic. The prefect is drawn away from the procession by the arrival of Bonnard, whose pocket is promptly picked by Dita. The prefect then takes Bonnard to look for Joe January, searching without success in several bars and brothels featuring sexualized dancers and young women for sale. The fleshy delights not only indicate January's debauchery but also reveal Timbuktu to be a city marked by dangerous, non-Western sexual temptations. In short, the Timbuktu of the film represents the cities and towns of Africa as treacherous, vice-filled places offering titillating yet depraved pleasures for adventurous Euro-American males.

Dita too, as a representative of the local culture, suggests the titillating exoticism of Africa, but her character collapses different cultural stereotypes that privilege a sexualized yet paternal Euro-American gaze and sense of responsibility. As played by Loren, Dita is both sexual and childlike, a world-weary prostitute who has seen the worst kinds of debauchery and yet is also a simple, innocent young woman in need of protection from the elements of the desert. She needs a moral guide who has faith in her ability to start a new life. Her character naturalizes and legitimizes the intervention of Western masculinities in the affairs of the non-Western world. Especially given Loren's reputation as a hypersexual screen goddess, Dita is represented as naturally sexual, a non-Western woman who exudes sexual charisma without trying and often without embarrassment. Her sexuality is alluring to the Western male (and having a European actress play the role softens anxieties about miscegenation), but her sexuality is also a source of tension, since it must be regulated and policed by bringing it in line with hegemonic structures like marriage and the family. Thus, the film suggests that without the intervention of the Western male, someone like Dita would succumb to the excesses of her exotic culture (the same excesses and exoticism, of course, that initially attracted the Euro-American male to Dita in the first place). Typically for the imperial adventure film, *Legend of the Lost* titillates the Western male imagination with clichéd images of female sexuality while simultaneously positioning the Western male as a necessary and paternal protector of femininity and morality.[2]

In most ways, therefore, the goals and attitudes of the film's U.S. and European representatives are mutually supportive, since both participate in a host of problematic assumptions about Africa and the inability of its people to self-govern, seeing African populations much as the film sees Dita: childlike innocents in need of protection and guidance.

IMPERIAL NEGOTIATIONS: U.S. VERSUS
EUROPEAN MODELS OF GLOBAL LEADERSHIP

While the film never wavers in its insistence on the necessity of western intervention in the space of Africa, much of the tension between Bonnard and January indicates a much deeper ambivalence about different models of international involvement in Africa. After all, Dita functions as a representative of the local cultures who needs protection and guidance, and much of the film centers on her choice between Bonnard and January and the different systems of involvement they represent. Bonnard's idealistic humanitarianism and January's rugged libertarianism dramatize and sensationalize the complex negotiation of power and decolonization in 1950s Africa.

The film addresses the tensions between U.S. foreign policy and European colonialism, tensions that began before World War II but intensified with the rise of U.S. global power after the war. As Melani McAlister points out, "In the years before World War II, US state policy and US businesses converged to promote the economic influence of US-based corporations as an alternative to conquest" (*Epic Encounters*, 30). Rather than engaging in colonialism based on military occupation and the establishment of colonial governments, the kind practiced throughout the nineteenth century and the first half of the twentieth by European powers, the United States in the postwar years for the most part expanded its international interests in the service of U.S. corporations and the export of U.S. goods. Focusing on the development of global capitalism as a system and the international consumption of U.S. goods, U.S. foreign policy advocated openly for an end to colonialism and for the establishment of independent nations, which would presumably enter more freely into international trade when colonial restrictions privileging trade with the colonizing nation were lifted. Freer trade would then allow for an "open" market (that is, one in which U.S. goods could dominate), one of the fundamental policies of economic globalization that is still hotly contested today.

The most prevalent example of the disconnection between American support of local autonomy and the imperialistic influence of European colonizers in this period was the Suez crisis of 1956. Since the 1880s, the Suez Canal had been an international waterway deemed neutral but protected by the British, who maintained a massive military outpost on the Suez into the 1950s. As the base became a source of tension with the Egyptian government in the 1950s (along with British support for the newly created state of Israel), the Egyptian and British governments reached an agreement in which British troops would eventually withdraw from the canal. Additionally, control of the Suez Canal Company—the company that regulates traffic on the canal—would be handed over to Egypt in 1968. But when Nasser nationalized the Suez Canal Company in July 1956 in order to exert more control in the region and secure the profits from the canal for Egypt, the combined forces of Israel, Britain, and France invaded the country. They argued that the canal was essential to international trade routes and should remain under the protection of European powers, which would keep goods flowing. The United States, however, disappointed its allies. Eisenhower intervened in support of Nasser, ending the invasion and keeping the Suez in control of Egypt. U.S. policy constructed itself as a major supporter of anticolonialism in the region while affirming Egyptian participation in a system of international trade, casting itself as the liberator and European colonialism as an outmoded and unnecessary system.

McAlister notes how Hollywood participated in these anticolonial discourses, pointing to DeMille's *The Ten Commandments* (1956) as a film that intersects with the public discourses of U.S. anticolonialism to loosely allegorize U.S. opposition to both the perceived domination of communism and the old European colonial system. Recognizing that the film is not a direct comment on the Suez crisis or an explicit affirmation of U.S. foreign policy, McAlister argues instead that the meanings and pleasures of a film such as *The Ten Commandments* (or other Hollywood epics) depended on their interactions with and juxtapositions to a host of complex cultural and political dramas like the Suez crisis (*Epic Encounters*, 43–47). Only when understood as one part of a broad historical context does the film resonate with U.S. anticolonialism.

Similarly, *Legend of the Lost* functions as one of many sites where U.S. and European models of global power were represented and contested in the mid-1950s. But given the film's status as a European coproduction, *Legend of the Lost* explores a more nuanced and complex set of associations concerning the role of Europe in the developing world than those evinced in McAlister's reading of *The Ten Commandments*. Rather than constructing European colonialism as a monolithic form of exploitation and racism, the film at first acknowledges the perceived humanitarian mission of uplift, even with its condescension and superiority. While Bonnard's mission in the Sahara is quite explicitly exploitative and functions as a metaphor for Europe's relationship to Africa—he is going into the desert to remove and extract an ancient treasure left there by native inhabitants—he does so not for his own wealth but to fulfill his father's dream of serving humanity. He wants to use the money to create "a refuge for the needy, a haven for the sick of soul and body, a monument to humanity rising out of the jungle." Bonnard's idealism and desires to help the needy set his vision of European involvement in Africa apart from superficial constructions of colonialism as exploitative and oppressive, even as his image of the monument rising out of the jungle condescendingly invokes ideas about Western humanitarianism towering over the immoral and needy developing-world jungle.

The early scenes of the film juxtapose Bonnard's humanitarianism and the corruption of colonial officials whose greed and exploitative behavior signify the oppressive excesses of the traditional colonial system. In the first scenes, the French prefect of Timbuktu halts and delays a local funeral procession so that he can attempt to squeeze some money out of the newly arrived Bonnard. And in the prefect's dealings with January, it is clear that he piles frivolous infractions one after another on the American to keep him in debt to the city so that the prefect can take a cut of January's earnings. In typical Hollywood fashion, the film uses body type to indicate character—the prefect's portly and slovenly appearance marks him as immoral and untrustworthy, a caricature of the corrupt colonial official seeking only personal gain and exhibiting the worst of the colonial system. The righteous and sensitive Bonnard, by contrast, dramatizes an alternative to the racist and corrupt system of colonialism as exploitation.[3]

Moreover, in contrast to Bonnard's optimistic appraisal of humanity and his desires to help others, Joe January is somewhat amoral and selfish, seeking only his own pleasure. He has made a life for himself in Timbuktu bouncing from bar to bar and brothel to brothel, often finding himself in jail. While likeable and heroic for his skills in the desert, in the early scenes of the film his cynical and practical wantonness stands in stark contrast with the grand idealism of Bonnard.

The differences between the men are on display when the travelers come across a band of Tuareg in the desert. The Tuareg have made camp next to an oasis that January, Bonnard, and Dita were planning to use, so the three travelers are forced to wait, hidden behind a sand dune, until the dangerous Tuareg leave. But it becomes clear that one of the Tuareg is ill, and in keeping with their traditions, they will wait there until the sick man dies. January, not wanting to interfere in their culture and not wanting to risk his life, is content to wait them out, but Bonnard immediately gets a small bag of medical equipment and rushes in to help. The Tuareg threaten Bonnard with guns but ultimately allow him to tend to the sick man and save his life while Dita watches on in awe and January expresses his admiration at Bonnard's courage. Enshrining the inherent goodness of Western medicine and science over the traditions of the Tuareg, the scene celebrates Bonnard's humanitarian instinct in contrast with the cynical and selfish individualism of January.

This construction of Bonnard's European humanitarianism reflects the complex manifestations of European colonialism in the 1950s. Colonialism as practiced by the European powers was often thought of as uniform and monolithic in its domination and exploitation of colonized lands and populations, but as Frederick Cooper points out, European colonialism was a "moving target" of sorts, shifting and changing its approach and attitudes regarding its colonies (*Africa since 1940*, 62). In the 1950s, the discourses of modernization and development that were dominating debates about international relations and the global fight against poverty and communism were integrated into the colonial mission. In what Cooper refers to as "modernizing imperialism," colonizers such as Great Britain and France tried "to relegitimize colonial rule, to increase African political participation in a controlled way, and to give Africans a stake in expanding production within the imperial economy" in the 1950s (62). There were clear limits to such processes. The expansion of colonial autonomy and development could never override European economic interests. So, for example, the Belgian government made vast improvements in social services and health care in the copper-mining regions of the Congo, but forbade trade unions and political organization among its colonial citizens in order to protect Belgian interests in the mining operations (63). Nevertheless, the culture of colonialism changed in the postwar years as more and more impetus was put on economic development, humanitarian projects, and local political autonomy. As Cooper puts it, the 1950s saw "a new world where [colonial] legitimacy was measured in terms of progress toward self-government and economic development" (66).

Bonnard's idealism and hopes of helping populations around the world can be seen as reflecting the 1950s attempts of colonial powers to redefine the colonial mission as essentially one of promoting the welfare and prosperity of African peoples. Of course, the redefinition of European colonialism was a sort of last-ditch effort to retain power and influence. With the looming threat of complete decolonization on the horizon, the changing focus of the colonial mission made more complex the buildup to decolonization, although in the mid-1950s, before the outcome and pace of decolonization was entirely clear, the project of modernizing imperialism was still up for debate. *Legend of the Lost*, then, allows for some debate, allows for Bonnard to represent a heroic and humanitarian model of European investment in Africa, but as the film progresses, Bonnard and his worldview come unraveled.

When Bonnard learns that his father abandoned his idealism and dreams of helping the impoverished in the developing world, and instead sought personal gain and pleasure with his lover, the political allegory of the film shifts. Throughout the film, Bonnard's faith rested on his father and his aspirations, but when the group comes across the dead body of the senior Bonnard, it becomes clear that Bonnard's father had murdered his lover and their desert guide, who had planned to run away together. The younger Bonnard turns to drink but continues to obsess over the treasure, reproducing his father's saga by running off with the gold and jewels and stabbing January in the back when he catches up with Bonnard in the desert. The shame of his father's true character destroys Bonnard's optimism, and he relives the sins of the father.

The intergenerational conflict in the film's resolution suggests that even present-day advocates of modernizing imperialism cannot overcome the dark and oppressive history of colonialism's past. By structuring Bonnard's break-

FIGURE 5.1. *January (John Wayne) and Dita (Sophia Loren) exploring the crumbling but grand Roman city in* Legend of the Lost *(Batjac/Dear Films Productions, 1957).*

down as a recognition of the true nature of the previous generation's relationship to Africa—that Bonnard's father, despite the humanitarian rhetoric, sought to extract precious resources from the expanses of Africa to spend on a lavish prosperity back in Europe—*Legend of the Lost* indicates the continuing legacy of past practices of colonial exploitation on the present generation. Bonnard's own breakdown and attempts to repeat his father's exploitation reveal that there is a fine line between humanitarian involvement and personal, selfish gain, a line that Bonnard is driven to cross.

The lingering history of imperial domination, after all, is spectacularly present when they find the lost city: it was not a legendary holy city that served as a beacon of hope and prosperity, but simply an old Roman metropolis lost to the desert.[4] As January and Dita wander through the Roman columns and vast coliseum and read the old Latin carved into the stone, they (and we) are reminded of the long history of conquest and domination in the region. The confrontation between January and Bonnard within the grand but crumbling city suggests not only the lingering presence of colonialism but also its inevitable decline as an outmoded system.

Moreover, as the three learned from the letters and effects found on the dead bodies, Bonnard's father would have brought his lover and treasure to Paris from the Sahara, a subtle but important reference to French colonialism that hints at continued French involvement in the region. In the mid-1950s, while France was fighting for control of Algeria against the independence movement there, the French government began granting more autonomy to its colonies. But with the outcome in Algeria unclear, the French quietly worked to retain influence in the Sahara, especially as more and more geological research pointed to extensive oil resources under the sands of the desert (and as the French realized the possibilities of the Sahara as a space to test nuclear bombs). The Sahara had always been more politically stable than other French holdings, thus the French in the mid-1950s sought to establish the Common Organization of Saharan Regions (Organisation commune des régions sahariennes, or OCRS), which would oversee Saharan territory from Algeria, Mauritania, French Sudan (Mali and Senegal), Niger, and Chad. Operating under the logic of modernizing imperialism, the French argued that oil revenues in the region would fund the modernization and development of Saharan peoples, but it was also clear that such a territorial reorganization would benefit French economic interests and keep the French government highly involved in the region. At first the OCRS only included the Algerian Sahara, then Niger and Chad joined the organization in 1959. The OCRS fell apart after Algeria won independence in 1962 (Sèbe, "Algerian War").

The OCRS represented an inconsistency in the U.S. anticolonial stance in Africa, since two successive U.S. administrations chose to ignore the organization and its neocolonial mission. Berny Sèbe details the complex reasons for U.S. nonreaction (including the possibility of U.S. oil revenues and the hope that political stability in the Sahara would be good for Africa), but the incident reveals the complex negotiations between the continued dominance of European colonialism and U.S. anticolonialism, suggesting a delicate balance between the imperialistic ideologies of development and the practices of European colonial exploitation.

Legend of the Lost's colonial allegory is tied to the history of French neocolonialism. Although Bonnard is never explicitly discussed as French (and Brazzi plays the character as ambiguously "European"), his name and the fact that his father wanted to take his lover to Paris draw connections between his humanitarian mission, which turns into violent and exploitative theft, and the historical context of French involvement in the oil-rich Sahara. Functioning as one part of a larger discourse about U.S. and European involvement in Africa, the film raises questions about the intentions of French and European investment in the Sahara. The film dramatizes the dangers of genuinely well-meaning humanitarian missions that slide into exploitation because of the weight of the past, exploring a possible critique of French involvement in the Sahara even as U.S. foreign policy remained conspicuously quiet. As January notes after Bonnard turns on them in the lost city, he has seen these kinds of "do-gooders" before, who end up doing more good for themselves. He calls out the hypocrisy of humanitarian missions in Africa and lumps Bonnard in with the long history of self-serving European uplift efforts in Africa, such as religious-conversion missions or attempts at forced modernization. By the end of the film, Bonnard is no better than the corrupt French officials in Timbuktu.

Since the film problematically constructs Dita as the representative of local cultures, it is ultimately her romantic rejection of Bonnard that solidifies the film's rejection of a kind of modernizing imperialism. Having lost faith in his father and his humanitarian mission, Bonnard abruptly decides that his romance with Dita will fulfill him instead, sneaking to her in the night as January sleeps. Hoping to make love, he is rebuffed by her. She cites his earlier optimism and his faith in her ability to become a moral person as reasons to avoid a tawdry affair. Bonnard then pleads with her, offering her the treasure and claiming that they could use the wealth to buy respectability for her, a prospect too close to prostitution for Dita, who hopes to start a new and enlightened life for herself.

Dita's rejection of Bonnard signifies a kind of local responsibility in the face of crumbling European leadership and domination, although one that still affirms the values of Western modernity and uplift. Having internalized the lessons of the optimistic European do-gooder, Dita is able to toss aside Bonnard and his slide into exploitation while still embracing the values that Bonnard once stood for. Much as the United States embraced the problematic condescension and paternalism of European colonialism—seeing African populations as childlike and in need of economic, political, and moral guidance—while still advocating for self-government and the end of European rule, Dita affirms the need for Western guidance while pushing aside Bonnard and the ghosts of European colonialism that haunt him.

Rather than indicating that she is truly taking responsibility for herself, Dita's rejection of Bonnard instead becomes an acceptance of Joe January and his individualistic and at times cynical worldview. Dita is never autonomous; she simply finds her way from one model of leadership and social relations to another. So just as Bonnard's once-admirable humanitarianism slips into exploitation, madness, and eventually violence, January's simple and at times crude individualism becomes more and more appealing as the film progresses, by the end offering the only sane option for Dita (and the audience) to identify with. In typical John Wayne fashion, January's perspective on the world is highly practical and based in rugged individualism. When Bonnard requests that no liquor be taken on the trek, January tells him, "I'll live my way, you live yours." When Bonnard stays up all night convincing Dita that she can change her life, January says that he is confusing her; he prefers that people stay out of others' affairs.

And throughout the journey, January's practicality and expertise at survival give his individualist worldview a sense of authority and legitimacy—as mentioned above, the American Wayne is more skilled in the desert than even the locals, legitimizing his presence and involvement in Africa.

January's model of participation in Africa becomes an affirmation of U.S. global leadership on the continent. Rather than the overly intellectual and condescending humanitarianism of Bonnard, who is knowledgeable about the desert but has only read about it in books while living in luxury in Europe, January has practical, on-the-ground experience and has spent years working as an entrepreneur in the Sahara. Unlike Bonnard with his lofty goals, January sees Africa as a space of commerce, somewhere he can make money with his skills. While January's individualism seems cynical and cold in contrast with Bonnard's inspirational sense of duty and obligation, as Bonnard falls apart, January's practicality becomes more sympathetic, even admirable, as his masculine knowledge and skills keep himself and Dita alive in the desert.

In the film's allegory, January becomes a stand-in for the United States and its self-proclaimed role as global leader. After all, he is played by Wayne — perhaps one the most famous Americans around the world in that period — and the film refers to January's patriotism and Americanism. When we first meet January, he is in the Timbuktu jail, where he demands free room and board, given his debt to the city. His most recent infraction, it turns out, was to have made "bombs" on the Fourth of July, a date of no significance to the French prefect. January's rugged Americanism provides a model of U.S. involvement in Africa that is supposedly egalitarian and individualistic — January is not there to offer anyone welfare, just to make a living — and that dramatizes the ideologies of a U.S.-inspired global leadership. Instead of grand ideologies of Western paternalism, the United States instead promoted a model of local and national autonomy and self-determination, but one based on international commerce and trade. It was a system in which foreign individuals or corporations were encouraged to participate in local and national economies.

By juxtaposing January's practical entrepreneurship with Bonnard's fall from grace, the political allegory of the film attempts to obscure the systems of inequality and dominance built into a U.S.-led system of global capitalism; in the end, it celebrates the down-to-earth and individualist notion of Africa as a space freed from the constraints of colonialism and ready for commerce and equal competition. But since Wayne as Joe January stands taller than most in the Sahara and benefits from the privileges of the Euro-American male produced by imperialism, his presence indicates how U.S. visions of anticolonialism still relied on many of the same ideologies and inequalities of Eurocentrism. In the final scenes of the film, as January lies wounded in the desert, he and Dita forgive Bonnard's lifeless body, crediting his optimism for giving them both a new appreciation for humanity and their own morals. So after Bonnard and the systems of paternalism and exploitation that he came to represent are finally put to rest, January expresses nostalgia for Bonnard's idealistic aspirations as a way of avoiding the obviousness of his own dominance in Africa and his relationship with Dita.

In the period just before massive African decolonization, John Wayne in *Legend of the Lost* typified the ideal of global capitalist masculinity, a model of

manhood and leadership that became dramatically more appropriate for relations with Africa than the shifting face of European colonialism. At a time
when the public discourses surrounding Africa and its relationship to both
Europe and the United States sought to balance European economic interests
with U.S. pressures to decolonize—while maintaining the persistent stereo-
type that African populations were too primitive, tribal, or undeveloped to lead
themselves—John Wayne as an icon of modern masculinity in the film managed these cultural and political tensions, articulating not only the "natural"
and practical role of U.S.-inspired capitalism in Africa but also the benefits and
pleasures of a skilled, entrepreneurial (and American) masculinity in ushering
Africa into the global economy.

HATARI! AND AFRICA AS A SPACE FOR CAPITALISM

Wayne returned to Africa in the early 1960s to shoot *Hatari!* with
Howard Hawks, a film shot entirely on location at several national parks and
big-game reserves in Tanzania. The film follows the exploits of Sean Mercer
(Wayne) and his team of big-game trappers, who traverse the African wilderness capturing wild game to be shipped to zoos around the world. The dynamics
of the team, however, are upset upon the arrival of a photographer from Italy
(Elsa Martinelli), who slowly forges a romantic relationship with Mercer. With
very little plot, the bulk of the film spends its time on action scenes tracking
Mercer's team as they speed across the African frontier trying to lasso giraffes
or run down grumpy rhinos (with many comic interludes detailing the bois-
terous camaraderie of the team also thrown in). And as in many other of the
Hawks-Wayne collaborations, such as *Red River* or *Rio Bravo*, the film's interpersonal relationships emphasize the gruff, masculinist exterior of Wayne's
character and the possibility of his being slowly opened up to romance and
sexuality by a woman willing to be one of the boys.[5]

Unlike Wayne's trip to Africa in *Legend of the Lost, Hatari!* suffers from
none of the existential crises surrounding decolonization and the relationship between the United States and Europe in Africa. While *Legend of the Lost*
slowly and methodically explores the crumbling worldview of European colonial intervention, dramatically negotiating the role of the United States versus that of Europe through January and Bonnard as their worldviews compete
for dominance, *Hatari!*'s relatively lighthearted African romp simply assumes
U.S. leadership; Mercer heads up a diverse group of mostly European followers
who are all happy to simply make a buck in Africa. Filmed in 1961 after a wave
of decolonization in Africa and around the world made it apparent that European colonialism was on its last legs, and filmed during the transition as Tanza-

nia (then Tanganyika) became independent from Britain, the film focuses on Wayne as the natural leader of his international crew of trappers. Almost comically diverse, Mercer's team is made up of a German race car driver (Hardy Krüger), a Mexican former bullfighter (Valentin de Vargas), a tribally ambiguous Native American named Little Wolf but simply called "The Indian" (played by a very white Bruce Cabot), a former New York City cab driver (Red Buttons), the French daughter of a team member who died long ago (Michèle Girardon), and a newly arrived French sharpshooter with a chip on his shoulder (Gérard Blain). So instead of philosophical questions about human morality and humanitarian goals, the film instead simply focuses on a band of mostly European and American men freed from the weight of colonial goals in Africa and undertaking their own exploitation of the land and its resources.

Legend of the Lost and *Hatari!* are very different films with different goals, so comparing the overwrought drama of the first with the comedic adventure of the second is not entirely fair, but in the trajectory of John Wayne's star text and his roles as an American overseas, the transition from *Legend of the Lost* to *Hatari!* makes clear the disappearance of certain discourses surrounding European colonialism. In their place is a vision of Africa in which capitalism and the entrepreneurship of hardworking men—be they European, American, Mexican, or Native American—will reign supreme as long as they follow the lead of the rugged and skilled American who leads the way. In this way, *Hatari!* completes the trajectory started in *Legend of the Lost* in which a humanitarian but condescending European colonialism gives way to the economic freedom and individualism of a U.S.-inspired global capitalism.

Which is not to say that *Hatari!* avoids the racist and Eurocentric assumptions of imperialism. In the film's logic, the white trappers (who here seem to include Mexicans and Native Americans) are clearly privileged and empowered over the local black Africans, who only play small subservient roles (anonymous helpers with the animals, butlers, and bartenders, for example). And while the trappers treat the tribes they encounter in the wilderness with a certain respect and admiration, the Africans are clearly primitive and exotic locals who don't seem to mind the local animals being trapped and shipped away. The fact that the animals are sent to zoos, moreover, links the film to a host of discourses privileging Western science and knowledge, forcibly and at times violently removing animals from around the world to be studied and categorized by Western researchers and to be displayed for the amusement of urban dwellers, a Eurocentric project the film has no qualms about. Indeed, zoos are a remnant of late nineteenth-century scientific thought that coincided with the ideological peak of imperialism, constructing the world as the natural domain of Western systems of knowledge. The ideologies of European colonialism linger in the film's affirmation of Euro-American privilege.

Thus, *Hatari!*'s tossing aside of European colonialism, rather than providing for local autonomy and prosperity, instead opens the door for American economic dominance, a narrative regarding Africa that the Hollywood studios were experiencing themselves. In attempts to develop and exploit more film markets around the world in the 1950s, the Motion Picture Export Association (MPEA, which was tasked with managing the major studios' international relations) turned to developing nations and Africa in the years before *Hatari!* was made. Hollywood had its eye on Africa, since decolonization meant that emerging African nations were no longer guided by the "imperial preference" import guidelines of European colonizers (by which, for example, British films were prioritized over U.S. films in British-controlled colonies). Late in the decade, the MPEA became more active in exploiting these markets; in 1959 an MPEA delegate was sent to tour West Africa, and in 1960 MPEA president Eric Johnston himself "toured the African market to survey exhibition facilities and to contact African government officials" about the elimination of trade restrictions (Guback, *International Film Industry*, 98–99). According to a press release from the MPEA dated September 6, 1960, the tactic was working: "The motion picture box office is jingling merrily in Ghana," with Johnston reporting: "There is only one way to describe the movie situation in this new nation of 6,500,000 persons . . . The people love the movies. Attendance is increasing all the time. New theaters are constantly under construction to accommodate the crowds."[6] The vision of U.S. global leadership and economic freedom in Africa dramatized in *Hatari!* closely mirrored Hollywood's own plans for Africa as a space for profit and new markets, a space in which Hollywood and other European industries could compete for new audiences outside the restrictions of any form of European colonialism.

As an emissary for both Hollywood and a U.S.-inspired global capitalism, John Wayne in the late 1950s and early 1960s modeled a kind of masculinity central to the ideologies of free trade and capitalist individualism in the new economic order: rugged, libertarian, skilled, and ready to profit from the land and resources of Africa once the oppressive restraints of colonialism were lifted. While still retaining the racial privileges and domination structured into the colonial system, John Wayne's Africa embraces the emerging values of economic freedom and freedom from colonial rule in order to construct the continent as one rife with possibilities and prosperity for those with the right kind of modern masculinity. And while Wayne's films in Africa clearly privilege white American males, the complex nature of race, ethnicity, and film identification suggests that Wayne's vision of African entrepreneurship may have broadly affirmed the pleasures and privileges of a global capitalist masculinity for those in Wayne's international audiences for whom Africa offered a new frontier for capitalist exploitation.

CHAPTER SIX

John Wayne's Japan

INTERNATIONAL PRODUCTION, GLOBAL
TRADE, AND JOHN WAYNE'S DIPLOMACY
IN *THE BARBARIAN AND THE GEISHA*

*A*T THE BEGINNING OF THE 1958 JOHN WAYNE HISTORI-
cal romance *The Barbarian and the Geisha*, Okichi (Eiko
Ando) — the geisha of the film's title, who provides the film's voice-over narra-
tion — insists, "This is my story too," while the film lyrically captures images of
traditional Japanese culture before Western contact. This forceful assertion of
narrative centrality and Okichi's powerful position as narrator challenge many
of the masculine and Western privileges normally associated with Hollywood
films, particularly those of John Wayne. In Wayne's cinematic world, he is most
often the center of the narrative: his subjectivity dominates the audience's perspective, privileging his position (and the position of white males in general)
over those of the women and people of color he dominates. Yet in *Barbarian*,
although Wayne still dominates the narrative, Okichi's voice-over establishes
that the film is from her point of view, contesting the centrality of Wayne's
(and the West's) perspective on the story. From the start, the film establishes
itself as a site of negotiation over whose film it really is and whose perspective
is privileged, for although it stars Wayne and Sam Jaffe, it was filmed in Japan,
with a largely Japanese cast and crew, and doesn't use English subtitles when
characters speak Japanese. Since this is Okichi's story too, a story about Japanese engagement with U.S. culture rather than simply an American story about
an exotic Other, *The Barbarian and the Geisha* explores the possibilities of local
cultures asserting their centrality to the dominant narratives about global cultural exchange and cross-cultural engagement.

Okichi's assertion of narrative centrality complicates a film that seems a
classic example Hollywood's racist and imperialistic construction of the non-
Western world. The film tells the story of Townsend Harris, a U.S. diplomat
who in 1858 traveled to Japan to open the country's ports, which had been

closed to foreigners for more than two hundred years. After landing in a small fishing village in the province of Shimoda, Harris must first win over the small community before the hostile local officials agree to take him to the capital to speak before the shogun. All the while, Okichi the geisha is sent to stay with Harris and spy on him, but she develops respect for Harris and his American ways, as does the governor of Shimoda, who must choose between adherence to traditional beliefs and his growing respect for Harris. The film's narrative therefore exemplifies many of the tropes of cinematic imperialism: it presents an exotic spectacle in which a Western male must navigate the alien spaces of a foreign culture while asserting his mastery over the sexualized and racialized woman who stands in as a reductive representative of the culture as a whole. Moreover, the film's use of CinemaScope wide-screen technology emphasizes Hollywood's spectacular construction of exotic locales for the visual pleasure of Western audiences, thereby participating in Hollywood's Orientalist construction of Asia in the 1950s.

To interpret *Barbarian* solely within the framework of Western imperialism and Orientalism, however, oversimplifies the film's complicated depiction of U.S.-Japanese relations within the context of global capitalism. The film was released at a unique historical moment when two former imperial rivals had to renegotiate their relationship within a globalizing economy and the context of "containing" communism. With the "loss" of China to communism, the U.S. government shifted its focus in the 1950s to rebuilding Japan into the ally and trade partner that China could not become (Dudden, *American Pacific*, 191–213). Meanwhile, during and after the 1945–1952 occupation of Japan by the U.S. military, the Japanese had begun to recognize the necessity of cooperating with their former enemies in order to revitalize the nation's economy and status in the world community. The rather swift reconsideration of their relationship on the part of both the Americans and the Japanese meant a substantial revision of the cultural stereotypes and racism within both cultures, which had resulted from years of dehumanizing propaganda before and during World War II (for example, see Dower, *War without Mercy*). Thus, the negotiation of the 1858 U.S.-Japanese trade agreement dramatized in *Barbarian* can be seen as an apparent allegory for the 1950s renegotiation of the Japanese as strategic allies and friends in both the American and Japanese cultural imaginations.

What is more, the film's production in Japan reflected the internationalization of Hollywood in the 1950s. Twentieth Century–Fox reportedly had more than $100 million in blocked funds in Japan, which the studio was trying to spend on Japanese productions and invest in the Japanese film industry (Beech, "Hollywood's Oriental Fad"). The $3.5 million that Fox spent on the production of *Barbarian* as part of that effort made *Barbarian* the most expensive film ever made in Japan at the time, perhaps because it was the first period piece

FIGURE 6.1. *Wayne as Townsend Harris coming ashore with his translator, Heusken (Sam Jaffe), in The Barbarian and the Geisha (20th Century Fox, 1958).*

attempted by Hollywood in Japan, requiring the elaborate transformation of modern Kyoto into a nineteenth-century Japanese fishing village (Scheuer, "'Barbarian' Leaves Japan"). The use of a large Japanese cast and crew suggests that the film's economic context required a negotiation of cultural exchange similar to that manifested in its narrative.

John Wayne at first glance seems an odd choice as arbitrator of these negotiations. Wayne is most often associated with American militarism and patriotism; his brand of rugged and violent masculinity can rarely be termed diplomatic. And yet as the world's most popular star in the 1950s, who represented not just Hollywood's vision of the United States but also a modern, capitalist masculinity being consumed around the world, Wayne in many ways was the perfect diplomat to oversee the integration of localities into global capitalism. Moreover, *Barbarian*'s unique production history complicates any attempts to see the film in simple terms of cultural domination—just like Townsend Harris, Wayne and the U.S. crew traveled to Japan in what was publicized as an attempt to foster cross-cultural understanding between the two nations. While such grandiose claims clearly obscured Hollywood's need to turn a profit from funds stuck in Japanese banks, it is nevertheless fruitful to see the film and Wayne's performance within the dynamics of cross-cultural exchange.

Mirroring the film's narrative, in which Harris encourages the Japanese to enter into international trade agreements despite Japanese concerns about cultural contamination, Wayne's performance showcases the delicate cultural negotiations that would allow Japan to embrace a kind of U.S.-led global capitalism while leaving open possibilities for uniquely Japanese modernities. Relying on (and at times modifying) the international cultural meanings surrounding John Wayne, *The Barbarian and the Geisha* dramatizes the necessity of reciprocal trade and mutual cultural understanding, rather than a straightforward affirmation of imperialist domination. The film showcases the important role of Wayne as a transnational star in managing certain kinds of historical tensions; at a crucial moment of geopolitical and cultural redefinition for both the United States and Japan, it was the complex construction of the John Wayne persona that could assuage anxieties while affirming the spectacle of a new economic and cultural order.

A PICTURE MADE "IN THE JAPANESE MANNER"

Wayne's performance in *The Barbarian and the Geisha* takes on added significance for understanding U.S.-Japanese relations in the context of global capitalism because of the film's unique position within Hollywood's expanding internationalization, particularly Hollywood's growing investment in international productions and international film industries. Throughout the postwar years, Hollywood increasingly turned its attention to exploiting film production around the world in regions where production costs could be kept lower than in the United States, where the industry could spend its money that had been blocked from leaving the country, and where coproductions could qualify for government subsidies for local film production (see, for example, Guback, *International Film Industry*). As a result, the number of Hollywood films shot internationally rose dramatically in the 1950s. Most of the productions were in Europe, but others were shot in Africa, Asia, and South America — films that often explicitly dramatized an emerging form of cosmopolitan identity in the postwar years (Schwartz, *It's So French!*). In fact, the director of *The Barbarian and the Geisha*, John Huston, was "the most traveled filmmaker in the period," making *The African Queen* (1951) in the Belgian Congo; *Moulin Rouge* (1952) in Paris; *Beat the Devil* (1954) in Italy; *Moby Dick* (1956) in Ireland, Madeira, and the Canary Islands; *Heaven Knows, Mr. Allison* (1957) in Tobago; and *The Roots of Heaven* (1958) in French Equatorial Africa, Uganda, and the Belgian Congo (Lev, *The Fifties*, 151). So although Huston was considered a top Hollywood director, he hardly ever worked in the United States during this period, traveling the world and exploiting Hollywood studios' increasing attention to international production.

For Huston, the production of *The Barbarian and the Geisha* was more about engaging with Japanese culture and the Japanese film industry than about exploiting Japan as an exotic locale for the consumption of Western audiences, or at least that is how he sought to construct his efforts in the press. He told the *Japan Times* in 1957 as he prepared to shoot the film: "The 'Townsend Harris Story' [*Barbarian*'s working title at the time] will not be just another American movie produced in Japan. I hope to make a Japanese picture in Japan, not an American one" (*Japan Times*, "Harris, Okichi Story"). He hoped to achieve that goal primarily by employing Japanese technicians on his crew. After seeing a number of films at a Japanese film festival, Huston originally intended to work with only a Japanese crew, seeking to hire the Japanese personnel employed on *Seven Samurai* (1954), *Rashomon* (1950), and *Gate of Hell* (1953). He told the Japanese daily *Mainichi* that Japan in the 1950s was making "the finest pictures in the world," thus he wanted to exploit the techniques and talents of the Japanese industry: "I would rather use Japanese cameramen and art directors than Hollywood men so that the picture I am going to make here in Japan can be more authentic" (*Mainichi*, "Huston Wants to Use Japanese Cameramen"). The studio, however, had concerns about using an all-Japanese crew, particularly given Japanese filmmakers' lack of experience with wide-screen technology such as the CinemaScope process used on *Barbarian*, and eventually Huston had to hire American counterparts for most of the Japanese technical crew he brought onto the project. When filming was completed, Huston still insisted, "We have made this picture in the Japanese manner" (Scheuer, "'Barbarian' Leaves Japan").

Huston and the film's producers, moreover, employed an entirely Japanese cast opposite John Wayne and Sam Jaffe (who plays Harris's Dutch interpreter), including Japanese actor Sô Yamamura, although their selection of Eiko Ando to play the role of Okichi caused some controversy. Huston told the *Japan Times* that he hoped "to use one of the very best Japanese actresses for the role of Okichi" (*Japan Times*, "Harris, Okichi Story"), and Huston cast the role in Japan, auditioning Japan's top actresses. By October 1957, Huston had settled on the Japanese star Yumeji Tsukioka to the play the role, but later he cast Ando, a former dancer who, according to studio publicity, performed at the famed Nichigeki Music Hall (but who, according to her critics, was a former striptease dancer). Ando had no acting experience, and the Japanese press was reportedly outraged not only because of her lack of experience but also because she was five-seven and didn't "look like a Japanese," indicating the extent to which the role was aligned with a sense of Japanese national identity (Beech, "Hollywood's Oriental Fad").

In addition to using a Japanese cast and crew, from the start *The Barbarian and the Geisha* was intended to market itself to Japanese audiences as a way to exploit the increasing importance of the Japanese market to Hollywood studios. In a memo dated June 7, 1957, from the Twentieth Century–Fox executive Harold Nebenzal to Huston and the film's producer, Eugene Frenke, Nebenzal outlines a marketing strategy for the film in Japan based on "the most successful picture released in Japan in the post war period," *Emperor Meiji and the Great Russo-Japanese War* (1957). Noting that both *Barbarian* and *Emperor Meiji* were period pieces, Nebenzal pointed out that the producers of *Emperor*

Meiji "banked correctly on the appeal this picture would have for mature audiences, but their concern was for those under 24 years of age who comprise 60% of movie audiences in Japan." To attract "youthful attendance" in Japan, the producers of *Emperor Meiji* produced a short "educational" documentary on the production of the film, and it was then shown in primary and secondary schools in Japan. Nebenzal wondered whether the same strategy might work as well to attract young people to *The Barbarian and the Geisha*.[1] It is unclear whether Twentieth Century–Fox followed through with that marketing device for the film, but the fact that the studio considered marketing the film through the Japanese school system (presumably on the grounds that the Townsend Harris story represented an important part of Japanese history) and that it based its marketing techniques on those developed by the Japanese industry indicates the extent to which *Barbarian*'s producers sought to engage the Japanese market, particularly by constructing the film and its content as part of Japanese history and U.S.-Japanese relations.

Huston's assertion that the film was produced "in the Japanese manner" reflects his own conceptions of what Japanese culture signifies, but the efforts taken to engage with Japanese culture and the Japanese film industry during the production of *Barbarian* suggest that the film is best understood as a negotiated encounter between Hollywood and Japan (although one privileging Hollywood). The supposed "goodwill" such an encounter can create was celebrated by Huston in a statement issued by the director on November 16, 1957, in which he touts the importance of international productions for engendering cross-cultural understanding. Huston notes that he once brought an English film crew to the south of Ireland, forming friendships between the British crew and the Irish locals that "will influence the years to come." Such "good feeling," Huston argued, was created in France, Italy, and Africa as well when he traveled there to shoot films, and the same was being created during his stay in Japan for *Barbarian*. Echoing the dominant discourses within the Motion Picture Export Association regarding the international distribution of films and mutual understanding between cultures, Huston argued that much like the picture itself, the context of its international production would work toward "cementing international goodwill." Thus, the subject matter of the first U.S. consul in Japan reflected the current necessity of "international goodwill" between Japan and the United States, a point Huston acknowledged in a letter dated October 4, 1957, to the mayor of Kyoto: "As you know, the arrival of Townsend Harris in Japan in 1853 represented a significant start in the opening of relations between Japan and the United States, and the reenactment on the screen of this period has, I think you will agree, taken on added meaning in view of the close and friendly relations that exist between our two countries today."[2]

The casting of John Wayne to play Townsend Harris took on added significance in the context of U.S.-Japanese relations, Huston argued, not only because Wayne was well known in Japan but also because he was known there as a famous representative of American culture. Noting in an undated press release from Japan during the shooting of the film that John Wayne's face "has probably been seen by more people than have viewed the Mona Lisa," Huston argued that it would not be necessary "to explain to the audiences of the world who he is and what he represents. He is Mr. America."[3] And as Huston explained later, Wayne's size and reputation for action made him perfect for signifying the United States of the 1850s: "The United States was a big and slightly awkward country, and Wayne has a size and scope to him, and a kind of innocence that probably represents the country at that time. As a diplomat in Japan, he'll react like a big Westerner, like a big American, and that's what I want" ("Director Huston Real Star of 'Townsend Harris Story'").

NEGOTIATING ALTERNATIVE MODERNITIES

Huston's characterization of Wayne as a big, somewhat naïve American tells only part of the story of Wayne's performance in the film, accurately capturing the visual spectacle of Wayne's body lumbering its way though 1850s Japan but failing to recognize that Wayne functions in the film as not just an icon of America, but also as an advocate for free trade and cultural exchange. With typical Wayne bravado, when Harris confronts a Japanese official in response to the claim that foreigners represent corruption, he proclaims: "Your country stands at the crossroads of the world. From both East and West men are finding an ever-increasing need for those roads. If in your desire for isolation you refuse to make them safe for peaceful traffic, the world will treat Japan as it would treat a band of brigands infesting a highway." Tough and resolute, Harris's proclamation reveals the no-nonsense John Wayne persona audiences might expect, and yet at stake in the speech is not simply U.S. domination but also a vision of the world as a web of cultural and commercial connections. Harris's rhetoric, with its emphasis on highways and the world's responsibility to keep the international flow of goods free from impediments, is indicative of a model of international trade invested in access to global "crossroads," perhaps even a vision of international trade based on the emerging economic regime of transnational corporate power in the 1950s that increasingly demanded "peaceful traffic" for goods across national borders.

For Wayne's diplomatic efforts (both the diegetic diplomacy of Wayne as Harris and the larger cultural diplomacy between the United States and Japan that the film engages in), the primary obstacle to Japan's entrance into the world of global flows is the issue of modernity. For Wayne-Harris as a representative of the United States and of global trade, how can he represent a kind of modernity that brings progress and social change without cultural contamination? And for the Japanese, how can they maintain cultural distinctiveness and pride while being assimilated into the modern, global crossroads?

The film attempts to answer these questions in complex ways, balancing its problematic appropriation and commodification of traditional Japanese culture with an acknowledgment of the existence of alternative modernities that might leave room for cultural autonomy. After all, Huston's interest in making a film that captures Japanese culture was not entirely disingenuous. In a narrative about the necessities of modernization, the film evinces an almost ethnographic fascination with the documentation of traditional Japanese customs.[4] The opening scenes focus on a traditional celebration and dance in the village of Shimoda before the Western ship carrying Harris appears ominously on the horizon; later in the film a group of geishas demonstrates a clapping game played on a tabletop while the camera almost awkwardly abandons the narrative to linger on the movements of the geishas' hands; when Harris is taken to the capital, he participates in a traditional dance en route; and when Harris finally arrives at the capital, he and the film's audience get a lesson on the workings of pre–Meiji Restoration Japanese political customs.[5] All the while, Harris introduces the Japanese to Western implements such as telescopes and meteorological devices, which, in one scene from Okichi's point of view, make Harris appear to be a sorcerer of some kind, the wind whipping through his dark cape as he checks his strange devices. The emphasis on documenting Japanese traditions while representing Western modernity from a Japanese perspective as bizarre and magical emphasizes the extent to which modernization and its relationship to traditional culture is at the center of the narrative.

The fascination with traditional Japanese culture is somewhat ironic given the recent brutal and highly modern warfare between the United States and Japan. Clearly, postwar Japan was not a new site of modernization, given the nation's swift emergence as a military and industrial power throughout the first half of the twentieth century. *Barbarian*, however, turns to a key moment of nineteenth-century modernization to dramatize an important twentieth-century vision of global trade and U.S.-Japanese engagement in a project of revisionist history. The reopening of international trade in Japan marked an important turning point in what was termed the Meiji Restoration, which "launch[ed] Japan on a dramatic course to abolish the anti-foreign remnants of feudal rule and modernize the nation toward world power." Japan "move[d] together with the United States and European powers toward the tumultuous events of the twentieth century" (Dudden, *American Pacific*, 19). However, *Barbarian's* dramatization of an important turning point in the nineteenth-century modernization process that put Japan on track toward a cataclysmic conflict with the United States refigures the modernization of Japan as being rooted in a cooperative U.S.-Japanese relationship. At a key juncture in U.S.-Japanese relations, the film goes back to the historical moment that foreshadowed the imperial conflict of World War II and reimagined it as one of a negotiated engagement between cultures. The revision constructs the brutal historical realities of the U.S.-Japanese war in the Pacific as a deviation from the "true" and cooperative nature of an American-inspired Japanese modernity based in global trade.

Rather than simply affirming the dominance and superiority of a U.S. style of modernity, *The Barbarian and the Geisha* offers a narrative about global capitalism and reciprocal cultural exchange that dramatically complicates the emerging vision of economic development and modernization. Within postwar academic, political, and economic discourses, the idea of "economic development" emerged as a means of addressing issues of poverty in the developing world (Arndt, *Economic Development*, 1). The wave of postwar decolonization made the supposedly undeveloped regions of the world important ideological battlefields in the Cold War, since the United States recognized the need to provide a rejection of colonial rule predicated on vast class inequality, lest the newly emerging postcolonial nations turn to communism (49–50). As a solution to the problem of poverty, modernization theory became increasingly prevalent within U.S. foreign economic policy. Developed and promoted by academics throughout the 1950s and 1960s, often while working in conjunction with the U.S. government, modernization theory argued that the solution to international poverty was to modernize the developing world. Although different theorists had different conceptions of what it meant to modernize, in general modernization was thought to occur through urbanization, industrialization, the development of bureaucracy, capitalism, and, perhaps most importantly, the replacement of traditional culture by Western-style rationalism. Although developed in the 1950s and 1960s, the ideologies of modernization theory as a perspective through which to understand developing-world poverty continue to resonate today.[6]

Echoing Daniel Lerner's foundational book in modernization theory, *The Passing of Traditional Society* (the book and Wayne's film both appeared in 1958), *The Barbarian and the Geisha* envisions the complex ways that people enter into and negotiate a sense of modern lifeways and embrace modernity as a worldview. Lerner's work emphasizes the importance of individual experience and lifestyle in the construction of modernity as a social system, recognizing that the shift to the modern entails a reorganization of not only social and economic structures but also the lived experiences and worldviews of people within those structures. Arguing that modernization means a "style of daily living with change" based particularly on physical mobility, Lerner was interested in ways to engender the modern human, paying particular attention to the role of the mass media in creating a "psychic mobility" that would aid one's ability to live with the social transformations of modernity (45–49).[7] Fulfilling Lerner's claim that U.S. mass media would play an important role in this transformation of lifeways, *Barbarian* offers up John Wayne as the ideal modern, cosmopolitan person, able to move through other cultures and maintain a modern worldview.

Consider, for example, the sequence in the film in which Harris inadvertently facilitates the entrance of Western sailors infected with cholera into the village of Shimoda. The village's traditional religion is ineffective in fighting the disease, so Harris decides that the only way to end the outbreak is to burn the village to the ground by force, against the wishes of the frantic Japanese. Although at first he is arrested, it soon becomes clear that his tactic worked and, in what could be read as a perverse allusion to the atomic bombing of Nagasaki and Hiroshima, his "modern" solution to burn away the contagion is ultimately celebrated by the village and the governor, who shows his gratitude by finally taking Harris to see the shogun. Of course, since cholera is not usually passed from person to person, being transmitted instead by poor sanitation practices in which waste makes its way into drinking water, the idea that the cholera-afflicted sailors could have immediately infected the village is highly unscientific, as is Harris's "cleansing" of the village by burning it to the ground. By forcefully contradicting traditional worldviews, Wayne's Harris helps the townspeople begin to accept modern lifeways. The film somewhat tautologically posits that Japan cannot hide from the contagion of modernization and therefore must embrace modern solutions to the problems of living in a globally connected world.

The pitfalls of remaining too invested in the customs and beliefs of traditional culture are also manifest in *Barbarian* through the figure of the governor of Shimoda, Tamura. Although Tamura seems to have some knowledge of the West (he speaks English and knows the history of previous U.S. involvement in Japan) and rejects the superstitions of his culture (at times even referring to other Japanese people as ignorant for their beliefs), throughout the narrative Tamura evinces a strict adherence to traditional values and social customs, keeping Harris from the capital lest he open Japan to new and foreign elements that would disrupt the existing, tradition-based social order. Yet his respect for Harris grows throughout the film, and he eventually relents and takes Harris to the shogun. After the national government there contentiously votes to sign a treaty with the United States and open Japan to international trade, Tamura's traditionalist clan orders him to assassinate Harris in a last-ditch effort to stop the treaty. Although "his heart was divided," as Okichi's voice-over tells us, he nevertheless orders Okichi to help him kill Harris. But Okichi tries to save Harris by putting herself in front of Tamura's sword. Seeing the sacrifice that Okichi was willing to make, Tamura spares them both and kills himself instead, since his values dictate that once his sword is drawn, it must be used. Despite his growing respect for Harris and the values of community and responsibility that Harris advocates, Tamura's worldview was so tied to his traditional beliefs that he had to end his life rather than adapt to the changes that modernization would bring to Japanese culture.

The Barbarian and the Geisha, however, also complicates the popular discourses of modernization theory by emphasizing the negotiation and compromise inherent in the kind of cross-cultural engagement that would make possible a vision of Japanese modernity compatible with global capitalism. Wayne's diplomacy in the film is actually diplomatic rather than an example of the masculine posturing, violence, and intimidation so essential to the John Wayne image in the period. In one scene, Wayne as Harris agrees to remove the U.S. flag from his residence in Shimoda, capitulating to Japanese demands rather than patriotically insisting on his right to wave the flag—the move contradicts the popular definitions of Wayne's hyperpatriotic persona. The emphasis on negotiation and compromise in the narrative suggests the necessity of a more nuanced reading of the film's representation of the tradition-modernity dynamic, indicating that *Barbarian* depicts not an imperialistic colonization of the margin on the part of the center, but an affirmation of the need for local cultures to engage with global capitalism, particularly in the context of U.S.-Japanese relations in the 1950s.

The delicate negotiations and compromises of the usually intractable Wayne, therefore, suggest not only a willingness on the part of U.S. culture to be flexible in its engagements with defeated former rivals within the logic of global capitalism but also the necessity of modifying constructions of Japanese masculinity and modernity. *The Barbarian and the Geisha* offers an alternative modernity from the one dominated by militarism and imperialism that had characterized Japan's modernization throughout the first half of the twentieth century. The film's concern with traditional Japanese culture, juxtaposed with Wayne's Western modernity, displays a Japanese renegotiation of nationalism and tradition in a world where modernization and fervent imperialism left the Japanese defeated and recently occupied by a Western power. Within the film, the Japanese traditionalists who want to see Japan remain closed to the contagion of foreigners are violent and xenophobic, ordering the failed assassination of Harris and killing a member of the government who supported opening the ports. Although the traditionalists are in favor of isolation, their construction as aggressive, violent, and intolerant perhaps links them to the aggressive and often-racist imperialism of Japan in Asia during its modernization. Rejecting that vision of modernity, the film insists on local cultures embracing modernization as capitalism and as global trade, and not modernization as national or imperial ambition. In other words, *Barbarian* supports a conception of nationality rooted in modernization defined as economic expansion through both unique cultural specificity and engagement with international trade markets, not the xenophobic and aggressive nationalism of traditionalists like Governor Tamura.

The negotiation of alternative modernities manifests itself in the representation of alternative masculinities in the film, particularly in the comical brawl between Harris and two men from Shimoda, one a massive, hulking, sumo-style fighter and one a diminutive, clownish character. While Harris easily knocks out the massive warrior, he is thoroughly bettered by the shorter man, who uses judo-style techniques to flip and throw Wayne's large body. The defeat of the prototypical, militaristic American male at the hands of a skillful Japanese character functions on a number of levels. To some extent, especially in relation to World War II–era U.S. propaganda against the Japanese, the idea of a small Japanese man getting the better of John Wayne affirms cultural stereotypes of the Japanese as sly, tricky, or crafty. But considering the broader context of the film's project in exploring international exchange, a number of other meanings become possible. The scene perhaps indicates a kind of postwar concession to Japanese audiences, who get to defeat the unwanted American presence in battle, while still engendering a kind of mutual respect—in the scene, Wayne is not enraged at the man for being sneaky, but rather surprised at and respectful of the man's skill. And the fact that the respect comes from a rejection of brute force and a tough masculinity (at which Wayne excels) while embracing a clever, flexible, adaptive masculinity indicates the kind of future that the film sees for Japan's relationship to modernity and militarism, that is, a rejection of militaristic and imperial aspirations. Moreover, the film in general offers Wayne as a model of cosmopolitan masculinity based in mobility and engagement with other cultures; so while Wayne's use of his diplomatic skills rather than force functions against his star text, the construction of Wayne as a figure of spatial and cross-cultural movement supports the masculine values Wayne conveys in his more typical roles in westerns. By placing this mobile and cosmopolitan vision of Wayne in the context of the two Japanese fighters, the film uses Wayne's star persona to affirm a vision of Japanese masculinity that supports a U.S. vision of U.S.-Japanese relations and global capitalism.

Another scene in the film allows Japan to interrogate the contradictions and hypocrisy of Western modernity, even if only superficially. When Harris is taken to the capital, he must submit to questioning from members of the national government before they vote. Over a ceremonial meal, various members of the shogunate question the benevolence and supposed superiority of the United States and its modern social system. One official, noting the size discrepancy between U.S. warships and fishing boats, accuses the United States of being too violent and going to war too often, of being more interested in fighting wars than in fishing and providing security for its people. Another official questions U.S. devotion to the supposedly modern social ideals of liberty and freedom, asking whether the United States sent ships to Africa to capture men and women to be slaves; this is perhaps a reference to the ways that in 1958 the increasing attention paid to U.S. civil rights problems weakened the country's position abroad as an advocate of democracy. And another openly questions Harris's utopian vision of modern development, asking him to define "progress." Of course, given the film's narrative, the scene is structured to support Harris's perspective and his responses to these questions as he argues for an international community and international responsibility, despite some of the moral shortcomings of the United States. Yet it is important that within a film addressing a transnational audience these questions are even asked, offering a moment when the supposedly benevolent and utopian visions of modernization and global capitalism proffered by the United States are interrogated and challenged by locals seeking to negotiate their place within such a system.

This need to reconfigure Japanese modernity and its relationship to the United States and global trade dramatizes the need to confront the existence of alternate, uneven, and non-Western modernities, rather than taking for granted, as modernization theory does, a monolithic modernization as westernization that subsumes the traditional. Given the existence at the time of an already-modernized Japan that could compete for dominance with Western powers, the film attempts to allay Western fears surrounding a monstrous, non-Western modernity. For example, the image of the kamikaze pilot in the Western cultural imagination is perhaps so horrific because of how it combines modern warfare technology and fundamentalist religious beliefs. Part of the horror for the West is the use of modernity and modern technology as a weapon against what the West perceives as the modern or civilized world, undermining modernity as a grand narrative by revealing the unevenness and reflexiveness of modernization. *The Barbarian and the Geisha,* however, reconfigures the monstrous alternative modernity of the Japanese in the Pacific war as an anomaly, reconstructing Japanese modernity as supportive of U.S. visions of global capitalism.

The film imagines the possibilities of uneven and alternative modernities even as an eastern culture engages with the West and global interconnectedness. The film's internal logic is based not on colonialist notions of the center dominating the margin, which are inherent in modernization theory, but on the logic of local communities enacting their relationship to the global flows of culture and commerce. Although they are not discussing the 1950s, Rob Wilson and Wimal Dissanayake note that one of the effects of contemporary globalization is the creation of "a new world-space of cultural production and national representation which is simultaneously becoming more globalized (unified around dynamics of capitalogic moving across borders) and more localized (fragmented into contestory enclaves of difference, coalition, and resistance) in everyday texture and composition" (*Global/Local*, 1). Neither the concept of the nation-state as an imagined community nor the colonialist control of land is central to this logic, which focuses instead on the interplay between, on the one hand, local affiliations, customs, and traditions and, on the other, the networks of global capitalism. In contrast with the colonialist perspective of modernization theory, which posits the necessary subordination of local traditions if a culture is to modernize and become a part of the global community, the focus on global-local dynamics emphasizes the dialectical relationship between local communities and the forces of global capitalism and other forms of globalization, asserting the necessity and vitality of locality and local specificity to the functioning of the world system.

So while *The Barbarian and the Geisha* still relies on the concept of the nation-state in the narrative (Harris must get the shogun and the national government to sign a treaty), the real negotiations that take place in the narrative are between Harris as a representative of global trade and the villagers of Shimoda. Harris officially represents the U.S. government, but the ideologies he promotes and the rhetoric he uses are those of free trade and cross-cultural understanding. Thus, when he finally meets with the shogun, the gifts he brings to honor Japan's ruler are not grandiose and opulent symbols of the United States but everyday objects such as a bottle of whiskey and a simple wooden chair, suggesting the local-level transformation of lifeways that free trade will bring to Japan. The villagers and the governor, moreover, seem less concerned about Japanese nationalism and more concerned about the effect of modernization on their everyday lives and the structures of traditional culture. At the core of a narrative about two nations signing a treaty, then, are the negotiations between a group of traditional villagers and a mobile westerner who wants them to learn about other cultures while he learns about theirs. So while I want to emphasize U.S.-Japanese relations as the historical context for the film, those relations took place within the context of the spread of global capitalism as the United States sought not colonialist hegemony but open, global trade for U.S.-based corporations. The film emphasizes locality and local traditions and the ways they can fit into global trade while still maintaining semiautonomy, dramatizing the concerns and issues of global capitalism rather than those of national or colonial domination.

This is not to suggest, as some scholars have, that localism necessarily operates against global capitalism as a mode of resistance. As Arif Dirlik argues, numerous approaches to globalization have constructed localism or locality as the primary site of resistance to global capitalism and domination in general, yet localism should be seen as a "site of predicament," given how transnational corporations in the era of globalization have appropriated the mantra of "think

FIGURE 6.2. *The procession to the capital, with U.S. insignias on objects of traditional Japanese culture in* The Barbarian and the Geisha.

locally, act globally": "ironically, even as it seeks to homogenize populations globally, consuming their cultures, global capitalism enhances awareness of the local" ("The Global in the Local," 23, 35). Or as Wilson and Dissanayake put it, "the local goes on being micromapped and micromined into so many consumer zones" (*Global/Local*, 2) in what Roland Robertson calls the process of "glocalization." Though localism often acts as a concrete site of struggle against the forces of global capitalism, it also functions to provide a new set of styles or values to be appropriated as part of global capitalism's fetishization of difference.

This is the kind of global-local nexus at work in *Barbarian*, which offers the exotic spectacle of Japan as a commodity for the consumption of Western audiences. Perhaps more importantly, however, the film constructs the Japanese as consumers rather than colonial subjects. When the villagers of Shimoda finally make peace with Harris and escort him to the capital, they provide a traditional procession with elaborate decorations. The villagers arrive with streamers, paper lanterns, and staffs, but with the U.S. golden eagle insignia printed on everything.

Earlier in the film, Okichi saw the symbol on a U.S. coin and asked Harris whether it was an American god, already indicating that "America" represented capitalism and the worship of money more than a national identity. The hybrid display of local tradition integrated with a U.S. insignia reveals not a kind of colonization but the creation of consumers of "America" in a small village in Japan. After all, Mitsuhiro Yoshimoto points out that as Japan became a global, postmodern nation, its Americanization in the postwar world was not due entirely to American cultural imperialism but also to the construction of America into a commodity for the postmodern consumption of Japanese people ("Images of Empire," 195). The consumption of America as a global brand that doesn't obliterate traditional cultures becomes a manifestation of global cultural flows rather than of the center colonizing the margin.

JOHN WAYNE AND THE ASIAN-CAUCASIAN ROMANCE

The most prominent indication of the balance between the needs of global capitalism and the local cultural anxieties of the Japanese comes through Wayne's participation in the trope of the Asian-Caucasian romance. Historically, as the U.S. government's concern with Asia grew throughout the twentieth century, the representation of interracial romance became central to U.S. imperialist ideology, either through the need to protect white women from Asian men, or through the sexual objectification of Asian women by benevolent white men, or even sometimes through the dangers of white men becoming victimized by hypersexualized Asian women. Hollywood's Orientalist constructions of Asia, in other words, "create a mythic image of Asia that empowers the West and rationalizes Euroamerican authority over the Asian other. Romance and sexuality provide the metaphoric justification for this domination" (Marchetti, "Yellow Peril," 6). Christina Klein, however, complicates that conception of Hollywood, arguing that middlebrow U.S. culture in the postwar years was deeply interested in "bridging differences" across class, race, and gender while disavowing racial hierarchies (Cold War Orientalism, 15). For Klein, Hollywood's construction of U.S. interests in Asia in the 1950s was based on "narratives of anti-conquest," which "legitimated US expansion while denying its coercive or imperial nature" by using sentimental appeals based on friendship, family, or community (13).[8] That mode of sentimentality, of course, "could serve as an instrument for exercising power" (15), providing an emotional, and most often gendered, appeal for U.S. and Western involvement in areas that the United States imagined itself sentimentally connected to. Klein focuses on what she calls a Cold War Orientalism that is more flexible, mobile, and adaptive than the model set forth by Edward Said in how it uses sentimentality to engage the West's interest in and exploitation of the East.

In the late 1950s, the Asian-Caucasian romance functioned as an important narrative device in both Hollywood and U.S. culture at large to dramatize both the necessity of U.S. involvement in Asia and the importance of U.S. cultural domination. In films such as Love Is a Many Splendored Thing (1955), The King and I (1956), Sayonara (1957), South Pacific (1958), and The World of Suzie Wong (1960), the melodrama of interracial romance often functions as a sentimental affirmation of U.S. foreign policy in Asia and the dictates of Western gender politics. In *Sayonara,* for example, Marlon Brando plays a troubled U.S. pilot who falls in love with an independent young woman who performs in the gender-bending Matsubayashi theater. In the film, he rejuvenates his ailing, Western masculinity by "saving" the woman from the "unnatural" gendered performance of Matsubayashi and integrating her into Western gender norms by taking her home to the United States to be a housewife (Marchetti, *"Yellow Peril"*). And in *South Pacific,* an American nurse, Nellie Forbush, must learn to forge cross-cultural familial ties with her French lover and his interracial children, allegorizing U.S. involvement in the Pacific. The film depicts a white female representative of the United States who "bestows her healthy sexuality" on a weary Frenchman while assuming educational and disciplinary responsibility for her new adoptive Asian children, indicating the extent to which U.S. interests in Asia replaced or at least reimagined failing European colonial regimes through discourses of maternal benevolence rather than military domination (Klein, *Cold War Orientalism,* 168).

In many ways, *The Barbarian and the Geisha* participates in these gendered imperialist ideologies. As in Klein's conception of a flexible Cold War Orientalism based in sentimental, cross-cultural emotional attachments rather than racial hierarchies and military force, *Barbarian* structures its narrative of U.S. interest in Japan around Harris's patient efforts to build friendships and mutual respect with the Japanese villagers, creating bonds based on racial equality rather than domination. Moreover, the budding relationship between Harris and Okichi constructs the relationship between the United States and Japan within discourses of romance and emotional engagement. The infantilization of Okichi in the film positions Harris as a benevolent, at times paternal protector (which is often how Wayne's characters relate to women in his other films).

But Wayne's global star persona dramatically complicates the romantic and cross-cultural power relations in *The Barbarian and the Geisha.* Wayne's masculinity, despite his associations with U.S. culture and national identity, was deeply ambivalent when it came to the settled structures of marriage and the family, which often act as metaphorical stand-ins for nations and empires. Wayne's vision of masculinity in the 1950s was rooted in the values of mobility and freedom, values threatened by the confining spaces of domesticity and the nuclear family. In his most popular films of the period—for example, *Red River, Hondo,* or *The Searchers*—Wayne offers a sensational fantasy of mobility and migration that is more comfortable outside the confining structures of marriage and often, by extension, nationhood, a kind of masculinity more tied to the necessary mobility of global capitalism. In short, the kinds of masculine values a union with Okichi would endorse—intimate connections with femininity and the domestic responsibilities of marriage and family—pose a challenge to the homosocial, mobile masculinity that Wayne most often embraced in his films and that reflected the emerging construction of a hegemonic masculinity within global capitalism.

It is not surprising, therefore, that the narrative resolution offered by *Barbarian* is the ultimate failure of the romance between Harris and Okichi. As in many other Wayne films, the temptation of marriage and domesticity is denied as Wayne pursues instead the grandiose masculine goals of empire building — or in this case, the establishment of global trade in Japan. *Barbarian* envisions the ultimate separation of Harris and Okichi at the film's end, using their romance as a way to imagine U.S.-Japanese relations but failing to impose the ideological structures of marriage or the nuclear family on the couple in order to dramatize a gendered vision of U.S. hegemony.

In the film, after the Japanese government has agreed to sign the treaty but before Governor Tamura attempts to assassinate Harris, the possibility of a settled, domestic existence for Harris and Okichi becomes an idealized fantasy for Harris. He tells Okichi that he must return to the United States for a brief time, but that when he returns they will never part. They will build a house together in the mountains overlooking a lake, he tells her, and despite all of Harris's rhetoric of neighbors and responsibility, he says that in this ideal world they will have no neighbors and will simply be alone to share their love. Within that image of a quiet, domestic existence, the romance between Harris and Okichi displays the potentially stifling and hegemonic role of marriage, envisioning a seemingly American manifestation of marriage and cohabitation alone in a cabin in the wilderness, cut off from the economic and cultural flows that Harris has worked so hard to establish. Deriving from Harris's romantic-paternal interest in Okichi, this potential resolution to their love story would affirm U.S. domination through the structure of marriage, since Harris would essentially "save" Okichi from her culture and situate her within the patriarchal structures of the Western nuclear family.

In the film, Okichi has no intention of being saved from her culture. After the suicide of Tamura, she too decides that she cannot turn her back on her culture, noting in her voice-over that if she is to live, she must do so by the beliefs of her ancestors. She leaves Harris to move on with her life, despite her love for him. Unlike Tamura, Okichi is able to negotiate both the demands of her culture and the new demands that modernity will bring, choosing to leave Harris because of her traditional beliefs but doing so as a newly freed and "modern" woman, because the death of Tamura no longer binds her to him as his geisha. Rather than simply moving from the unconditional loyalty inherent in her traditional relationship with Tamura to the supposedly more egalitarian yet potentially stifling and isolating paternalism of a Western marriage with Harris, Okichi instead chooses her own path within her culture. And yet it is clear that

Okichi can't go home again, so to speak. The cultural transformations of modernization cannot be undone as she seeks her new, modern existence.⁹

Okichi's separation from Harris suggests that the film's vision of cross-cultural, international relations is one based on temporary engagements that result in better understanding but take place outside the bounds of colonial domination. In many ways, the transitory romance between Harris and Okichi fits into the vision of mobility offered by Wayne's star text; the film emphasizes a momentary connection between people brought together by the flows of global capitalism that Harris seeks to institute in Japan, but a more permanent union would impede those flows with the stifling structures of marriage and family, nation and colonialism. Their fleeting romance seems an appropriate representation of the global's mobile and often temporary engagement with local concerns and the local's negotiated interface with global flows.

Barbarian's insistence on a kind of local autonomy rather than a hegemonic imposition of Western modernity is made clear when it is compared with *The King and I*, a film that shares *Barbarian*'s vision of an interracial romance that fails because of the cultural strain between tradition and modernity. Unlike *Barbarian*, *The King and I* privileges the totalizing forces of modernization. In *The King and I* (in a narrative that mirrors that of *The Barbarian and the Geisha* but with a gender reversal: a modern white woman teaches a traditional Asian male about modernity), romantic love becomes the primary vehicle through which modernization occurs. The king of Siam desires modernization and yet resists it, since the process would undermine his power and identity. But when Anna (the schoolteacher brought in to modernize the education of his children) insists that his affection for her take place on the modern terms of romantic love and mutual respect rather than the traditional terms of his despotic power, he finally embraces—and is destroyed by—modernity. Luckily for Siam, his children, through their familial and cross-cultural affection for Anna, embrace a modern worldview.

Compare the final scenes of both films. In *The King and I*, as the king lies dying from the destabilizing influence of modernity on his traditional worldview, he instructs his son to make Siam a modern nation based on the teachings of Anna. As the king dies, his son assumes command and immediately begins to construct his rule on "modern" principles of equality, instructing his brothers and sister that people no longer need bow before him. Instead, he orders them to stand tall, shoulders back in a neat line in front of him. The image is striking not only because of how it completely embraces the eradication of local culture in the modernization of the developing world, but also because of how it envisions a supposedly egalitarian modernity with highly militaristic iconography. Indeed, the film doesn't question the right of the king's wealthy and privileged young son to rule Siam; it simply constructs his rule, and the vision of a "modern" developing nation, as a militarized dictatorship, clearly reflecting how the West's need to modernize and dismantle traditional culture in the non-Western world is rooted in a need for Western rationality, bureaucracy, and strict social order rather than the sentimental goals of democracy and egalitarianism.

The final scenes of *The Barbarian and the Geisha*, on the other hand, emphasize the retention of local, traditional cultures even as the culture embraces its entrance into the flows of global trade. In the last scene of the film, as Harris is swept up in a celebratory procession through the streets of the capital, the audience's perspective stays with Okichi, who watches Harris's triumphal moment anonymously from within the crowd. Rather than structuring this final victory of Western modernity from the West's perspective, the point of view remains firmly with Okichi as a representative of local culture defining her relationship with the global. Rather than being a part of the flow of the procession through the streets of the capital, and thereby embracing a position within the flows of global trade that would bring modernity to Japan, Okichi chooses to stay tied to the local after her temporary engagement with Western modernity during her time with Harris. Instead of depicting the totalizing transformation of traditional culture through the processes of modernization, the final shots position the audience within the crowd with Okichi, watching as global capitalism flows through the culture while she remains emotionally tied to the local as a site of identification, although the local will now begin to change and transform just as Okichi has from her time spent with Harris. The final shot of the film offers a poignant close-up of Okichi as her voice-over notes that Harris passed into Japanese history but never from her heart, ending the film by emphasizing her subjectivity and her autonomy to determine her level of engagement with Harris's Western modernity, even as that vision of modernity transforms Japanese culture.

THE KING AND I, SOUTH PACIFIC, AND SAYONARA ARE PRODucts of the same Hollywood industry that produced *The Barbarian and the Geisha*, but because of *Barbarian*'s unique position within Hollywood's internationalization, that is, as an internationally produced and internationally marketed film that explicitly set out to engage with the Japanese film industry and Japanese film markets, *Barbarian* goes further than the others in challenging the hegemonic vision of modernization theory, offering a negotiated and more complicated sense of how local cultures can relate to modernity. Within *Barbarian*, the beginnings of a transformation in how global power is structured and organized in the second half of the twentieth century can be seen as the militaristic and colonial dominance of Western nations begins to reorganize itself into a regime of transnational corporate power based on the free (yet clearly inequitable) flow of goods, ideas, money, media, and people across national borders. Although marketed as egalitarian in the film, that transformation clearly served the interest of powerful Western nations such as the United States. After all, despite Harris's intention to learn about Japanese culture, it is clear in the film that Japan must adapt to the demands of modernization, that Japan will be transformed from its engagement with the United States and global interconnectedness, not vice versa.

Thus it was the international star power of John Wayne that helped manage the cultural tensions associated with the transition as the United States renegotiated its relationships to old adversaries such as Japan. At a vital historical moment, the swagger of Wayne as he walks through 1850s Japan (rather than the dusty cow towns of the American West also on the verge of modernization) became a resonant image of not only the United States abroad but also the kinds of masculinity and modern identity that would thrive within the nomadic flows of the global economy. As a transnational star, Wayne could be a kind of diplomat, a spectacular and dynamic image inspiring trust in the film's vision of cross-cultural exchange and nascent globalization, even if such an exchange clearly privileged the United States and the West.

CHAPTER SEVEN

Men at Work in Tight Spaces

MASCULINITY, PROFESSIONALISM, AND POLITICS IN *RIO BRAVO* AND *THE ALAMO*

A S THE SIEGE OF THE LOCAL JAIL RAGES ON IN HOWARD Hawks's *Rio Bravo* (1959), Nathan Burdette (John Russell), a powerful rancher attempting to violently break his brother out of jail, pays the band at the cantina across the street to play a tune over and over again to send a message to the sheriff, played by John Wayne. Proving his intelligence despite his young age, Colorado (Ricky Nelson), a young man who has stayed out of the conflict up to that point, explains that the song is called "El Degüello," or "The Cutthroat Song." As Colorado explains it, "The Mexicans played it for those Texas boys when they had them bottled up in the Alamo." Finally understanding the reference, the sheriff remembers the significance of the song: Santa Anna played it to indicate that no quarter would be given to anyone surviving the battle, the message that Burdette wants to send. As the action plays out in *Rio Bravo*, the song foreshadows Wayne's next major role as Davy Crockett in the project Wayne had been working for years to bring to the screen, *The Alamo* (1960). In fact, Wayne used the same tune (which Hawks had Dimitri Tiomkin rewrite for *Rio Bravo* because he thought the historical "Degüello" was too banal) in his version of the famous Texas siege, linking the two films' cinematic sieges through the haunting melody (Arnold, "My Rifle," 270–271).

While the two films are rarely grouped together for analysis—Hawks's film is a darling of film critics and historians who see in it the master director at his best (even when critical of its values), while Wayne's *The Alamo* is often dismissed as reactionary jingoism because of Wayne's personal politics—the two films share much in common. Among other similarities, both dramatize the plight of different forms of masculinity that are brought together by a violent conflict but must be combined into a cohesive unit, both eschew the open horizons typical of the western genre in favor of the closed and confining spaces of a siege, and both explore what it means to be a man in the face of oppressive power, whether wielded by an out-of-control capitalist tycoon or a despotic military ruler putting down revolts.

As the 1950s came to a close, the John Wayne persona became increasingly associated with such tensions in the construction of masculinity, exploring the kinds of masculinity that thrive while under siege and "bottled up." Although Wayne was associated with contexts of crisis and danger, and was celebrated for his violent skills and practical know-how as they helped resolve the competitive crises of the frontier (often between white settlers and Native populations), the crises of *Rio Bravo* and *The Alamo* took the typical dangers of the frontier to the extreme, envisioning a world in which Wayne was backed into a corner by powerful foes, cut off from the open spaces of the frontier so fundamental to the construction of his body and its mobility.

Both films use the collapsing of space and mobility to intensify their consideration of masculine identity within a competitive and dangerous world, and to create highly pressurized contexts defined by tight spaces in which men must find a way to articulate a vision of manhood that seems authentic and worthwhile in the face of powerful forces of individual alienation, such as the excessive greed of capitalism or the tyrannical military might of an authoritarian leader. In *Rio Bravo*, the action dramatizes the possibilities of authentic connections between professional men in a world marked by commodified relations and the abuse of power by the wealthy, a narrative that can be historicized within the global spread of wage labor and the construction of capitalist masculinities. *The Alamo*, on the other hand, explores the kinds of authentic masculine leadership that can embody the ideals of capitalist self-interest while still cultivating the necessity of self-sacrifice and individual submission to a grand ideological mission, a project that reflects the geopolitics of decolonization and U.S. global power. In short, both films attempt to articulate modern male subjectivities that can negotiate the gendered tensions of a rapidly changing world, offering, on the one hand, a model of professional masculinity that seeks homosocial intimacy and authenticity while largely downplaying the unethical values of capitalism, and, on the other hand, a model of modern political leadership that touts freedom and egalitarianism while insisting on the "natural" abilities of certain men to lead the community. As the sun set on the 1950s—the decade that saw both the meteoric rise of Wayne as a global sensation and the rapid internationalization of the world economy—Wayne's most iconic and popular roles continued to examine what it means to be a modern man amid the cultural transformations and disjunctures of capitalism and democracy.

RIO BRAVO: MASCULINE PROFESSIONALISM
AND HOMOSOCIALITY

It has become a tradition of sorts among film scholars to understand *Rio Bravo* as Howard Hawks and John Wayne have told us to: as a response to Fred Zinnemann's *High Noon* (1952). Both Hawks and Wayne have described *Rio Bravo* as an attempt to remake Zinnemann's tale of a local marshal seeking help, but getting none, from the cowardly townsfolk for his impending showdown with a gunslinger recently released from jail. As Hawks puts it, "*Rio Bravo* was made because I didn't like a picture called *High Noon*. . . . I didn't think a good sheriff was going to go running around like a chicken with his head off asking for help, and finally his Quaker wife had to save him. That isn't my idea of a good western sheriff" (quoted in McBride, *Hawks on Hawks*, 130). And for Wayne, the idea that the marshal would toss his badge on the ground and grind it into the dirt with his boot (even though he only tossed it on the ground) was "un-American." He criticized the film in his famous 1976 *Playboy* interview for being an allegory condemning the Hollywood blacklist, as the film is often seen (Lewis, "Wayne: Interview"). In response, *Rio Bravo* was supposed to provide a more heroic vision of the Old West and the authority of the local sheriff, who refused to ask for help (but got it anyway).

The two films, then, are often considered political opposites. *High Noon* provides a leftist and liberal attack on McCarthyism and the cowardice of people who fail to stand up and fight for what they believe in, and *Rio Bravo* is supposedly a reactionary affirmation of government authority, embodied in John Wayne. *High Noon* offers an introspective examination of violence and society, and *Rio Bravo* supposedly celebrates Wayne's fascist machismo and masculine posturing.[1] But as Robin Wood has pointed out in his foundational work on *Rio Bravo*, those politicized readings do not hold up when one analyzes the films. Even though *High Noon* is supposedly an allegory of McCarthyism (as its writers and directors may have intended), its allegory is so loosely constructed that the film's narrative can represent any number of contexts (in fact, it is just as easy to read *High Noon*'s Marshal Kane [Gary Cooper] as McCarthy himself, a lone crusader facing an impending evil threat and finding himself surrounded by cowards unwilling to help stave off communism). The openness of *High Noon*'s political allegory is evident, since conservatives such as Dwight Eisenhower and Ronald Reagan have celebrated the film's vision of Kane's courage and dedication to duty. It is also difficult to find textual evidence that *Rio Bravo* supports conservative politics and anticommunism. Wood suggests that *Rio Bravo*'s nuanced questioning of Wayne's masculine authority makes it the more "liberal" film of the two. Whereas Kane asks for help, he ultimately affirms his masculine skill and independence by fighting off all the bad guys on his own (with only a little final help from his wife). *Rio Bravo's* Sheriff Chance, on the other hand, repeatedly refuses the help of amateurs and outsiders, but must be saved time and time again—by a drunk, an old man with a limp, a young man, and a woman gambler—suggesting the limits of his idealized masculinity (see Wood, *Rio Bravo,* 10–12).[2]

The real site of contention between the films is not a politicized left-right split but rather some of the key issues in Hawks's work as a director: masculine professionalism, labor, and male-male relationships within capitalism. Concern for those qualities is at the core of Hawks's critique of *High Noon*: Kane's desire to draw amateurs into his fight against the gunslinger didn't sit well with Hawks's vision of professionalism and male identity. For Hawks, *Rio Bravo* became a site in which to explore a common theme: a group of men with a strong sense of professional duty working together in dangerous context. Hawks's sheriff wants help not from amateur townspeople but from real professionals.

Thus, capitalism and its construction of male identity provides the most salient context within which to understand *Rio Bravo* and the articulation of John Wayne in the late fifties—the belief that identity is tied not just to one's profession but by one's professional skill. While the construction of masculinity has been central to the critical discourse surrounding *Rio Bravo* (see, for example, Peter Lehman's discussion of the film in *Running Scared*), the film's exploration of male identity cannot be separated from its complex vision of capitalism, mobility, and space. In a narrative that condemns amateurs but villainizes the power of the wealthy, *Rio Bravo* dramatizes men carefully negotiating their relationships with one another in contexts of commodified personal relationships. In the global context of the 1950s—when capitalism increasingly insisted not only on wage labor and the selling of one's bodily resources as central components of male identity but also on increasingly homosocial contexts of such labor—a film such as *Rio Bravo* dramatized the ability of men, thrust together in tight spaces and dangerous labor, to develop meaningful personal relationships with one another while maintaining the ethics of professionalism. The John Wayne star persona served as an ideal site for Hawks's continuing exploration of a kind of masculinity that was not simply professional but demonstrated a unique form of capitalist subjectivity for the period.

In the film, Wayne plays a sheriff named John T. Chance. He has arrested Joe Burdette (Claude Akins), the brother of a powerful local rancher and businessman, after Joe casually kills an unarmed man in the film's opening scene. Chance holds Burdette in the border town's small jail with the help of deputies played by Walter Brennan, Ricky Nelson, and Dean Martin, the last a former deputy who is now a drunk and needs to be cleaned up. Meanwhile, Nathan Burdette, the powerful rancher, is buying hired guns from around the territory to close off the town while Chance holes up in the dilapidated jail and tries to keep order in the town, waiting for days on end for a U.S. marshal to arrive to take Joe to court. Unlike *Red River*, which explores the importance and necessity of mobility to create economic stability, *Rio Bravo* dramatizes the inequalities of mobility: those with power close down space and attempt to destroy local communities. After *Rio Bravo*, Wayne and Hawks collaborated on *El Dorado* (1966) and *Rio Lobo* (1970), two more films that focus on responsible professionals (whether sheriffs or gunmen) who find themselves under siege by powerful capitalist interests.

As others have noted, *Rio Bravo* is a complex exploration of masculine identity. All of Chance's deputies attempt to prove their masculine worth, whether by overcoming alcoholism (Dean Martin as Dude), proving themselves despite their youth (Ricky Nelson as Colorado), or proving their continued worth despite old age and bodily impairment (Walter Brennan as Stumpy). But as Arnold explains in his astute reading of the film's music, the film consistently questions traditional masculinity, its relationship to femininity and domesticity, and the "tenuous formation of homosocial relationships" ("My Rifle," 268). Although Wayne functions as the yardstick by which the men measure their masculinity, the film explores the intimate friendships between the men, with Wayne acting as "a nurturer, a kind of burly, well-armed mother hen who administers doses of tough love to his variously compromised fragments of men who surround and purport to assist him in the task of maintaining civil order" (268). Meanwhile, Chance must address the tension posed by Feathers (Angie Dickinson), a young woman gambler who falls in love with Chance but only slowly wins him over. Feathers carefully and systematically opens Chance to a vulnerable romantic engagement by getting him to divest himself of certain kinds of masculine authority; in a film centered on the tension between excess and control, Feathers allows Chance to control his excessive adherence to masculine hardness and allow room for an eroticism and emotional vulnerability that ultimately makes him a better sheriff (Thomas, "John Wayne's Body" 83). Within the film, there is a concerted effort to negotiate the extreme rejection of femininity at the core of the Wayne star text, an attempt to balance Wayne's hard masculinity with eroticism and romance, or at least to carve out a space for femininity within the homosocial world that Wayne inhabits.

But the construction of masculinity in the film cannot be separated from the tenets of professionalism and capitalism. The ideal and hegemonic form of manhood proffered by *Rio Bravo* is based on what Wood broadly calls "self-respect" but really refers to a kind of professional competency and skill (*Rio Bravo*). As opposed to the westerns of Ford, in which masculinity is defined in relation to femininity and the (at times ambivalent) need to protect and promote "civilization," there is no suggestion of that theme in *Rio Bravo*. In fact, as Wood illustrates, the film goes out of its way to suggest very little beyond the borders of the small town, offering no interest in the fact that there might be any "civilization" to protect beyond the dusty borders of the town (56). Instead, the men in the film are motivated by a desire to prove themselves and their abilities: "The development of civilization means nothing to them [the film's heroes]. They need a cause (fighting the predators of power, defending the helpless and the law-abiding), but only really as a pretext . . . They undertake their duties as a test, to prove themselves to themselves, and for that they need the acknowledgement of others" (58).[3]

Thus, Chance, Dude, and Colorado throughout the film belabor the idea of being "good," discussing, for example, whether they think Colorado is good enough to help them, or if Dude can ever be good again, using the vague idea of being good over and again to suggest a sense of expert proficiency that must be measured against that of other men and in fact thrives off of the conflict in the film as an important context to prove how good they are. The self-respect the men seek through their actions is deeply tied to their labor as professionals, an inherent desire to judge their actions in an economy of skill and ability in which they must constantly execute their duties with the greatest of expertise.

Examine, for example, the tense scene in which Dude ferrets out a wounded gunslinger from the saloon filled with Burdette's hired men. After one of Burdette's men shoots and kills Chance's friend Wheeler (Ward Bond), who was passing through town and publicly offered to help Chance, Chance and Dude chase the assassin out of a barn, with Dude clipping the man and noticing that he stepped in a mud puddle as he ran into the saloon where Burdette's men are gathered. Chance and Dude decide to enter the hostile bar and drive the man out, but when Chance starts to head over to the bar, Dude says he is ready to take the lead and work the room over himself, looking for the man with muddy boots. As Dude handles the men, disarms them, and looks them over (all while Chance looks on, evaluating Dude's performance), his confidence is tested when none of Burdette's men have muddy boots and they start to laugh at him, accusing him of seeing things and being a drunk. One man even tosses a coin in the spittoon for Dude to fish out, mirroring Joe Burdette's humiliating gesture from the film's opening scenes that sets the plot in motion. But then Dude notices drops of blood dripping into a beer on the bar and seamlessly spins, shoots, and kills the man, vindicating his professional skills and masculinity.

Wood singles the scene out as one of the best in *Rio Bravo*, citing the professional craftsmanship of Hawks as a director and his ability to dramatize the film's theme of self-respect (*Rio Bravo*, 51). But the pleasures of the scene are equally rooted in the pleasures of professionalism in general, the aesthetics of a complex job executed expertly. Just as Hawks is meticulous in his cinematic construction of Dude's labor (carefully establishing the scene, Chance's perspective as observer, and the slow awareness that the guilty party is watching from above), the scene offers up a meticulous attention to detail in the carrying out of the task, methodically examining the details of Dude's job, from how he has the men take off their guns to his expert instincts in making sure the bartender doesn't move and alter the strategic scale of the room. While the scene dramatizes the tensions of self-respect and whether Dude can be as good as he used to be, it suggests as well the simple pleasure of watching someone who is good at his job, the ultimate professional who is smart, thinks strategically, and can act spontaneously and effectively when tested.

The film's conflation of masculinity and the need for constant professionalism dramatizes one of the tensions of wage labor within capitalism: the pressure to execute one's labor well over and over again in an endless routine. In the film, being good at one's job means always being the consummate professional, always being good, day in and day out, in order to stay alive. This need for constant professionalism is what nags at Dude, who notes that when he is sober, he is the best, but can he keep his sobriety up throughout his withdrawals? Or will he lapse and let Chance and the others down? Indeed, the pressure to maintain professional awareness and skill is the crux of the narrative: How long can Chance be on guard and ward off Burdette's men? Will he or his deputies make a strategic mistake, or will they execute their duty until the end? Such pressure, in a way, is the pressure of capitalist labor in general, the pressure to perform professionally day in and day out over long periods of time, a pressure often seen as alienating and dehumanizing (and that, for laborers in certain professions, can be physically quite dangerous). *Rio Bravo* dramatizes that anxiety, showing the dangers of letting one's professional guard down (imminent death at the hands of paid guns) in a way that might give voice to the alienating and dangerous pressures of capitalist labor. And yet those anxieties ultimately serve only to provide the context within which one's masculinity can be tested and proved. To endure such pressure and continue to perform with professional expertise and acumen, in Hawks's world, is the ultimate benchmark of modern masculinity.

This sense of professionalism is key to the meanings of John Wayne throughout the 1950s. Without trying to be reductive or to downplay the spectacle of Wayne's immense bodily skill on-screen, one of the attributes that make the Wayne persona so appealing is a general sense of basic competency, a reassuring sense that he knows how to do his job well and with the utmost professionalism. While that competence is called into question in a film such as *Red River*, where his intractability leads to tyranny, throughout the decade he played characters who evince an assured ability to manage well all the details and nuances of their jobs. In his cavalry films with John Ford, for example, it is not Wayne's skill on horseback or with a rifle that marks him as a capable leader, but rather his ability to manage his command and its personalities effectively, to be able to make the best strategic decisions possible for the good of the troop. Similarly, in *Sands of Iwo Jima*, even when Wayne's Sergeant Stryker is critiqued for his hard-nosed approach to his troops, his professional abilities are never called into question, and he is validated as an effective teacher. Even in *The Searchers*, a film in which the audience is invited to question the dark and racist tendencies of Ethan Edwards, Wayne is constructed as more capable at tracking and wandering the frontier than Ward Bond's Reverend Clayton or Harry Carey's Brad Jorgensen. This is not to suggest that Wayne alone signified such competence — indeed, it is a quality that Hollywood often uses to characterize and venerate its leading men — but rather to emphasize that proficiency and professional competency were central components of Wayne's roles and his star persona more often than they were for, say, Jimmy Stewart or Cary Grant, or even Gary Cooper.

Importantly, in *Rio Bravo* such professionalism remains separate from a capitalist desire to accumulate wealth and power, which leads to greed and the abuse of power. Those values characterize Nathan Burdette, the powerful rancher who uses all his money and influence to spring his brother Joe from jail. Whereas Chance and his deputies operate within an economy of self-respect and professional skill, Burdette epitomizes all the excesses of capitalism by placing self-interest above the needs of the community, dominating others with his wealth, and assuming special social status. Moreover, his immaculate and stylish appearance, especially in contrast with the rough and utilitarian garb of Chance and his men, marks his masculinity as narcissistic and invested in a consumerist model of status and privilege. (The leather riding crop that dangles, whiplike, from his hand in all his scenes suggests a certain sadism and possible sexual perversity as well, much as the silver-tipped whip used by Liberty Valance in *The Man Who Shot Liberty Valance* suggests the sadism of lawless capitalism.) Burdette signifies "an embryonic form of corporate capitalism" by operating with a power that "can buy anything (including people), the power that, in its extreme but logical forms accrues such names as Fascism, Nazism, totalitarianism, and is absolutely central to the current phase of our civilization, the phase we call consumer capitalism" (Wood, *Rio Bravo*, 13, 58). Although modern and capitalist, Burdette's masculinity represents a materialistic and irresponsible counterpoint to Chance's modern professionalism based in self-respect and commitment to individual duty.

Burdette's unethical power finds its most resonant manifestation in his ability to commandeer space for his own benefit. Rather than using the wide-open horizons of the frontier to provide a backdrop for riders on horseback exploring borderless space, *Rio Bravo* dramatizes a cramped and claustrophobic space; most of the film takes place in the small and often dark sheriff's office or as Chance patrols the dark streets, unsure of what might be lurking in the shadows. As the characters note throughout the film, the town is "bottled up" by Burdette and his hired guns, with no one getting out and no one coming in to help. Much of the film, therefore, unfolds in medium shots of the characters within the sheriff's office and the jail, often with three or four characters in the frame to illustrate how confined the space is. The sparse and utilitarian set—from the bland stone walls to the black iron bars—suggests that the office is as much a jail for the sheriff and his deputies as it is for their prisoner.

The action in the film evokes a sense of confinement as well. Rather than involving chases through space on horseback, as seen in films like *The Searchers*, or elaborate shootouts within complicated natural spaces like rocky crags seen in films such as the Anthony Mann westerns *Winchester '73* (1950) and *The Naked Spur* (1953), the violent action in *Rio Bravo* involves the careful negotiation of tight, shadowy spaces throughout the town, such as a dark barn or Burdette's saloon. *Rio Bravo* constructs a cramped sense of tension amid a claustrophobic space. For audiences used to seeing Wayne galloping on horseback through the frontier, gun in hand, the tense, confined action of the film as he lurks through the streets must have felt new and restricting.

The spatial politics of the film, of course, were not new to the Hollywood western, which often focused on the spatial tensions between powerful ranchers and those who would create settled communities out of the open spaces of the frontier. The forces and excesses of capitalism, in fact, often function as a nefarious threat to the possibilities of movement and mobility in the western. The open spaces of the frontier are always populated by disreputable gunslingers for hire, rustlers, and evil, power-hungry cattle barons. In a film like *Shane* (1954), for example, the struggles of homesteaders to settle the territory is threatened not by Native Americans with claims to the land but by powerful ranchers who don't want to see the territory fenced off. To advance their cause, the ranchers hire evil gunslingers to threaten the homesteaders. The narrative of conflict between ranchers and homesteaders—between powerful people who want to exert control over space while keeping it open and borderless, and those who want to create a settled community—is a common one throughout the genre, used frequently in B westerns and in A westerns such as *My Darling Clementine*, *Shane*, and *The Man Who Shot Liberty Valance*. It is echoed in Walter Brennan's only dramatic turn in *Rio Bravo*, in which he reveals that Nathan Burdette drove him off of 460 acres of land—not much to Nathan, but "a lot of country to me." Rather than celebrating the freedom of movement and borderless space, narratives such as these dramatize the potential for powerful capitalist interests to commandeer and threaten space.

The claustrophobic sensations of *Rio Bravo* mirror the anxious transformations of space within global capitalism, dwelling on the tensions of immobility in a world where movement is power. The spatial dynamics of *Rio Bravo* paint a picture of global capitalism run amok, of powerful business interests using mobility and capital to thwart the "justice" of freedom of movement by blocking Chance's connection to the larger world and any possible professional support. Burdette is essentially a powerful capitalist who exploits the freedom of movement his money buys him (he rides in and out of town at will, whereas Chance and his men work on foot), allowing the free flow of men and guns for himself while blocking the mobility and social connections across space that Chance needs in order to operate. That particular construction of space reflects the experiences of modernization as both a kind of freedom of movement to create social relations across space and simultaneously the dominance of such transnational flows by those with power and influence.

The consummate professionalism of Chance and his deputies might stand in for an ethical vision of capitalism, an adherence to one's duty and occupational obligations without the pursuit of excessive power, wealth, or status that marks global capitalism. They are capitalist professionals, but without the implications of massive inequality that are central to the functioning of global capitalism. This professionalism should not be confused with social responsibility. Other than their friendship with Carlos (Pedro Gonzalez-Gonzalez) and Consuela (Estelita Rodriguez), the Mexican hotel owners, neither Chance nor any of his deputies show any real concern for the broader community or even with the ideal of justice, which is ironic considering their jobs as protectors of the communal good. Instead, the ethics of the film are highly individualized; the men's commitment to their duties is based not on external factors—love of community, ethical ideals, and so forth—but rather on internal desires—the need to prove how good they are at what they do. One gets the sense from the film that they are holding Joe for the U.S. marshal not necessarily because his unethical behavior is bad for the community (although he is seen as a bad seed) but because of mere professional obligations, which provide a context for practicing their well-honed skills.

Examine, for example, Chance's explanation for becoming the sheriff in *Rio Bravo.* When Feathers asks him how someone gets to be a sheriff, Chance says: "He gets lazy. Gets tired of selling his gun all over. Decides to sell it in one place." While there is a certain element of self-deprecation here that makes the line witty, and indeed most likely indicates Chance's desire to avoid meaningful conversation about his past and his emotions through reductive one-liners, his description of his labor centers around himself and his skills, not the community that he took an oath to protect. In fact, his line suggests that Chance sees little difference between his professional skills as a sheriff and those of his nomadic, gunslinging past, and without further explanation one must wonder in what contexts he "sold his gun." Was he once like the anonymous horde of gunslingers that Burdette has brought to town, paid guns also just doing their jobs? Chance's line emphasizes the commodification of his skills, the extent to which he can be reduced to a set of bodily resources that he must exchange for money. Ethics are removed from the equation as Chance describes it; he is responsible only for the execution of skills, regardless of context. This is not to say that Chance is unethical—despite the reduction of his skills to "selling his gun around," Chance is vaguely concerned with the maintenance of order and justice in the town—but that the film is concerned with a system of professional self-respect and the dynamics of wage labor in which one's personal worth is tied to the worth of one's skills, rather than with the broader social context in which those skills are exercised.

The real ethical considerations of the film focus on the development of authentic relationships between men within contexts of professional skill. Despite Chance's affirmation that the town of Rio Bravo is just another context within which he sells his skills, his relationships with Dude, Stumpy, and, to some extent, Colorado differentiate the four of them from Burdette's hired men, whose relationships with one another and with Burdette are grounded solely in economic exchange. The film consistently uses the economic relationship between the Burdettes and their hired guns as a counterpoint to Chance's friendships with his deputies, emphasizing throughout the cost of doing the Burdette's dirty work (at first, one fifty-dollar gold piece, later two) and the rationale of Dude, who just wants to regain his self-respect and to help his friend Chance. As Wood points out, the distinction comes to a head as Nathan visits Joe in the jail, claiming that he is not responsible for anything that Joe's friends might try. But Chance tells him that Joe "hasn't got a friend in the world—and he won't have any unless someone buys 'em for him at fifty dollars a head." While Burdette and his men are capable only of professional interactions, seeing their relationships with one another and their employer only in economic terms, Chance and his deputies are able to retain their professionalism while still developing and maintaining authentic and emotional interactions with one another.[4] Thus, Chance's team of professionals uses nicknames for one another (as Wood tells us, although Chance's real name is Chance, it still sounds like a nickname), suggesting a playful sense of camaraderie among buddies.

The real resolution of the narrative, then, is not the final shootout at the Burdette warehouse on the edge of town, in which Chance and his deputies capture and arrest Nathan Burdette. Rather, the famous song sequence in which the crooning skills of Martin and the teen heartthrob Nelson come together for a duet in the jailhouse resolves the personal tensions of the film and offers a utopian vision of men simply hanging out on the job. The narrative conflict with the Burdettes merely provides the backdrop within which the male melodramas of Dude's alcoholism, Colorado's initiation into the homosocial, professional world, and Stumpy's need to prove his continued use can unfold, making the final shootout narratively necessary to wrap up loose ends but thematically an afterthought. Instead, the laid-back and comfortable sing-along with Stumpy on the harmonica and Chance looking on with paternal approval "serves to announce a period of unparalleled solidarity among the major characters" (Arnold, "My Rifle," 272). The men crystallize into a coherent homosocial unit: Dude overcomes his withdrawal; Colorado, by helping Chance and killing some of Burdette's men, is now unequivocally involved in the standoff; and Stumpy "for once is out front and involved instead of bitching about having to do all the cooking and cleaning" (272).

The utopian camaraderie of the songs suggests the triumph of friendship over the purely economic relationships of Burdette's men, providing a vision of men who retain their professionalism and duty to their occupation but still find a sense of homosocial intimacy with one another. In this way, *Rio Bravo* dramatizes the importance of authentic and intimate relationships between men in contexts of labor and professional interaction. The structures of wage labor, which (thanks to the globalization of capitalism and the pressures to modernize in the 1950s) increasingly enforced around the world a homosocial separation of a male public sphere of labor and a female private sphere of domestic household chores, supported and created constructions of masculinity based in professional identity and the skilled accomplishment of daily labor, rather than those organized around relationships with women, the family, and domestic life. But such constructions of professional masculinities yield interpersonal tensions too: how to maintain a sense of authentic interaction and connection when relations become increasingly commodified. The insistent emphasis on friendship in *Rio Bravo* negotiates those tensions, providing a vision of professional masculinity that can find pleasure in the homosocial contexts of labor and celebrating men just hanging out at work, enjoying each other's company, singing together.[5]

The central relationship triangle in the film between Dude, Chance, and Feathers dramatizes these tensions in the construction of masculinity, balancing a desire for homosocial intimacy between Dude and Chance with the need to integrate Chance into structures of heterosexual romance (really, the need to integrate Feathers and the idea of heterosexual romance into the all-male world of the protagonists). As described in detail in Chapter 1, the need to envision the possibilities of heterosexual romance and nuclear-family ideologies for Wayne's characters and to simultaneously justify the creation of all-male worlds of action and adventure is one of the defining traits of Wayne's persona, and in *Rio Bravo* the dichotomy pulls Chance in opposite directions. While Feathers works throughout the film to open Chance to the possibility of romantic and emotional engagement in what Deborah Thomas refers to as Chance's "erotic education" ("John Wayne's Body," 78), Chance in the meantime is putting his emotional labor into the rehabilitation of Dude, using a host of sometimes cruel and humiliating tactics to slowly reinitiate Dude into the structures of professional masculinity, putting Dude back into the habiliments of masculine authority (returning to him his old guns, his old clothes, his old hat) as Dude's sense of self-respect gets rebuilt. In essence, Feathers does all the work in pursuing Chance, while Chance's time and efforts are devoted to his rehabilitation of Dude, indicating the general trajectory of Wayne's star persona and its flight from heterosexual and familial entanglements.

Indeed, the interactions between Feathers and Chance seem unduly awkward and lacking chemistry (perhaps because of the vast age difference between Wayne and Dickinson). Even at the end of the film, he can express his affection for her only in the professional terms of the sheriff, saying he will arrest her rather than let her dance for money in a skimpy outfit. Chance's interactions with Dude, on the other hand, are more nuanced and reciprocal, particularly the highly charged moment when Chance gives Dude his old guns back, bestowing upon him phallic symbols in a scene ripe for queer analysis. Within the film's gendered dynamics, Feathers's storyline is an important reference to the lure of heterosexual romance—and as Wood points out, Feathers functions as a significant figure in deflating and poking fun at the masculine posturing characteristic of John Wayne (*Rio Bravo*, 46)—but the ability of Chance and Dude to carve out a space for male intimacy within contexts of professionalism provides the emotional core of the film.

Like the recommitment of Kirby and Kathleen Yorke at the resolution of *Rio Grande*, the union of Feathers and Chance can occur only by "evading the problem of the home" and the domestic while lingering in the homosocial spaces of male violence and professionalism (Thomas, "John Wayne's Body," 87). Those tensions find explicit manifestation in the spaces of the film. As Arnold notes, Carlos and Consuela's hotel (interestingly named the Hotel Alamo in a reference to another famous siege) functions as the most domestic space in the film for Chance. There, he can dabble in the comforts of domesticity, either vicariously through Carlos and Consuela or by engaging in his own emotional entanglement with Feathers, who never leaves the hotel (Arnold, "My Rifle," 275). But we never lose sight of the fact that the hotel is a hotel, a temporary place of lodging that might resemble a home but will never be one (except, of course, for Carlos and Consuela). It is, rather, a way station, a space where people like Chance, Feathers, Chance's friend Wheeler, and others passing through town can meet and socialize, a space that might resemble the domestic but will always be transient in nature. The hotel functions, as Thomas explains it, as "a non-domestic space which is neither wilderness *nor* marital home that both men and women can inhabit together" ("John Wayne's Body," 87).[6]

The semidomestic space of the hotel is contrasted with the "untrammeled, undomesticated masculine rapacity" of the saloon, where Burdette's men wait for their opportunity to strike (Arnold, "My Rifle," 275). Chance's jail functions as an intermediary space between these poles, a space that is marked both by masculine professionalism (swearing in and paying the deputies, holding the prisoner, storing guns and ammo) and by the emotional, homosocial connections between men. The space of the jail, while the site of labor and professionalism, is constantly constructed as a domestic space, with Stumpy functioning as a stereotypical maternal caregiver: cleaning, cooking, nagging Chance to be nicer to Dude or to show him some appreciation (which Chance eventually does by kissing Stumpy on the head, prompting Stumpy to playfully swat him on the bottom with a broom). After all, "Wayne's characters generally prefer to nudge out alternative familial spaces away from the domestic (in the cavalry, the army, on the range, and so on), even when a woman is part of the package" (Thomas, "John Wayne's Body," 78). So just after the cathartic crooning of Martin and Nelson, it is not surprising that Chance's epiphany about how to finally resolve their problems is to move all the men into the jail together, to gather bedding, food, cigarettes, and beer and hole up for the last few days until the marshal arrives. The real solution, once the friendships and intimacy between the men have been resolved, is for the transformation of the professional sphere into a domestic one, just without women. The plan backfires when the hotel's domesticity gets in the way: when Feathers helps Dude take a bath at the hotel before the men all move in together, Burdette's men get the drop on them and eventually take Dude hostage, revealing the dangers posed by a feminized domesticity and the necessity of masculine professionalism and readiness.

At the core of the film's vision of professionalism is not simply the ability to be good and prove one's worth through skilled labor but also the ability to create alternative worlds of authentic friendships and intimacy out of the homosocial sphere of men's labor.

THE ALAMO: DECOLONIZATION, DEMOCRACY, AND MASCULINE LEADERSHIP

In his next major role, Wayne found himself similarly under siege, only this time at the hands of a despotic military ruler who can move freely through space while Wayne and his cohorts are forced to hunker down and fight an idealistic battle. In *The Alamo*, Wayne plays Davy Crockett, fresh from his turn as a U.S. congressman, traveling south to Texas (then a part of Mexico) with a band of friends and followers from Tennessee. Crockett's followers don't know that Crockett is leading them south to help the local "Texicans" declare independence from Mexico and establish the Republic of Texas. Crockett and his men wander into the small town of San Antonio de Bexar and find themselves enmeshed in a struggle for power and respect between Colonel William Travis (Laurence Harvey), the educated and regulation-minded soldier who was put in charge of the mission turned fort known as the Alamo, and Colonel Jim Bowie (Richard Widmark), the legendary frontiersman who settled in Texas and leads a large band of soldiers in the fight against Mexico. After some manipulation at the hands of Crockett, his freedom-minded Tennesseans volunteer to help the small fort fight off the Mexican army, and Crockett's presence helps smooth the relationship between Travis and Bowie. The fort is vastly outnumbered by thousands of well-trained and polished Mexican troops under the command of General Santa Anna, but the men remain at the Alamo and embrace certain death in order to hold Santa Anna at bay long enough for the Texas army to be assembled north of the fort. All the men die at the film's end, and they are celebrated as brave men who chose to die for the ideals of democracy.[7]

We can see in *The Alamo* an attempt by Wayne to import the Hawksian conception of professional subjectivity not only into the cinematic narrative of *The Alamo* but also into the cultural narratives of U.S. global leadership within modernization and global capitalism. Through the figure of Crockett and his juxtaposition with Travis and Bowie, Wayne as a director articulates not simply a conservative political message about the need for the United States to stave off communism internationally (as the film is often interpreted) but rather an examination of the role of capitalism and democracy within the kinds of masculine identities that can thrive within the global economy. For example, in the film's celebration of Crockett as leader, *The Alamo* doesn't simply present him as a hyperpatriotic, tough-minded politician; instead, the film uses Crockett to illustrate an ideal vision of capitalist subjectivity that should be the model for modern masculinity and political leadership.

So while *Rio Bravo* concerns itself with the ideal of a professional self-respect that doesn't slide into capitalist greed and commodified personal relationships, *The Alamo* focuses instead on self-sacrifice, dramatizing the ordeal of individuals whose beliefs in personal freedom and self-interest lead them to (somewhat ironically) sacrifice themselves for the ideals of democracy and free-market capitalism. But as in *Rio Bravo*, the core of *The Alamo*'s appeal lies in the pleasures of men at work, backed into a corner and under siege, deciding what kinds of men they really are. Wayne's vision of masculine leadership in *The Alamo*, like Hawks's in *Rio Bravo*, dramatizes how different kinds of masculinity can (and must) come together in highly dangerous contexts to ensure the supposed "common good." But while *Rio Bravo* centers on the dangerous context of an out-of-control capitalism able to commandeer space in ways that those without power cannot, *The Alamo* dramatizes the dangerous spatial geopolitics of decolonization and the role of U.S. global power in a rapidly transforming political landscape, offering a spectacular representation of the kinds of capitalist masculinity that conservatives like Wayne saw as essential to democracy and the global economy.

The Alamo was a personal project of Wayne's, a film that he had tried to get produced since the late 1940s and one that he directed himself. As Garry Wills describes in his critical biography of Wayne, the Alamo mythology was "the closest Wayne came to having a real religion, one for which he would sacrifice himself" (*John Wayne's America*, 204). And sacrifice himself he nearly did: the film's production was a financial and logistical disaster. Wayne produced the film himself in partnership with United Artists, which distributed it, so both Wayne's reputation as a new director and a great deal of his money were on the line. Following the lead of big studios, Wayne originally sought to shoot the film overseas in order to capitalize on cheap labor, in either Mexico or Panama. But the prospect of shooting the founding Texan myth abroad was too controversial, and Wayne looked to locations in Texas, which led his original investors to pull out of the project. Wayne was forced to seek out Texan investors, whose patriotic sensibilities he appealed to in his quest for funds.[8] The production itself was also rocky: Wayne had a contentious relationship with costar Richard Widmark; John Ford showed up on set and undermined Wayne's role as director; a fire broke out at the office of Wayne's production company; one of his actresses was murdered; and Texas oil executives flew their planes over the shoot in order to get a better look, thereby ruining Wayne's shots (216–227). And although the film was profitable and was nominated for several Academy Awards, including Best Picture, it was widely panned by critics dismissive of Wayne's personal politics.

Because Wayne is so associated with right-wing politics (often fairly, sometimes not), *The Alamo* is most often lumped together with Wayne's other personal endeavors, particularly *The Green Berets* (1968), Wayne's cinematic argument in favor of the Vietnam War. The comparison is in some ways apt: it is difficult to avoid the explicit anticommunist message of the film. The men of the Alamo sacrificing their own lives to contain Santa Anna's forces long enough for a larger army to be assembled allegorizes the necessity of holding the communists at bay in far-flung locales such as Korea (and soon Vietnam), even if doing so means sacrificing U.S. lives.[9] Thus, it is popularly believed that the film is a straightforward affirmation of reactionary conservatism, and has even been seen as a mouthpiece for the John Birch Society and the politics that led Wayne to support Barry Goldwater (which is ironic, since the film supports international interventionism).

But overall the film is a much more complex and contradictory muddle of political values and rhetoric. Reflecting the contradictory discourses of U.S.

global power in the late 1950s and early 1960s, the film attempts to balance libertarian celebrations of individual freedom in the face of a tyrannical government with a celebration of military camaraderie and the necessity of U.S. intervention overseas. *The Alamo* attempts to valorize extreme, rugged individualism and self-interest while still affirming the importance of self-sacrifice for the government's military efforts. The film envisions an extreme egalitarianism and distrust of hierarchies while still insisting that certain "natural" leaders must be followed. In short, the film is a hodgepodge of conservative political ideals supporting not only hyperconservative individualism and freedom but also the projection of U.S. power overseas to bring democracy and capitalism to the world's peoples (for their own benefit and protection, as the argument went). While many of those ideals might be characterized as essentially American in nature, the contradictions that the film attempts to bridge also reflect a host of international contexts regarding modern subjectivity, national identity, and individual rights.

One way of understanding the film's construction of Crockett's last stand, then, is to see the film in the context of modernization and U.S. interventionism in the late 1950s and early 1960s. Stanley Corkin, for example, situates the film with other westerns of the period such as *The Magnificent Seven* (1960), which depicts U.S. gunslingers aiding an undeveloped Mexican village in its fight against a ruthless, Mafia-style baron. Corkin argues that *The Alamo* is about the necessity not only of drawing a line in the sand against communism but also of U.S. intervention in the affairs of typically nonwhite, undeveloped nations (*Cowboys as Cold Warriors*, 184–204). Crockett's Tennesseans, after all, do not have to get involved in the affairs of the Texans; as one of the Tennesseans puts it, "It ain't our oxen being gored." But Crockett makes the case for containment: "A fellow gets in the habit of goring oxen, it whets his appetite. He may come up north and gore yours." Thus, moral responsibility knows no geographic boundaries; Crockett articulates a vision of U.S. foreign policy in which U.S. military might has a responsibility to intervene around the world. As Corkin puts it: "Wayne's Texas becomes much like Hungary in the fifties or Vietnam in the fifties and sixties in the imagination of US conservatives—nations made up of freedom-loving people . . . who need to be rescued from despotism in order to benefit from free markets and Christianity" (196).

The need for such intervention was heightened in the early 1960s because of the wave of decolonization that had increased since the 1950s, creating a spate of nations that (from the perspective of the United States and the former imperial powers) needed to be integrated into a system of global capitalism. The year 1960, in fact, was the high-water mark of the decolonization process, when eighteen African colonies attained independence (Strang, "Patterns of Decolonization," 437). All the while, the French war to retain colonial power in Algeria raged in North Africa, Tibetans staged an unsuccessful revolt against the Chinese, and colonies outside Africa, such as Cyprus, attained independence. The year 1960 was a watershed historical moment for the breaking down of European colonialism and for revolts against colonialism in general.

This wave of decolonization yielded massive social and political tension for the crumbling European empires, the newly decolonized, and the United States as the self-proclaimed leader of global capitalism and liberal economics. For those experiencing decolonization, the massive shift in political power often meant a negotiated realignment of political and national identity as territories created by European interests negotiated, at times, a new sense of national identity or, at times, a new sense of political opposition, as when postcolonial regimes simply reproduced the structures and ideologies of the European colonizers. Indeed, as Frederick Cooper points out, the early processes of decolonization, while marked by intense feelings of hope and empowerment, saw the rise of what he terms "gatekeeper states": postcolonial national governments that sought to maintain power by mirroring the dynamics of late colonialism. Such states limited the possibilities of advancement for populations beyond an elite, privileged group, a tactic that helped maintain power but also, ironically, made such states vulnerable to coups and regime changes (*Africa since 1940*, 5).

For those witnessing decolonization, especially foreign-policy makers in the United States, the transition of power became a moment of opportunity and danger (as discussed in Chapter 5). As largely undeveloped nations, the newly decolonized figured into U.S. and European economic strategy as the processes of modernization (implemented through institutions such as the World Bank and the IMF) sought to draw the new nations into a system of modern capitalism based on free trade and open borders. The push to enshrine modern capitalism as the world's economic system felt countervailing pressures from communism, particularly in the late 1950s and early 1960s with the rise of communism in Cuba in the backyard of the United States. The historical moment of *The Alamo*, therefore, was marked by a host of tensions concerning decolonization and the implementation of global capitalism.

At this peak of decolonization and Cold War tensions, it isn't surprising that Crockett, Bowie, and Travis in the film are fighting for a vision of individual freedom that closely resembles global capitalism. Indeed, Travis's description of the oppression Texans will face unless freed from the grip of Mexico centers on individual freedom and, in particular, free trade: "no access to markets for our goods, forbidden to trade with the North." And Crockett's lengthy explanation for wanting to help Texas form a democratic republic evinces a strong, libertarian notion of freedom: "Republic. I like the sound of the word. It means people can live free, talk free, go or come, buy or sell, be drunk or sober, however they choose." As in the discourses dominating U.S. foreign policy at the time (and also today), the rhetoric of democracy and freedom is deployed in the film to indicate free markets and a laissez-faire approach to government and the economy (in much the same ways that the modernization of Japan depicted in *The Barbarian and the Geisha* is framed within the discourse of international trade and consumption; see Chapter 6).

And yet *The Alamo*, like *Rio Bravo*, is suspicious of purely self-interested capitalism, which finds its cinematic expression in Emil Sande, a greedy and slick war profiteer who is selling guns and anything else he can to Santa Anna while also attempting to blackmail a local woman with large family landholdings into marrying him. When Travis orders the confiscation of all the guns and powder from all the merchants of the town, Sande hides his in the local church in an attempt to keep his goods and make a higher profit off them. Yet he insists in private that he will find a way to be acceptable to the Texas leaders should they find themselves victorious, in essence refusing to fully take a political stand and thereby maximizing the possibilities for financial gain. As is typical of U.S. visions of class and labor, *The Alamo* is deeply invested in the values and ideologies of free-market capitalism, but villainizes Sande as a stereotypical vision of excessive capitalist greed concerned only with status and power. In attempting to disavow the inherent inequalities and unethical behavior within a capitalist system (in reality, a war profiteer like Sande is central to the functioning of global capitalism and is not an unethical outlier), the film attempts to assuage the tensions of a capitalist system. *The Alamo* celebrates individual self-interest, free choice, and a form of competitive, capitalist masculinity while simultaneously constructing the consolidation of power in the hands of a few dominating individuals as an aberrant outcome that results from the actions of deviant personalities such as Sande, rather than as being foundational to the structures of power. While such a disavowal is important to the functioning of the U.S. class system, such narratives must be considered important also within the contexts of global capitalism and international audiences experiencing firsthand the inequalities of a globalizing capitalist system.

In contrast with such deviant personalities, *The Alamo* offers up several different models of Western masculinity as possible forms of leadership around the world, leading Corkin to insist that the film is an unapologetic imperialist project linked to Eurocentric assumptions of modernization theory, which considers Western modernity the standard by which other cultures can be measured and posits the natural leadership of white Europeans and Americans in the nonwhite world. The individualism and egalitarianism in the film (especially evident in the band of Tennesseans) naturalizes and celebrates the leadership of men like Davy Crockett. Crockett leads his men not because of position (he refuses to use his title of colonel) nor because of his wealth. Instead, he is simply a natural and unpretentious leader whose wisdom and intelligence mark him as special. In contrast with the Texans of Mexican heritage (Tejanos), who are practically nonexistent at the fort or whose advice is publicly dismissed, Anglo figures such as Crockett and Bowie stand out as natural leaders in the fight against oppression.

But the film's celebration of U.S. intervention abroad seems to tell only part of the story. The cinematic pleasures of the film that helped make it internationally successful suggest a broader set of issues and anxieties than simply those of white American conservatives. Examine, for example, the battle imagery used throughout the film, in which a ragtag group of untrained soldiers takes on a massive, well-equipped army. As Santa Anna's army closes in on the Alamo, the film makes sure to contrast the soldiers of the Alamo, who wear sloppy, frontiersman clothing and have little formal training as soldiers (with the exception of the Tennesseans) with Santa Anna's army, which forms up in precise lines while wearing colorful uniforms. The Alamo's soldiers repeatedly remark on the spectacle of the Mexican army, with one calling it "the prettiest army I've ever seen." The imagery of a large and disciplined army in European-style uniforms taking on a small band of untrained but idealistic rebel freedom fighters seems to offer a set of pleasures that would resonate in many contexts, especially at a historical moment that saw not only a wave of decolonization but also battles for colonial independence, such as the one raging in French Algeria. Since cinematic identification often crosses racial and ethnic lines, the spectacle of *The Alamo* in some contexts might offer a tale of resistance to colonial power or even resistance to emerging postcolonial regimes styled on European models.

Moreover, like *Rio Bravo, The Alamo* offers the sensations of claustrophobia instead of the pleasures of mobility, suggesting the confining anxieties of those without power within the context of capitalism and decolonization. With the exception of a few incidents in which Crockett leads a small band under cover of darkness to attack the approaching Mexican army, the bulk of the film and its action unfold in the closed and often cramped spaces of the Alamo. The replica of the Alamo built for the film constructs the space as an old, decrepit mission, often filled with shadows. The arches of the mission often provide internal framing for the characters, suggesting a sense of confinement for them and their plight. For example, in one scene after Bowie and Crockett have violated one of Travis's orders by clandestinely destroying one of the Mexican army's large cannons, Travis and Bowie confront each other in a dark and shadowy corner of the mission. The low-key lighting and crowded frame create a cramped and uncomfortable sense of space as the men challenge each other and agree to duel after the battle is over.

It seems telling that a film supposedly celebrating and extolling the virtues of U.S. intervention abroad would use the story of the Alamo and the sensations of claustrophobia. The story of men under siege who choose certain death in order to defend their ideals is heroic, but also suggests a certain level of anxiety and apprehension about mobility and borderlessness. Unlike other westerns of the period such as *Gunfight at the OK Corral*—which, as Corkin points out, dramatizes modern law enforcement sweeping through the frontier without regard to borders or jurisdiction (*Cowboys as Cold Warriors*, 166–172)—the sensations of *The Alamo* make clear the inequalities of borderlessness as a despotic army seeks to draw populations under the banner of a nationalism that they do not want to embrace. Although the film's narrative and dialogue enshrine freedom of movement and free markets as fundamentally good for people and communities, the film's imagery explores a sense of apprehension about open space and the threats to free movement and free markets posed by those with too much power.

In this way, the film's resonance in the historical context of decolonization is appropriate. Mirroring the upheavals of decolonization, in which imperial or emerging national identities are in flux, the film tells the story of a population that no longer sees itself as part of a national or imperial community and seeks their independence and own identity as Texicans (or Texians). In a time of rapid decolonization, in which the swift removal and rejection of imperial subjectivity was unevenly replaced with sometimes new and novel forms of national identity, *The Alamo* expressed the tensions and confinement of negotiated spatial identities.

The film makes it clear that the men choose their confinement at the Alamo as a highly symbolic gesture of self-sacrifice. The mobile guerilla tactics advocated by Bowie, after all, are quite effective: the men pull off several successful raids on Santa Anna's army, stealing beef and disabling the Mexican army's large cannons. But instead of pursuing the empowering and heroic mobility inherent in such tactics, the men all decide to embrace certain death in the closed spaces of the fort, to die for their political ideals. In the political world of the film, that decision is the only way to bridge the gap between the values of self-interest and the need for self-sacrifice: the men must exercise their freedom by choosing to protect the freedom of others, even at the cost of their own lives. Self-interest can go only so far in a world full of oppressive dictators. It seems clear that Wayne as a director intended the narrative of self-sacrifice to highlight the importance for U.S. conservatives, the military, and the government of the need to stand up to communism—thus making the film's highly patriotic message hard to swallow for more critically minded reviewers and critics.

But just as *High Noon*'s supposedly liberal but open-ended allegory against the blacklist can be read in a number of ways, we should consider how the message of self-sacrifice might function outside the context of U.S. politics. Is the idea of drawing a line in the sand, choosing to die for one's values and ideals, really endemic only to U.S. conservatism, or might we understand the international popularity of a film like *The Alamo* as part of a broader discourse on violent masculinity and political conflict? In the latter context, we can analyze Wayne as representing not simply an American ideologue but also a model for a kind of masculinist political leadership with implications for a wide range of political contexts, say, anticommunist struggles in Hungary, anticolonial revolts in North Africa, or even the communist revolution in Cuba. The final moments of Davy Crockett in the film have him heroically ignite the fort's power kegs, destroying himself, the powder that might be used against the Texas army, and a host of Mexican soldiers in a death that is active and rebellious, an image that suggests a broad sense of violent resistance to tyrannical oppression.

As this suggests, the film goes out of its way to construct Wayne's Davy Crockett as a model not only of U.S. global leadership but also of a modern masculine political subjectivity, one able to mediate and hold together conflicting masculine personalities and leadership styles and model democratic political conviction.

In *The Alamo*, Crockett negotiates the alternative masculinities of Travis and Bowie. Resembling *Fort Apache's* Colonel Thursday, Colonel Travis in *The Alamo* is a strict commanding officer who places a high value on military regulations and professionalism. He is educated and at times highly condescending—such as when he rudely dismisses the mayor of the town, who brought him information of Santa Anna, because the mayor is simply a civilian, or when he scoffs at the folksy demeanor of Jim Bowie. He has no qualms about lying to or misleading his men in order to keep them from abandoning their posts in the face of certain death. But while his faults put him at odds with Bowie, the film shows a certain sympathy for him, revealing his flaws to be part of a style of leadership full of bravado and superiority in the service of bolstering morale and commanding the respect of the men. His support of Texas, after all, is wholly ideological; unlike Bowie, who is a wealthy landowner in Texas with a great deal to gain economically from Texan independence, Travis is a poor professional soldier who believes in democracy and freedom (just not within his command). Played by Laurence Harvey, a Lithuanian-born star from the British cinema, Travis exudes a European or East Coast sensibility with a hint of effeteness in his posture and demeanor, suggesting forms of bureaucratic and urbane masculinities.[10]

In contrast with Travis is Jim Bowie, the legendary U.S. frontiersman, providing a plainspoken, rough-around-the-edges, hard-drinking foil to the teetotaler Travis. While Travis adheres strictly to military regulation, Bowie is drunk when Sam Houston arrives at the beginning of the film to dispense orders. While Travis marches around the fort dispensing erudite orders, Bowie slouches and drawls as he talks things over with his volunteers. And while Travis fights for democracy as an ideology, Bowie fights because he has developed a relationship with the land and its people. After a night of drinking, he tells Crockett about the wonders of the Texas landscape and the simple pleasures that the Texas people take in living life, sounding a great deal like an early 1960s modernization theorist who loves the land and the people and wants to help Texas become a modern state, which, of course, he would also profit from because of his landholdings. Rather than by barking orders and demanding obedience, Bowie earns the respect of his men because of his honesty and reputation. So while Travis plans to gallantly hold the fort as long as possible, even to his death, in order to give Sam Houston time to build an army, Bowie initially sees such a stand as foolhardy, preferring to lead the small band of troops in guerrilla warfare against Santa Anna in order to save the lives of his men and slow Santa Anna down. Bowie, then, functions as a practical, down-to-earth, rural masculinity that values directness and common sense over rank and education.

Wayne's portrayal of Davy Crockett mediates those competing masculinities and facilitates their partnership at the fort. Although his folksy charms and drunken behavior would seem to align Crockett with the rough-and-tumble Bowie, he also develops respect for Travis, who sees from their first meeting that Crockett's plainspoken ways are somewhat of a façade that hides a deep intelligence and eloquence. Travis learns early on that Crockett is a fellow idealist, someone who traveled south to fight not for personal gain but to support democracy and freedom (and free trade). Crockett's eloquent yet plain egalitarianism makes him an ideal form of modern masculinity, someone who embodies democratic ideals and fights for the rights of others. In an early scene in the film, Wayne as Crockett helps save a local woman from being forced into marrying Emil Sande, the unscrupulous war profiteer, saying that he can't stand people being forced into anything. Within that sequence, he makes sure that Sande gives a gratuity to the small Mexican child who carries his bag up a flight of stairs, insisting repeatedly that the boy's efforts be rewarded. Thus, Crockett fights not only for individual rights but also for free enterprise and entrepreneurship, linking a melodramatic scene of oppression with the everyday ethics of capitalism.[11]

Crockett's inherent sense of natural rights, rejection of pretentiousness and formal titles, and ability to empathize with the political plights of others leads Corkin to argue that Wayne as Crockett embodies the ideal modern personality that modernization theorists such as Daniel Lerner saw as necessary to facilitate the transition from traditional to modern societies (Corkin, *Cowboys as Cold Warriors*, 191). As Corkin notes, neither Travis nor Bowie is shot in the low-angle medium shot of the cinematic hero, but Crockett is consistently depicted as the heroic everyman of the film. From the first shots of Crockett as he rides into town, side by side with his men, his style of egalitarian masculinity is celebrated as vital to the success of modern societies and political systems.

But this vision of egalitarian masculine leadership is also contradictory, balancing a sense of equality with the valorization of Crockett's natural superiority to his men. In one scene, in fact, Crockett allows one of his men to punch him in the face, a game that they play to see who can punch the hardest. Travis, watching on, is appalled by the lack of discipline and the breakdown of hierarchies. But Crockett is happy to have his men engage him in competition, especially since he apparently never loses. While his burly companion punches him hard enough to faze Crockett, he doesn't fall over; at that point, his men know the game is over, since no one can punch harder than Crockett, who effortlessly floors the man. The scene is able to extol the virtues of egalitarian leadership, but only because Crockett is naturally superior to his comrades (much as the United States was constructed as advocating democracy and equality around the world but assumed a natural superiority that justified inequalities).

Moreover, like Travis, Crockett is a master manipulator. His casual egalitarianism, while somewhat genuine, is also a strategy he employs to construct his image and lead his men. When Wayne as Crockett gives his often-quoted speech about the beauty and importance of democracy and a republic (at which point Travis recognizes that Crockett's backwoods demeanor is an act), it becomes clear that Crockett's vision of egalitarianism is predicated upon his ability to pander to an audience, whether using bad grammar and folk expressions to convince voters that he is an everyman or forging a letter from Santa Anna to goad his fellow Tennesseans into joining the fight at the Alamo (he later admits to forging the letter, although by that time his men have already accepted his idealistic argument). Rodney Farnsworth characterizes Crockett's leadership style as Jeffersonian; in contrast to the elitism of Travis's Hamiltonian leadership and Bowie's populist, Jacksonian style, the cinematic Crockett balances the ideals of egalitarianism with the necessity of intelligent and naturally gifted government paternalism ("Epic of Contradictions," 29). Farnsworth's American-history metaphor situates the film within U.S. discourses of masculinity and governmental authority, but that idealized vision of leadership also characterizes the projection of U.S. global power and also finds resonance in the general construction of international political masculinities and the ideals of democratic leadership being negotiated in contexts of decolonization.

Given Wayne's investment not only in the film but also in the character of Crockett, this vision of political leadership and the necessity of a naturally talented and interventionist masculine authority is difficult to separate from Wayne's constructed masculinity in the 1950s. Most accounts of the film note that Wayne didn't want to play Crockett himself, but was forced to do so by his investors, who knew that the drawing power of Wayne would ensure the film's profitability. But it is difficult to imagine anyone other than Wayne playing Crockett, and indeed the part seems to be written for him, with its emphasis on his physical size and violent abilities, imposing yet paternal presence, and libertarian political soliloquies. Wills even suggests that the idea of Crockett as someone who puts on a plainspoken manner that obscures depth, sensitivity, and intelligence is meant by Wayne the director to highlight the emotional depths hidden behind the common perception of him as a simpleminded cowboy (*John Wayne's America*, 221). Wayne's Crockett becomes a surrogate for how Wayne wanted to see himself and his public persona, a kind of masculinity that balances the public projection of rugged strength with an inner eloquence and intellect in a global world marked by crucial political crises.

THE CLOSING OF SPACE IN
THE JOHN WAYNE WESTERN

Taken together, *Rio Bravo* and *The Alamo* complete an increasingly cynical trajectory regarding open space and borderlessness in the John Wayne western. The spaces of the western genre are predicated on the dialectical sense of utopian freedom of movement set against intense competition and danger, sensations that, as I argue in Chapter 2, are also fundamental to the spatial relations of global capitalism and modernization. But early in the fifties, films such as *Red River* or Ford's Cavalry Trilogy privileged the utopian possibilities of open space and movement, celebrating the economic opportunities of borderlessness and the formation of diverse communities in the face of the dangers of the open frontier. By mid-decade, those possibilities had become more ambivalent, as films such as *Hondo* and *The Searchers* explored the racial tensions and antisocial tendencies of wandering and mobility. Finally, in *Rio Bravo* and *The Alamo*, space is bottled up by the powerful, leaving ordinary folks to fend for themselves or else be overrun by the wealthy or by dictators. This isn't to deny that there is something clearly utopian about the male camaraderie in *Rio Bravo* and *The Alamo*, or that this spatial trajectory dominates all of Wayne's westerns; certainly, films such as *The Sons of Katie Elder* (1965) or *True Grit* (1969) return to the themes of wandering and mobility. But for Wayne's most popular and resonant films of the fifties (before his star persona began to shift through age and the changing culture of the 1960s), the pleasures of the films are converted from those rooted in the possibilities of open space and movement to those of seeing men in tight spaces, cut off from the openness and mobility of the powerful, either by force, in *Rio Bravo*, or by idealistic choice, in *The Alamo*.

Through their narratives as well as the visual construction of space on screen, both *Rio Bravo* and *The Alamo* cultivate the feelings and sensations of claustrophobia, a stark contrast to the fantasy of free movement and labor usually on display in the John Wayne western. The overwhelming feelings produced by both films are of men working closely in a confining space, whether it is a dark and dank small-town jail or a dilapidated old mission turned into a makeshift fort on the Texas frontier. While both *Rio Bravo* and *The Alamo* emphasize the typical construction of Wayne's middle-aged body—large, still quick and graceful when it needs to be, able to endure pain and pressure—the spaces that his body occupies as the decade comes to a close restrict his mobility and require that he endure the torments of closed borders.

Such apprehensions about open space may be linked to the tumultuousness of the period, especially with regard to decolonization and the integration of newly formed nations into a system of global capitalism. The fifties were a period of immense economic prosperity for most of the world's population, and yet also a period of intense social, economic, and political tension, particularly since the end of the decade saw the rapid decolonization of European empires. So it should not be surprising that the John Wayne western—as one of the most globally pervasive forms of popular culture in this period—reveals a deep ambivalence and anxiety about borderlessness, mobility, and even the implications of the free market, offering narratives that explore the oppressive possibilities of unregulated capitalism and the plight of populations faced with having to accept a national identity they do not embrace. As films such as *Rio Bravo* and *The Alamo* indicate, the modern capitalist man may find himself enmeshed in economic oppression, political turmoil, and nationalist struggles that limit the possibilities of an open and borderless world. Such tensions suggest an emerging sense of claustrophobia and restricted access in a world once optimistic about mobility and open space.

Conclusion

THE MAN WHO SHOT LIBERTY VALANCE AND
NOSTALGIA FOR JOHN WAYNE'S WORLD

*A*FTER FOURTEEN YEARS AS AN INTERNATIONAL SU-
perstar defined by dynamic body movement, an uncanny skill
and speed with a weapon (despite his aging body), and a rugged masculinity
capable of enduring hardships and torment, John Wayne's emergence in *The
Man Who Shot Liberty Valance* (1962) charted new territory for the star. The first
we see of his character, Tom Doniphon, is the simple wooden coffin that contains his dead body. The film opens with Ransom Stoddard (Jimmy Stewart),
a former governor, senator, and U.S. ambassador, and his wife, Hallie (Vera
Miles), arriving by train in the small western town of Shinbone, where they
met. They tell the local newspaper that they have come for the funeral of Tom
Doniphon, an old, poor rancher whom the reporters have never heard of. When
pressed by the local newspaper editor about why such a prominent politician
would come all the way from Washington for the funeral of an inconsequential
rancher, Stoddard relates the story of his arrival in Shinbone decades earlier and
his relationship to Doniphon, the flashback that forms the bulk of the film. In
the frame story, we never see Doniphon's body, only the coffin, but his presence
haunts Stoddard, Hallie, and the other characters who knew the role he played
in Stoddard's rise to power and the creation of law, government, and modernity in Shinbone.

In a narrative that explicitly takes on the role of the nation-state in matters
of open space, individual mobility, and the economics of borderlessness, Wayne
takes on a role much different from those seen in *Red River, Fort Apache, Hondo,
Rio Bravo*, or his other popular westerns. Instead of a triumphant masculinity
heroically succeeding in the competitive spaces of the frontier, in *The Man Who
Shot Liberty Valance* Wayne becomes a nostalgic throwback to a time gone by,
an out-of-date masculinity yearned for by those in the present. It is in this film
that Wayne's star text begins to chart a new direction, shifting Wayne's articula-

tion of a modern masculinity away from an active celebration of a mobile, capitalist manhood and toward the nostalgic invocation of a rugged individualism incompatible with the changing culture of the 1960s and 1970s.

Liberty Valance is the perfect vehicle to initiate that transition because the film explicitly takes on the chronology of modernization rather than simply dwelling on the pleasures and spectacle of an uneven modernity stretched across the landscape. The flashback not only narrates the relationship between Stoddard, Hallie, and Doniphon but also dramatizes the events that led to the modernization of the town and the institutionalization of government in the territory. The flashback begins with Stoddard, a young man fresh from law school, traveling to Shinbone by stagecoach. The coach is robbed, and Stoddard is brutally beaten and left for dead by the psychopathic outlaw Liberty Valance (who carries a silver-tipped whip and is played with a certain camp sensibility by Lee Marvin). Tom Doniphon finds Stoddard in the desert and takes him to Shinbone to be cared for by Hallie, the beautiful and illiterate daughter of the local immigrants who run the town's restaurant. Everyone assumes that Hallie and Tom will marry, and Tom is even building an addition onto his house for Hallie, but he has yet to propose. Stoddard vows to use the law to put Liberty Valance in jail, but Doniphon insists that only a gun and violence will stop Valance, especially since the town is presided over by the cowardly and timid marshal Link Appleyard (Andy Devine). Stoddard begins working for the town newspaper and running a school, where he teaches Hallie to read and write and teaches the citizens of Shinbone about the merits of law and democracy. Valance has been hired by powerful ranchers to the north of town who want to keep the territory from becoming a state (and thus keep the space open for the cattle range). When Stoddard is elected delegate to the territorial convention, where he plans to fight for statehood, Valance confronts Stoddard. Rather than running away, Stoddard faces Valance in the dark streets of Shinbone and miraculously shoots and kills him despite having no real skills with a gun, a feat that makes him a local hero and leads to his nomination as representative for the territory. Later at the territorial convention, Stoddard finds out that Doniphon, who was hiding around a dark corner, actually killed Valance by shooting him at the same time that Stoddard pulled the trigger. Doniphon tells Stoddard that Hallie is Stoddard's girl now and that he had better accept the nomination and give Hallie a more prominent life than Doniphon can provide for her.

Between Doniphon's acquiescence in Stoddard's request (as well as in his view of the West) and the nostalgic frame narrative foregrounding Doniphon's death, the film explores the passing of older structures of power and the coming of modern systems of society, in ways that deviate from the classic western of the 1950s. As noted in Chapter 2, despite the emphasis on wilderness giving way to civilization in theoretical discussions of the western genre, most of the westerns of the 1950s are more concerned with space than with time, with dramatizing a moment of uneven modernization than with showcasing the temporal processes of development. *Hondo*, for example, provides an elaborate spectacle of an incomplete modernity, with little care for the coming of modern institutions such as the law or statehood. But *Liberty Valance* explicitly takes on the temporal narrative of the western frontier and the stages of modernization, a tendency in the genre that emerged in the early 1960s in films such as *Ride the High Country* (1962) or *Hud* (1963) and continued as a part of New Hollywood's critical examination of the mythology of the West in films such as *Butch Cassidy and the Sundance Kid* (1969) or *The Wild Bunch* (1969). *Liberty Valance* seems to recognize that the genre was changing as the culture changed in the 1960s, that the idea of the western itself was becoming more and more nostalgic and reflexive about the celebration of masculine violence and mobility in the genre's past.

For the film's director, John Ford, the tale of Doniphon's role in the modernization of the territory became the perfect vehicle with which to explore a growing apprehension about the promise of civilization and the pleasures of the wilderness of the past. Ford's ambivalence about the project of civilization, as opposed to the natural freedoms of nature and individualism, had been part of his westerns as early as *Stagecoach* (1939), in which Wayne as the Ringo Kid flees the confining and hypocritical structures of society along with Dallas, a good-hearted prostitute, preferring to create new lives for themselves in the wilderness of the open frontier. And throughout the fifties, Ford's Cavalry Trilogy, along with westerns such as *The Searchers*, explored the same tensions, examining the lives of people attempting to create settled social structures amid the dangerous but alluring open space of the frontier. But *Liberty Valance* articulates Ford's ambivalence more cynically than his previous work, dramatizing both the harsh violence that civilization is built upon and the ways that modern society, while admirable, slowly saps the freedom and vitality that the premodern wilderness nurtured.

It isn't surprising, then, that Ford, chose to shoot *Liberty Valance* primarily on back lots and soundstages rather than in Monument Valley, which he had famously used as a setting in the late 1940s and 1950s. Stylistically, the crags and spectacular rock formations of Monument Valley provided the backdrop for narratives about mobility, open space, and the masculine heroics necessary to survive in such a space, but the somewhat flimsy-looking sets of *Liberty Valance* forecast the restrictions on space and mobility that a more complete modernity and nation-state provide. Monument Valley provided a space that facilitated Wayne's heroics and matched the monumental sensations of Wayne's body in action, but the sets of *Liberty Valance* hem in his large frame, which looks out of place, as if he might accidentally knock over a wall. He is already a masculinity out of his element and on the verge of extinction. Indeed, as Sue Matheson argues, Ford's use of studio rather than location shooting (along with the film's use of film noir techniques and strange discrepancies within the mise-en-scène) was part of an effort to deconstruct the mythology of the western genre, to offer in the early years of the Kennedy administration a critique of the kinds of New Frontier rhetoric that appealed to U.S. youth ("Ford on the Cold War").

If, in this interpretation, Ransom Stoddard functions as a kind of stand-in for the youthful values of Kennedy (whose idealistic rhetoric is based on the misrepresentation of history in Ford's vision of the film), then Wayne is constructed as he would be for the rest of his career: as the heroic and masculine counterpoint to the excesses of youthful liberalism. In the film's narrative structure, Wayne acts as the shared term of two dichotomies (Doniphon-Valance and Doniphon-Stoddard), a function that leads to his disappearance and obscurity as the two dichotomies collapse into a single and inaccurate one (Stoddard-Valance) that defines Stoddard's popular and political success. First, as the title suggests, Doniphon functions as the man who shot Liberty Valance, the counterbalance to Valance's mayhem and chaos. Valance represents all that is irresponsible about the open spaces of the western frontier. He uses his skill with a weapon to dominate others and secure his own power and privilege, taking advantage of the absent bureaucracies of law and order to intimidate others. Valance is aligned with the cattle-ranching interests much like the powerful rancher Burdette in *Rio Bravo* (or the ranchers in a film such as *Shane*). The cattlemen in *Liberty Valance* resist statehood and want to keep the spaces of the frontier open, borderless, and without the kinds of government oversight and regulation that statehood would bring. Valance as villain explores the anxieties of a borderless capitalism that is out of control, exploitative, and irresponsible.

Valance and Doniphon both function within the same vision of libertarian individualism, but Doniphon does so with a sense of ethics and personal responsibility. Both Valance and Doniphon see the world as a place of violence and individual skill. For Doniphon, law and government are unnecessary because there are men like him around, men with enough violent skill and courage to make sure that Liberty Valance doesn't get away with too much. But Doniphon sees the world only in light of his own interests. For example, when Valance trips Stoddard in the restaurant, making him drop a steak, Doniphon steps in and protects Stoddard from Valance's violence, but only because it was *his* steak that was ruined. His personal interests dictate his involvement. When Doniphon is nominated to be the delegate from Shinbone, he declines because he wants to focus on starting a life with Hallie. Doniphon supports statehood, but his own interests keep him from representing the community more broadly.

So while Valance and Doniphon represent two poles on the same libertarian spectrum (one vicious and domineering, the other responsible and ethical), Doniphon functions also as the opposite of Stoddard, who abhors the law of the gun and instead fights for civilization: bureaucracy, education, democracy, and the law. While Doniphon insists that only a gun will stop Valance, Stoddard for much of the film insists that Valance must be arrested. What is more, Stoddard starts the first school in Shinbone, teaching not only the town's multiethnic children but also several adults, including Doniphon's sidekick (and possibly slave) Pompey, about the Constitution and democracy. Doniphon is more concerned about the practical realities of his small ranch. Stoddard offers idealism and participation in the national discourses of democracy and modernization, while Doniphon offers practicality and the protections of violent skill.

When Doniphon's killing of Valance is attributed to Stoddard, Doniphon's role in the process is obscured, and what emerges is a somewhat false dichotomy of Stoddard versus Valance in which law and order triumph over wilderness and lawlessness — the false narrative that facilitates Stoddard's rise as a popular public figure. And Doniphon's obscurity is cemented when, in one of the film's most famous scenes, the editor of the newspaper refuses to print the story that Doniphon actually shot Liberty Valance, saying, "This is the west. When the legend becomes fact, print the legend." But the mythic narrative oversimplifies history and glosses over the role that Doniphon and his individualistic violence played in the town's and territory's progress, revealing that Stoddard's idealized notions of progress and civilization are rooted in the extralegal violence and masculinity of men such as Doniphon, who are the real forces of modernization and nation building.

The film critiques the processes of modernization and democracy that Stoddard represents. As Corkin points out in his discussion of the film's nostalgia, the frame narrative makes sure that the film's representatives of modernity and progress are old and frail when we first see them, a stark contrast to the strong vitality of their memories of Tom Doniphon. And Stoddard's recent service as U.S. ambassador to England associates him with a kind of refined, European masculinity that is meant to be more effete than the large and violent Doniphon. Moreover, between the newspaper editor's participation in political mythmaking and the ridiculous spectacle of the territorial convention (full of empty rhetoric and showmanship — a rider on horseback enters the auditorium with a campaign sign), the processes of democracy fail to live up to Stoddard's idealistic standards, offering superficial and insincere posturing rather than engaged justice and democracy (Corkin, *Cowboys as Cold Warriors*, 224–229).

The film's critique of mythmaking and government produces nostalgia for Tom Doniphon and the rugged, individualist masculinity of John Wayne. Rather than celebrating the processes of modernity and the building of nation-states, the film looks fondly back on the days when Doniphon's powerful but responsible masculinity ruled the territory. While Stoddard became a legend on the back of Doniphon's violent skills, for Stoddard and the film itself it is Doniphon's masculinity that proved mythic and haunting as it vanished in favor of refinement and the trappings of civilization.

For critics such as Corkin, nostalgia for Wayne's Doniphon explores the cultural yearning for the seemingly simpler era of U.S. imperialism before the weight of Vietnam and the cultural turmoil of the 1960s burdened the U.S. cultural imagination. In pointing out that the film's release in 1962 coincided with increased U.S. involvement in Vietnam, the beginnings of the youth counter-culture movement, the Cuban missile crisis, and a monetary crisis that led to soaring U.S. trade deficits, Corkin argues that films such as *Liberty Valance, Lonely Are the Brave* (1962), and *Ride the High Country* (1962) reveal a change in the U.S. national mood, a "general sense that the glorious days of moral clarity and uninterrupted growth had passed" (*Cowboys as Cold Warriors*, 211). By locating a sense of national triumph in the past rather than the present, those early-1960s westerns were "elegies for a simpler time and for a world in which narratives of decline have not replaced stories of conquest" (211).

Liberty Valance explores as well a nostalgia regarding masculinity and individualism in the face of nation building and modernization. This is not to say that the nostalgia for Wayne was somehow nostalgia for premodern social organizations, a yearning for a time before modernization and capitalism had transformed the landscape. Rather, the nostalgia for Wayne that began with *Liberty Valance* and continued throughout the rest of his career indicated a yearning for the pleasures and spectacle of an uneven modernization full of optimism and a sense of possibility about borderlessness and entrepreneurship. As shown throughout the book, Wayne throughout the 1950s offered a masculinity that expressed the tensions but also the pleasures of modernization and global capitalism, and those are the pleasures yearned for in *Liberty Valance*: not necessarily a simpler time, but one marked by the optimism of an open frontier, even if such a frontier is fraught with danger and tension. *Liberty Valance* is nostalgic for a world of individualism and intense competition—nostalgia based on our identification with characters like Doniphon and a masculinity such as Wayne's. Such a vision of competition on the frontier can be appealing only via the raced and gendered privileges of men such as Doniphon.

Moreover, as the processes of modernization increased in the 1960s and decolonization increasingly yielded political instability and struggling nation-states around the world, *Liberty Valance*, with its emphasis on burgeoning governments and an unstable process of democracy, might easily have produced a critique of emerging national regimes and a nostalgia not for colonial rule but for an individualist masculinity that succeeds through skill and toughness rather than through bureaucracy. Although *Liberty Valance* idealizes Stoddard's principles, the film's nostalgia is a condemnation of the kinds of emasculating bureaucracy that ideals such as the law and government rely on. As the film ends and we see the aging Stoddards on the train back to Washington, they sit quietly, Hallie gazing into the distance, suggesting a sense of both nostalgia and regret, a continued yearning for Doniphon and the world that he represented. As they discuss all the changes in Shinbone and in the territory that have come because of Stoddard's work in government, Hallie wistfully says to Stoddard, "This land was once a wilderness. Now it's a garden. Aren't you proud?" But it comes off as an accusation; they both recognize that the modern "garden" has replaced the vitality of the past, that bureaucracy and other structures of modernization have eliminated the kinds of action-oriented masculinity that were necessary in the dangerous but exhilarating state of uneven modernization that Doniphon flourished in.

As it did throughout the 1950s, Wayne's cinematic image in *Liberty Valance* offers a fantasy of tough and skillful masculinity that is modern, mobile, and competitive in the spaces of uneven modernization. But starting with *Liberty Valance*, that masculinity is constructed on-screen as somehow out of date in a world of increasing government and increasing bureaucracy, even as people around the world flocked to experience its pleasures. Starting in the early 1960s, Wayne's star persona began to shift. His roles increasingly reflected a nostalgic construction of his masculinity, seeing him as an older figure who doesn't fit into the changing times rather than as a heroic figure whose masculinity provides a model for modern life. In *McLintock!* (1963), he plays an aging father figure who oversees not only his estate but also his children's entrance into romance and marriage. In *In Harm's Way* (1965), he plays a father figure during World War II whose tense relationship with his son dramatizes the generational conflicts of the escalating Vietnam War. In his Oscar-winning performance in *True Grit* (1969), he plays an aging U.S. marshal who is out of touch with the changing world but whose violence still helps a young girl. He plays an aging rancher who is estranged from his own sons and so hires young boys as his cattle hands and teaches them the values of the past in *The Cowboys* (1972). He reprises his role as the out-of-date U.S. marshal from *True Grit* in *Rooster Cogburn* (1975). And his last performance, *The Shootist* (1976), offers the ultimate nostalgic construction of Wayne, using footage from Wayne's 1950s westerns as the backstory of J. B. Books, a gunslinger dying of cancer who teaches a young man that the time of gunslinging and violence in the frontier is over. In his most prominent films after 1962, which clearly reflect his advancing age, Wayne is defined by the same complex nostalgia that marks *The Man Who Shot Liberty Valance*.

Wayne still took on roles in traditional western and war films in the 1960s and 1970s, roles that celebrate his skill and violence. Films such as *The Sons of Katie Elder* (1965), *The War Wagon* (1967), *The Green Berets* (1968), *Chisum* (1970), *Rio Lobo* (1970), and *The Train Robbers* (1973) affirm the characteristics of Wayne's masculinity developed in the 1950s, constructing his body, its labor, and the spaces of the frontier in ways similar to Wayne's 1950s westerns such as *Hondo* or *Rio Bravo*. But especially as Wayne grew older, the sense of nostalgia and the idea that Wayne was a figure whose time had passed appeared in most of his films. For example, in another collaboration with Hawks, *El Dorado* (1966), Wayne plays an aging gunslinger caught in the middle of a range war between a family and a powerful rancher. In a key plot twist, a shooting leaves a bullet lodged next to his spine, which at times causes paralyzing seizures. While Wayne is still rugged, tough, and quick on the draw, the plot device highlights his aging body and its periodic failures, especially because the film constructs Wayne and Robert Mitchum as old-timers whose vulnerability is contrasted with the youth and vitality of Wayne's sidekick, played by James Caan. The final scene of the film, in fact, shows Wayne, partially paralyzed, limping off into the horizon with a limping Mitchum (whose character had also been injured), a striking image of aging masculinity enduring against time and the elements. So Wayne's body after 1962 still signified the sensations of speed, violent skill, and the ability to endure the elements, all of which defined his rise to international prominence in the late 1940s. But in the mid-1960s, his body began to dramatize the retention of those bodily attributes into old age, especially in the context of Wayne's public bout with lung cancer in 1966.

Moreover, it was in the context of a prominent, liberal youth culture and the international youth-based cultural revolution of the 1960s that Wayne began to be associated with the conservative, older generation. Wayne's politics— particularly his strong support for the Vietnam War—became a much larger part of his star persona, since they provided an appropriate foil for the youth culture. It was at that moment in the mid-1960s that Wayne took on the characteristics that still define how we view him today. It was then that Wayne became an icon of conservative politics, a figure used by the Right to celebrate conservative values and by the Left to mock his simplistic view of the world. And Wayne actively cultivated that aspect of his persona. When invited to speak by the highly liberal, satirical publication the *Harvard Lampoon*, Wayne rode into campus on a tank borrowed from the military, clearly relishing the perception of him as a warmongering old cowboy.

This is not to say that the nostalgic and conservative construction of Wayne wasn't popular in the United States and abroad. While the meanings surrounding Wayne shifted in the 1960s as cultures around the world continued to experience dramatic cultural and social changes, Wayne remained a top international star. The nostalgia for Wayne's masculinity, which was structured into his films in the 1960s and 1970s, continued to draw audiences around the world to the spectacle of his body in action in the spaces of the frontier, suggesting the appeal of nostalgia in dramatizing the pleasures and tensions of the processes of modernization and the globalization of capitalism. As the pace of modernization increased and capitalism continued to transform social structures and mobility, a nostalgic appreciation for Wayne resonated with international audiences throughout the last decade and a half of his career. It is unclear whether that resonance reflected a generation gap, or whether his continued popularity was due to movie attendance by an older generation finding pleasure in remembering the days when a masculinity such as Wayne's was celebrated and emulated, or whether young people around the world found something enjoyable about the idolization of a masculinity that transgressed structures of bureaucracy and legality, even if it was out of date.

In the fifties, Wayne offered a dynamic spectacle of action and mobility that explored the promises and the anxieties of the changing world, a model of modern masculinity that helped manage the ideologies and often-harsh realities of modernization and capitalism, and a style of inhabiting a world of uneven modernization. John Wayne provided a globally ubiquitous set of images and narratives that reflected the kinds of masculinity and social relations that resulted from the massive reorganization of power as structures of colonialism gave way to the flexible and exploitative systems of global capitalism. The common conception of Wayne as an icon of U.S. national identity has fundamentally hindered our understanding of Wayne and Hollywood in the 1950s, for whereas Wayne was certainly associated with America in this period, the America he represented was (somewhat ironically) not the dominating military hegemony of a jingoistic United States, but rather a set of styles and values at the core of an American-style capitalist modernity. It is only by unthinking the assumptions and biases that have oversimplified Wayne among film scholars and the culture at large that we can fully understand the complex vision of modern masculinity that circulated around the globe in Wayne's world.

Notes

1. There has been only a trickle of scholarship exploring the cultural implications of the John Wayne star persona in the last thirty-five to forty years of modern, institutionalized film and cultural studies, despite the fact that Wayne remains popular with audiences around the world well after his death as well as a potent icon of masculinity. Some of the scholarship on Wayne, moreover, has simply perpetuated his identification with a reactionary conservatism rather than exploring the ambivalence of his vision of masculinity (see, for example, Bentley, "Political Theatre of John Wayne"; Jefferson, "Wayne: American Icon"; Loy, *Westerns in America*). But several recent works have begun to examine the complexities of John Wayne and the cultural and ideological implications of his vision of masculinity, interrogating (among other things) Wayne's relationship to heterosexuality and the institution of marriage, the cultural signification of Wayne's body, and the significance of his place within discourses of masculinity and disability (see, for example, Wexman, *Creating the Couple*; Thomas, "John Wayne's Body"; Sanderson, "*Red River*"; Luhr, "Wayne and *The Searchers*"; Freedman, "Post-Heterosexuality"; Meeuf, "Wayne as 'Supercrip'"; Rawlins, "This Is(n't) John Wayne"). One scholar has gone so far as to connect Wayne's 1950s star persona with the existentialism of the hardboiled detective in film noir (Matheson, "West—Hardboiled"). Additionally, the work of French auteur critics who idolized directors like John Ford and Howard Hawks in the 1950s and 1960s saw complexities in Wayne that contradicted and complicated their definition of Wayne as a conservative political icon.

2. Faced with a host of protectionist trade restrictions around the world—including import quotas, blocked currencies (i.e., currencies that cannot be converted to other currencies because of exchange controls), and subsidies for national film companies—Hollywood studios internationalized their operations in this period, investing heavily in other international film industries and reestablishing their dominant international distribution network in the wake of World War II. If, for example, the UK wanted to restrict the number of U.S. films distributed in the country, then Hollywood would begin

purchasing interests in British film companies, which could distribute U.S. films in the UK. If Japan wanted to limit the quantity of U.S. dollars leaving the country, then Hollywood would begin shooting films in Japan and spend its money there. If Italy wanted to give subsidies to native film production, then Hollywood would coproduce films with Italian companies and thereby qualify for subsidies for their "Italian" films. In short, despite the attempts of many countries around the world to protect national cinemas, national borders and cultural identities became more porous and flexible within the international film industry as Hollywood became intertwined with international film industries, sought out international production opportunities, and continued to dominate international film distribution (Guback, *International Film Industry*).

3. For a detailed examination of another star of the western genre in the context of U.S. media globalization, see Michael Kackman's examination of the international reach of the Hopalong Cassidy brand in the 1940s and 1950s ("Nothing on but Hoppy Badges").

4. Recent work on the historical exhibition and reception of Hollywood internationally often makes the claim that Hollywood films were (and are) situated within a complex set of local cultural negotiations rather than simply dominating local cultures. For Richard Maltby, the research on Hollywood abroad doesn't provide "descriptions of hapless audiences deceived by irresistible texts into abandoning their cultural patrimony to become 'temporary American citizens'"; rather it "describe[s] the activities of local agents accommodating and adapting Hollywood movies to the cultural topography of their immediate environment" ("Americanisation of the World," 7). For specific examples of such research, see the essays in Maltby's anthology *Hollywood Abroad: Audiences and Cultural Exchange*.

5. This perspective on the Hollywood-Europe relationship is echoed by Ian Jarvie. As he puts it: "Overseas audiences saw displayed in American movies mores, values, and attitudes they took to be subversive of local custom and political arrangements. American films were marked by an aggressive egalitarianism in dress, speech, action, relations between the sexes, and access to the basic necessities of the good life" ("Free Trade as Cultural Threat," 34).

CHAPTER ONE

1. This chapter is particularly indebted to Eve Kosofky Sedgwick's discussion in *Between Men* of homosociality as a form of social organization. Sedgwick details the construction of different forms of homosociality and same-sex interactions in different historical and cultural contexts, exploring the slippages between same-sex interactions and same-sex eroticism. This conception of homosociality, I argue, is tied to globalization and capitalism. The increased cultural need to articulate and explore homosocial relations between men (particularly in films and other media) is a reflection of the changing socioeconomic conditions of global capitalism, which first insisted on a gender-segregated workplace and then later disrupted the hegemonic masculinities based on that segregation by taking on the seemingly gender-neutral ideologies of neoliberalism.

2. Robert Sklar has discussed the ways *Red River's* construction as an aesthetic masterpiece within film criticism has obscured the centrality of capitalism to the film's narrative (*"Red River"*).

3. Connell's explanation of a world gender order and the shifting constructions of gender in response to social, economic, and geopolitical changes foregrounds the importance of analyzing and understanding gender on a global level. As the processes of imperialism and globalization transform social relations around the world, we can trace the increasingly global patterns of gender relations and gender definitions in the wake of those changes. These global patterns, of course, are not a uniform and standardized set of gendered expectations for men and women; there is not a homogenous gender order that exists for every culture affected by imperialism, modernization, and globalization. But what has emerged is a complicated and interrelated set of gender relations that connects the socially constructed ideas about gender in the developed and developing worlds.

4. Of course, Connell notes that transnational business masculinity is not homogenous. Different manifestations and variations exist in different national and local contexts, but it nevertheless remains the dominant pattern of masculinity within the decolonized and neoliberal world of global capitalism.

5. Steven Cohan, for example, describes Wayne as an "established" star in his analysis of *Red River*, suggesting that we should view Wayne's vision of masculinity as a nostalgic one and Clift's as a "new" manifestation (*Masked Men*).

6. Wexman claims that Wayne embodies the ideal of dynastic marriage, a vision of marriage and coupling central to the projection in westerns of U.S. national identity and the dominance of the land by white men (*Creating the Couple*). Central to the articulation of dynastic marriage is the trope of the family on the land, the vision of a white patriarch, wife, and children occupying territory and legitimizing the "natural" right of white men to control land and exercise authority over women and any racial Others also on the land. Because of his size and adeptness at physical violence, Wayne is an ideal mate within this imperialist vision of families, someone who can protect women and children from the threats of the frontier, endure the hardships of "mastering" the land through physical labor, and impart to his sons the patriarchal values of "hard" masculinity.

7. Moreover, Hirsch as well as Padilla and his coeditors foreground the role of the media in promoting and transmitting the modern ideal intimacy and emotional fulfillment through love (*"'Love Makes a Family,'"* and *Love and Globalization*). Because Hollywood has spectacularly displayed a modern, bourgeois vision of romantic love and companionate marriage since it attained international dominance in the 1910s, it seems that the fantasy of romantic love within modernity resonated with international audiences well before the 1980s, suggesting that love played a prominent role in the world gender order throughout much of the twentieth century, even as it contrasted with traditional definitions of gender and marriage.

8. This vision of masculinity was not always part of the Wayne star text. Throughout the 1940s up until *Red River*, Wayne played a variety of roles but was commonly cast as an object of female desire, the desirable frontier cowboy. In *Tall in the Saddle* (1944),

for example, Wayne is at the center of a love triangle with two women: a proper, aristocratic good girl and a tomboyish, fast-on-the-draw bad girl. The film resolves itself with the coupling of Wayne's character with the newly feminized tomboy, and the union of her ranch with the ranch Wayne inherits at the end of the film. In *Angel and the Badman* (1947), Wayne plays a dangerous yet charming gunslinger who falls in love with a Quaker girl and gives up his violent lifestyle to marry her, even facing his nemesis in the final shootout unarmed in order to not violate the Quaker creed (only to be saved by the town sheriff, played by Harry Carey). Moreover, Wayne was constructed in the fan magazine *Photoplay* within discourses of love and romance, focusing on his desirability to female fans or his romantic courtship of his second wife, Esperanza Baur (Meeuf, "Wayne as 'Supercrip'"). Wayne's association with romance and female desire would change after Hawks's *Red River*. Wayne's construction as a suitable object of female desire essentially ended in *Photoplay*, and his roles became marked by the same anxiety about the role of femininity within the masculine endeavors of capitalism and empire building manifest in *Red River*.

9. It seems ironic that one of Freedman's illustrations in "Post-Heterosexuality" is an image of Wayne shoving a massive pistol into the mouth of another man in *The Shootist* (1976), revealing how the homoerotic elements of Wayne's violence cannot be repressed even in Freedman's essay denying homoeroticism. And in *Red River*, moreover, it is difficult to deny the homoerotic charge of the cattle drive and Wayne's relationship with Matt. Steven Cohan has artfully teased out the queer interactions between Matt and Cherry Valance as they perform a "soft" and sexually flexible masculinity in contrast to the "hard" masculinity of Dunson, particularly in the scene where each playfully offers the other his gun and they size each other up.

10. In other westerns, this role as domestic caretaker is often given to a nonwhite male (such as the Asian cook in the television series *Bonanza*), revealing how the all-male worlds of the western create a racial hierarchy that corresponds to the gender hierarchy in U.S. culture.

CHAPTER TWO

1. Jim Kitses makes most explicit these dualities within the genre, with a large table listing the various dichotomies that mark the western, many of which are spatial distinctions (Kitses, *Horizons West*, 12).

2. As this suggests, the spatial relations of the cinematic frontier have always been in the forefront of criticism on the western. According to Philip French, "This contrast between open land and the town . . . between a relaxed association with nature and a tense accommodation to society, lies at the roots of the genre" (*Westerns*, 107). Robert Warshow similarly highlights the "'cinematic elements' which have been long understood to give the western theme its special appropriateness for the movies: the wide expanses of land, the free movement of men on horses," elements exploited fully in the 1950s western's use of wide-screen and color technology ("Movie Chronicle," 47). And yet for these critics, time still trumps the spatial relations. John G. Cawelti, for example,

notes that in the western town the "rickety wooden buildings with their tottering false fronts help express the tenuousness of the town's position against the surrounding prairie; nonetheless we do not see the town solely as an isolated fort in hostile country . . . but as an advance guard of an oncoming civilization" ("Savagery, Civilization," 59).

3. Most often, space is understood as a neutral concept, the backdrop within which the actions of history and everyday life unfold. But such an assumption obscures the complex ways that space and spatial relations are actively produced through history, capitalism, and social relations. Echoing the work of Henri Lefebvre, Neil Smith notes, "The notion that things happen 'in space' is not just a habit of thought but of language too . . . By its actions, this society no loner accepts space as a container, but produces it; we do not live, act, and work 'in' space so much as by living, acting, and working we produce space" (*Uneven Development*, 116). For Smith and other scholars, the idea of space is a social construction; cultural discourses and social power structures produce not just the spatial relations of the constructed, modern world (urban environments, architecture, routes of transportation, and so forth) but also our conceptions about space, nature, and society.

4. My discussion of cinematic space is informed by several innovative analyses of the construction of space on film, from Deborah Thomas's close readings of space in classic Hollywood (*Reading Hollywood*) to Yingjin Zhang's analysis of the construction of locality in Chinese cinema (*Cinema, Space, and Polylocality*). Particularly informative for my work is Vivian Sobchack's application of Bakhtin's chronotope to the spatial logic of film noir, in which Sobchack links the spatial sensations of cinema to the experience of space in the material world ("Lounge Time").

5. The title of this section is borrowed from Charles Ramirez Berg's excellent essay on Ford's westerns, "The Margin as Center." But while Berg refers to the cultural margin (ethnic others such as the Irish) and the cultural center (the WASP mainstream), his terminology clearly indicates the spatial dynamics of those cultural negotiations.

6. See Berg, "The Margin as Center," for a more detailed explanation of Ford's construction of ethnic identity.

7. The cultural impact of these spatial transformations has been discussed by a host of scholars investigating the deterritorialization of culture and the ways that cultural identity has been uprooted from place-based definitions. For an explanation of these dynamics in relation to an analysis of the spatial dynamics of cultural texts such as film, see Lawrence Grossberg, "The Space of Culture, the Power of Space."

8. See Chapter 6 for a more detailed discussion of modernization theory and its proponents. Also, this approach to modernity has been widely critiqued as not only condescending and imperialist but also an inaccurate assessment of the totality of modernity. See, for example, Appadurai's analysis of an uneven and irregular "modernity at large."

9. Giddens's analysis of the spatial dynamics of modern social interactions in *The Consequences of Modernity* is similar to a variety of approaches to global-local dynamics within the spatial structures of globalization. See, for example, Arif Dirlik's discussion of globalism and localism in "The Global in the Local."

10. In Western cities, Anthony D. King notes, suburban growth cannot be separated from the internationalization of the economy or from imperialism and colonialism; the

accumulation of capital via imperialism and global capitalism spurred the growth of both the urban centers of Western Europe and the migration of their populations to the suburban peripheries of the cities. And the growth of suburbs in former European colonies was likewise based in colonialism and the organization of colonial urban space, which "was subsequently to provide the spatial infrastructure for post-colonial kinds of suburban development, including the influx of foreign companies, tourist hotels and residential developments for the new indigenous as well as international elite" (*Space of Global Culture*, 100).

11. The popularity of the genre led to numerous international films inspired by Hollywood westerns: the British *Diamond City* (1950); the Brazilian *O Cangaceiro* (1953); the Italian films of Pietro Germi, such as *The Road to Hope* (1951) and *The Outlaw of Tacca del Lupo* (1952); several German films starring Hans Albers, such as *Wasser für Canitoga* (1939) or *Sergeant Berry* (1938); a Czech puppet satire of Hollywood westerns called *Song of the Prairie* (1952); several prominent western-inspired films such as Kurosawa's *Seven Samurai* (1954); the so-called spaghetti westerns of Sergio Leone in Italy; and the Indian "curry western" *Sholay* (1975); for more discussion of international westerns, see Fenin and Everson, *The Western*, 319–329. More recently, several playful appropriations of the genre's form have emerged, including Takashi Miike's *Sukiyaki Western Django* (2007), the South Korean *The Good, the Bad, and the Weird* (2008), and *The Warrior's Way* (2010), a martial arts western filmed and produced in New Zealand and directed by the South Korean Sngmoo Lee.

12. My approach to modernity here privileges space over temporality. The concept of modernity—for my purposes, referring to urbanization, rationalization, industrial technology, capitalism, and bureaucracy—has most often been defined as a historical and temporal one; in the grand theories of Western social science, modernity assumes its own totality as a system that marks a distinct moment of historical rupture between the past and the modern. (Thus, even the name "modernity," which is applied to this constellation of social and economic phenomena, frames the concept as a temporal one). And yet a host of groundbreaking research by sociologists, geographers, and critical theorists has challenged the primacy of history and temporality to modernity and modern capitalism, analyzing space as a critical concept in understanding social, economic, and political relations within modernity (see, for example, King, *Spaces of Global Culture*; Wallerstein, *Modern World-System*; Smith, *Uneven Development*; Soja, "History: Geography: Modernism"; Lefebvre, *Production of Space*; Massey, *Space, Place, and Gender*; Castells, *Rise of the Network Society*; Harvey, *Condition of Postmodernity*; Giddens, *Consequences of Modernity*). From this spatially conscious perspective, modernity refers not simply to a "new" mode of social and economic organization but also to a reorganization of space and the ways that people inhabit and think about space. The literal transformation of space through urbanization, city planning, and modern architecture; the fundamentally spatial nature of modern capitalism and neo-imperialism as the world is divided by a geographic division of labor and uneven levels of development (Wallerstein, *Modern World-System*; Smith, *Uneven Development*); the new ways that people think about space because of technologies that "compress" space and facilitate distanci-

ated social connections (Harvey, *Condition of Postmodernity*; Giddens, *Consequences of Modernity*) — the transformations of modernity are largely spatial.

CHAPTER THREE

1. For an overview of Wayne's participation in Hollywood's anticommunist policies and the Motion Picture Alliance for the Preservation of American Ideals, see Roberts and Olson (*John Wayne: American*) for a rather apologetic description, or Gary Wills (*John Wayne's America*) for a more critical description.

2. For a history of the Hawaiian Islands emphasizing the role of imperialism and U.S. foreign policy, see Arthur Power Dudden's *The American Pacific*.

CHAPTER FOUR

1. The 3-D version was later scrapped, and a 2-D version made from the "left eye" camera was used for the theatrical release.

2. The press releases mentioned in this paragraph are stored at the Warner Bros. Archive, University of Southern California, Los Angeles.

3. Max Westbrook argues, in fact, that the emotional pleasure of Wayne dancing with Shirley Temple in *Fort Apache* obscures the problematic politics of the film ("John Wayne Danced").

4. Luhr notes that Wayne's relaxed and restrained mannerisms developed in the 1950s. In much of his 1940s work, and in particular in a film such as *Red River* (1948), Wayne played overly ambitious men who barked orders quickly and "radiated tensions and provocation" ("Wayne and *The Searchers*," 78). In the 1950s, Wayne's persona became quieter and more restrained, "like a panther waiting to pounce" (78).

5. For an analysis of Wayne's star image that explores these patriarchal and gendered ideologies, see Wexman, *Creating the Couple*.

6. Since Wayne was constructed as a star to be watched and admired by men, the affective pleasures of Wayne cannot be separated from a homoerotic appreciation of Wayne's body — and indeed, the homoerotics of the male body in action-oriented genres has long been analyzed in film scholarship; see, for example, Neale, "Masculinity as Spectacle." I am not pursuing a necessarily queer reading of Wayne here, but the popularity of Wayne's body nevertheless revolves around the sensations aroused when men watch Wayne engaged in violence, sensations that surely range from the mundane to the erotic.

7. The film's resolution — with Hondo embracing romance and the nuclear family and creating a settled existence for his new family — seems to privilege the daily labor of domesticity, but the film doesn't really resolve this tension. Instead, the film represses it through the spectacle of Wayne engaged in violent action. Although Wayne, Mrs. Lowe, and Johnny embrace a happy domestic future together in California, they secure that

future through Wayne's heroic violence against the Apache. Hondo is able to use his brutal skills to help the homesteaders escape from the war-torn territory, but his new domestic life with Mrs. Lowe and Johnny remains in the offscreen future. The ending thus offers the spectacle of Wayne's graceful violence without representing the new domesticity of Hondo's life.

8. These socioeconomic changes affect not just constructions of masculinity but also the sensations and textures of everyday life within modernity around the world. The ways that wage labor restructures daily routines and relationships, the spatial reorganizations of urbanization and suburbanization necessitated by the new regimes of gender and labor, the actual sensations and textures of both wage labor and white-collar office work: the transformations of modernization and global capitalism underway in this period created not simply new political, economic, and bureaucratic structures but also new sensations and lived experiences of the physical world. As Appadurai notes about growing up in Bombay in the 1960s, modernity for him was a rather synesthetic experience, something to be felt through a range of transnational images, products, and ideas such as blue jeans, Hollywood B movies, and the smells of Right Guard deodorant as much as a structural, political transformation (*Modernity at Large*).

9. The emphasis on suffering pain through labor, moreover, exemplifies Steve Neale's argument in "Masculinity as Spectacle" that the homoerotic implications of the overt display of the male body can be repressed through sadomasochism, punishing the body for its exhibition.

10. The emphasis on the relationship between cinematic sensation and the material sensations of modern life is supported by Vivian Sobchack's examination of film noir, in which she argues that the spatiotemporal sensations of homelessness within noir chronotopically mirror the literal and cultural feelings of homelessness in postwar America ("Lounge Time").

11. These terms come from David Harvey's discussion of the compression of space (*Condition of Postmodernity*) and Anthony Giddens's discussion of the distanciation of space within modernity (*Consequences of Modernity*).

12. The novelty of air travel and its relationship to the complex connectivity of global culture are made evident in the Wayne airline-disaster film *The High and the Mighty* (1954).

13. Perhaps one reason why Wayne's fantasy of borderless movement is so appealing is that it offers a vision of mobility often tied to responsibility and community in contrast to the disconnection from community and responsible action at the root of global capitalism's "space wars." The Cavalry Trilogy films, for example, emphasize the creation of new social relations among a diverse group of people brought together by migration and movement. And even in films in which Wayne's character doesn't quite fit in with the community, in *Red River* (1948) or *The Searchers* (1956), his mobility in the end works to affirm the construction of communities, often through the heterosexual coupling of a younger comrade. Wayne offers an assurance that freedom of movement in the end supports the greater good.

14. Sue Matheson interprets Wayne's psychological turmoil in the film in the context of "blood pollution": the lingering traumatic symptoms of veterans who have returned

home from war. For Matheson, Ethan's psychological voyage is not simply about race and miscegenation, but rather about the effects of war on his psyche, issues clearly relevant to U.S. audiences in the years after World War II and the Korean War ("'Let's Go Home'"). This astute reading of the film suggests as well the film's relevance for international audiences, in light of the many international military conflicts of the period.

15. For a detailed and astute analysis of Wayne's performance in *The Searchers*, see Luhr, "John Wayne and *The Searchers*." Analyzing how the film both relied on and deviated from the existing Wayne star persona, Luhr describes Wayne's role in developing Ethan's complex character.

16. In the popular novel tied to the film, the character of Hondo Lane is much more ethnically ambiguous.

17. See, for example, Christopher Sharrett, "Through a Door Darkly."

18. Slotkin makes a similar case about *Rio Grande*, arguing that the film allegorizes the tensions of the Cold War in the early 1950s (*Gunfighter Nation*).

19. The trope of the white man on the frontier who adeptly learns the survival skills and culture of the Native peoples by "going native" is analyzed by Shari Huhndorf, who argues that this trope facilitates the oppression of indigenous populations (*Going Native*). But as I note above, that view of Wayne is complicated by JoEllen Shively's research on Navajo and Anglo perceptions of *The Searchers*, in which she notes that many Navajo people identify with Wayne as a strong male character who is close to the land and has the skills to survive in the wilderness ("Cowboys and Indians").

CHAPTER FIVE

1. Algeria was a unique case in that French authorities did not consider Algeria a colony; the region was classified as an official department of France. That status helps explain the French government's hesitancy to hand over power in the region to political organizations such as the Front de Libération Nationale. But the violent resistance to French occupation in the mid to late 1950s in Algeria made it very clear to the French government that its power in Algeria was understood locally as imperialistic.

2. For a detailed analysis of the tropes of the imperial adventure film and the ways in which Western cinema perpetuates the ideologies of imperialism, see Ella Shohat and Robert Stam, *Unthinking Eurocentrism*.

3. The distinction between a callous and oppressive colonialism and a more sensitive desire to help native inhabitants is not a new narrative trope, one that often critiques a superficial notion of "bad" colonialism while still indicating the need for Western supervision. See, for example, Richard Dyer's discussion of *Simba* (1955) in *White* as another film that explores different visions of white relations with black Africa while still villainizing out-of-control black bodies.

4. Interestingly, Wayne refers to the Roman city in the desert as Timgad, which was the name of the Roman ruins in Libya that were used for location shooting, ruins very far away from the Sahara. That kind of loose approach to geography is characteristic of a Eurocentric mindset—all cities in Africa are essentially interchangeable exotic

locales—but also ties the diegetic Roman city with the history of imperialism in Libya, which had recently earned its independence.

5. See Chapter 1 for an overview of Wayne's star persona and its complex relationship with structures of romance and the family. Throughout this period (and through much of Wayne's career after 1948), Wayne continually played characters most comfortable in the company of other men, despite the cultural pressures of the hegemonic nuclear family. This tendency, I argue, indicates the tensions between nuclear-family domesticity and the necessity of homosocial wage labor on a global scale in this period.

6. The press release is kept at the Margaret Herrick Library of the Academy of Motion Picture Arts and Sciences, Beverly Hills, California.

CHAPTER SIX

1. The memorandum is kept at the Margaret Herrick Library of the Academy of Motion Picture Arts and Sciences, Beverly Hills, California.

2. Huston's press release and his letter to the mayor of Kyoto are in the Margaret Herrick Library of the Academy of Motion Picture Arts and Sciences, Beverly Hills, California. The goodwill that the production of *Barbarian* in Japan was supposed to generate was threatened when the film crew attempted to film a small fishing vessel on fire in the harbor and accidentally set fire to most of Kyoto's fishing fleet, inciting a small riot that Wayne and Huston had to help settle (*Mirror*, "John Wayne Pacifies Mob").

3. The press release is kept at the Margaret Herrick Library of the Academy of Motion Picture Arts and Sciences, Beverly Hills, California.

4. My use of the term "traditional" is not to suggest that Huston and the film's crew created an accurate representation of Japanese culture and traditions in *The Barbarian and the Geisha*. Their conception of traditional Japanese culture is based in Orientalist models of exoticism. Moreover, as numerous scholars in folklore and anthropology point out, the idea of a static "tradition" against which modern changes can be measured is itself a problematic idea that doesn't address the fluidity and adaptability of traditions and traditional culture. Nonetheless, I use the terms "tradition" and "traditional" to indicate the construction of an idea of Japanese traditional culture with which Harris's Western modernity is compared.

5. Interestingly, it was reported that some of the footage Huston shot of supposedly traditional fishing techniques came when a dolphin run started in Kyoto and most of the film's extras rushed to start fishing in their period costumes, shutting down shooting on the film for three days (Beech, "Hollywood's Oriental Fad").

6. Modernization theory has been widely critiqued for its problematic and condescending view of the non-Euro-American world. Modernization theory is premised on a universal, linear, temporal progression of societies that constructs the "undeveloped" as somehow more antiquated and "out of date" than the United States and Europe (for example, see Rostow, *Stages of Economic Growth*). W. W. Rostow sees all societies within a progressive vision of development that moves from a "traditional society" to one manifesting the "preconditions for take-off" to the "take-off" itself to a "drive to

maturity" and culminating in an "age of mass-consumption." By constructing the developing world in such temporal terms, modernization theory reified the racist and imperialist position that Euro-American modernity is not only the yardstick by which to measure the rest of the world but also the "natural" result of the "progression" of history, regardless of the cultural contexts of other societies (see also Huntington, *Political Order*).

7. For more on Lerner's views regarding mass media and modernization, see Hemant Shah, *The Production of Modernization*.

8. The term "narrative of anti-conquest" is from Mary Louise Pratt, *Imperial Eyes*.

9. Within the film, Harris attempts to describe Western gender dynamics as being more egalitarian than those in Japan. When Okichi asks about girls in America, she is shocked to learn that women in the United States are allowed to walk beside their husbands rather than being required to walk behind them. That vision of gender equity in the United States was vastly exaggerated. With perhaps unintentional irony, Wayne joked in an interview with Hedda Hopper in 1957 that 1950s Japanese men "have it made" because of the strict gender hierarchy requiring their wives to walk behind them (Hopper, "Wayne Awes His Fans").

CHAPTER SEVEN

1. For an example of this divisive approach to *High Noon* and *Rio Bravo*, see Jeffrey Meyers's review of Jim Hillier and Peter Wollen's *Howard Hawks: American Artist* (London: British Film Institute, 1996), in which he celebrates the sensitive vision of *High Noon*, as opposed to the "mindless machismo" of John Wayne ("The Big Sleep"). Meyers's distinctions are also referred to in Arnold, "My Rifle, My Pony, and Feathers."

2. Wood suggests that the film subtly invites the audience to question Wayne's character's "quasi-fascism," which comes from too much dedication to duty and a strict adherence to violence, arguing that Dude (Dean Martin) stands as a counterpoint to the brutal Chance (*Rio Bravo*).

3. Wood's argument here is similar to one made by Will Wright in his structuralist study of the Hollywood western, *Six Guns and Society*. Wright singles out *Rio Bravo* as the first example of the "Professional Plot," in which the chief dynamics of the film are between the men as professionals and do not concern their relationships to the larger social world.

4. The one exception to this comes near the end of the film when one of Burdette's hired guns tells Chance that some of the men Chance killed in the standoff were friends of his, providing the only sense of noncommodified relations between Burdette's men. For Wood, this is an intriguing moment when the film's generally casual vision of violence is called into question (*Rio Bravo*, 80–81).

5. See Arnold's analysis of the film for a more detailed examination of the songs themselves and their construction of homosociality ("My Rifle").

6. Whether Feathers (and Hawks's typical heroine in general) can be read as progressive, or even feminist, is complex and beyond the scope of this essay. Wood argues

that the relationship between Feathers and Chance, with its emphasis on friendship instead of dominance, should be understood in terms of women's liberation (*Rio Bravo*). Similarly, Naomi Wise has famously argued that Hawks's women defy the standard stereotypes of the action and adventure genre ("Hawksian Woman").

7. In this essay, I use the shorter version of *The Alamo*, which was used for widespread, international release, not the longer, road-show version that Wayne preferred.

8. According to Rodney Farnsworth, the excessively patriotic rhetoric that Wayne used to describe the project was due to his need for Texas financial backers ("Epic of Contradictions"). To convince Texas businessmen to help fund the project, Wayne appealed to their patriotic sense of duty, using rhetoric that Farnsworth suggests might not have been as prominent in Wayne's framing of the film had he been able to use his original backers and shoot the film in Mexico or Panama. Farnsworth suggests that the unscrupulous war profiteer in the film, Emil Sande (Wesley Lau), was a thinly veiled dig at Wayne's Texas backers, whom he had to beg for money.

9. Randy Roberts and James Stuart Olson support this interpretation of *The Alamo* in their celebratory biography of Wayne, *John Wayne: American*, seeing the film as a heroic statement of conviction and duty.

10. This understanding of Travis as a more urbane form of masculinity was no doubt underscored by the fact of Laurence Harvey's bisexuality, which was fairly widely known.

11. Corkin interprets Crockett's insistence on a gratuity for the boy as a condescending act of U.S. paternalism, suggesting the necessary role of a benevolent U.S. protector for the childlike inhabitants of the developing world.

References

Acker, Joan. "Gender, Capitalism, and Globalization." *Critical Sociology* 30, no. 1 (2004): 17–41.

Acland, Charles R. *Screen Traffic: Movies, Multiplexes, and Global Culture.* Durham: Duke Univ. Press, 2003.

Ambler, Charles. "Popular Films and Colonial Audiences in Central Africa." In *Hollywood Abroad: Audiences and Cultural Exchange,* edited by Melvyn Stokes and Richard Maltby, 133–157. London: BFI, 2004.

Appadurai, Arjun. *Modernity at Large: Cultural Dimensions of Globalization.* Minneapolis: Univ. of Minnesota Press, 1996.

Armitage, Susan, and Elizabeth Jameson, eds. *The Women's West.* Norman: Univ. of Oklahoma Press, 1987.

Arndt, H. W. *Economic Development: The History of an Idea.* Chicago: Univ. of Chicago Press, 1989.

Arnold, David L. G. "My Rifle, My Pony, and Feathers: Music and the Making of Men in Howard Hawks' *Rio Bravo.*" *Quarterly Review of Film and Video* 23, no. 3 (2006): 267–279.

Bauman, Zygmunt. *Globalization: The Human Consequences.* New York: Columbia Univ. Press, 1998.

Beech, Keyes. "Hollywood's Oriental Fad." *Saturday Evening Post,* May 10, 1958.

Belton, John. "John Wayne: As Sure as the Turning o' the Earth." *Velvet Light Trap* 7 (Winter 1972–1973): 25–28.

Bentley, E. "The Political Theatre of John Wayne." *Film Society Review* 7–9 (1972): 51–60.

Berg, Charles Ramirez. "The Margin as Center: The Multicultural Dynamics of John Ford's Westerns." In Studlar and Bernstein, *John Ford Made Westerns,* 75–101.

Berlant, Lauren. "Intimacy: A Special Issue." In *Intimacy,* edited by Lauren Berlant, 1–8. Chicago: Univ. of Chicago Press, 2000.

Bloom, Peter J. "Beyond the Western Frontier: Reappropriations of the 'Good Badman' in France, the French Colonies, and Contemporary Algeria." In *Westerns: Films through History,* edited by Janet Walker, 197–216. New York: Routledge, 2001.

Bulcroff, Kris, Richard Bulcroff, Linda Smeins, and Helen Cranage. "The Social Construction of the North American Honeymoon, 1880–1995." *Journal of Family History* 22 (1997): 462–490.

Burns, James. "John Wayne on the Zambezi: Cinema, Empire, and the American Western in British Central Africa." *International Journal of African Historical Studies* 35, no. 1 (2002): 103–117.

Castells, Manuel. *The Rise of the Network Society*. Malden, Mass.: Blackwell, 1996.

Cawelti, John G. "Savagery, Civilization, and the Western Hero." In *Focus on the Western*, edited by John G. Nachbar, 57–63. Englewood Cliffs, N.J.: Prentice Hall, 1974.

Citizen-News. "Wayne Most Popular in Japan, Says Actress." September 14, 1950. Accessed at the Margaret Herrick Library of the Academy of Motion Picture Arts and Sciences, Beverly Hills, California.

Cohan, Steven. *Masked Men: Masculinity and the Movies in the Fifties*. Bloomington: Indiana Univ. Press, 1997.

Connell, R. W. *The Men and the Boys*. Berkeley and Los Angeles: Univ. of California Press, 2000.

Coontz, Stephanie. "The Radical Idea of Marrying for Love." In *Sociology: Exploring the Architecture of Everyday Life Readings*, edited by David M. Newman and Jodi O'Brien, 158–68. 7th ed. Thousand Oaks, Calif.: Pine Forge, 2008.

———. *The Way We Never Were: American Families and the Nostalgia Trap*. New York: Basic Books, 1992.

Cooper, Frederick. *Africa since 1940: The Past of the Present*. Cambridge: Cambridge Univ. Press, 2002.

Corkin, Stanley. *Cowboys as Cold Warriors: The Western and U.S. History*. Philadelphia: Temple Univ. Press, 2004.

Cott, Nancy F. *Public Vows: A History of Marriage and the Nation*. Cambridge, Mass.: Harvard Univ. Press, 2000.

de Grazia, Victoria. *Irresistible Empire: America's Advance through Twentieth-Century Europe*. Cambridge, Mass.: Belknap Press of Harvard Univ. Press, 2005.

"Director Huston Real Star of 'Townsend Harris Story.'" ca. 1957. Unknown source. Accessed at the Margaret Herrick Library of the Academy of Motion Picture Arts and Sciences, Beverly Hills, California.

Dirlik, Arif. "The Global in the Local." In *Global/Local: Cultural Production and the Transnational Imaginary*, edited by Rob Wilson and Wimal Dissanayake, 21–45. Durham, N.C.: Duke Univ. Press, 1996.

Dower, John W. *War without Mercy: Race and Power in the Pacific War*. New York: Pantheon, 1986.

Dudden, Arthur Power. *The American Pacific: From the Old China Trade to the Present*. New York: Oxford Univ. Press, 1992.

During, Simon. "Popular Culture on a Global Scale: A Challenge for Cultural Studies?" *Critical Inquiry* 23, no. 4 (1997): 808–833.

Dyer, Richard. *Stars*. London: BFI, 1979.

———. *White*. New York: Routledge, 1997.

Eckstein, Arthur M. "Darkening Ethan: John Ford's *The Searchers* (1956) from Novel to Screenplay to Screen." *Cinema Journal* 38, no. 1 (1998): 3–24.

Edgerton, Gary. "A Reappraisal of John Wayne." *Films in Review* 5 (1986): 282–289.

Farnsworth, Rodney. "John Wayne's Epic of Contradictions." *Film Quarterly* 52, no. 2 (1998): 24–34.

Fenin, George N., and William K. Everson. *The Western, from Silents to the Seventies.* New York: Grossman, 1973.

Freedman, Carl. "Post-Heterosexuality: John Wayne and the Construction of American Masculinity." *Film International* 5, no. 1 (2007): 17–31.

French, Philip. *Westerns: Aspects of a Movie Genre.* New York: Oxford Univ. Press, 1977.

Giddens, Anthony. *The Consequences of Modernity.* Stanford, Calif.: Stanford Univ. Press, 1990.

———. *The Transformation of Intimacy.* Stanford, Calif.: Stanford Univ. Press, 1992.

Grossberg, Lawrence. "The Space of Culture, the Power of Space." In *The Post-Colonial Question: Common Skies, Divided Horizons,* edited by Ian Chambers and Linda Curti, 169–188. London: Routledge, 1996.

Guback, Thomas H. "Hollywood's International Market." In *The American Film Industry,* edited by Tino Balio, 463–486. Madison: Univ. of Wisconsin Press, 1985.

———. *The International Film Industry: Western Europe and America since 1945.* Bloomington: Indiana Univ. Press, 1969.

Harvey, David. *The Condition of Postmodernity: An Enquiry into the Origins of Cultural Change.* Oxford: Blackwell, 1989.

Hayden, Dolores. *Redesigning the American Dream: The Future of Housing, Work, and Family Life.* New York: Norton, 2002.

Hirsch, Jennifer S. "'Love Makes a Family': Globalization, Companionate Marriage, and the Modernization of Gender Inequality." In *Love and Globalization: Transformations of Intimacy in the Contemporary World,* edited by Mark B. Padilla, Jennifer S. Hirsch, Miguel Muñoz-Laboy, Robert E. Sember, and Richard G. Parker, 93–106. Nashville: Vanderbilt Univ. Press, 2007.

Hollywood Reporter. "French Award to Wayne." August 2, 1951.

———. "Hayward, Wayne Win Foreign Poll." February 16, 1953.

Hopper, Hedda. "John Wayne Awes His Fans in Japan." *Los Angeles Times,* December 27, 1957.

Huhndorf, Shari. *Going Native: Indians in the American Cultural Imagination.* Ithaca, N.Y.: Cornell Univ. Press, 2001.

Huntington, Samuel P. *Political Order in Changing Societies.* New Haven, Conn.: Yale Univ. Press, 1968.

Japan Times. "Harris, Okichi Story Plans Aired by Huston." May 9, 1957.

Jarvie, Ian. "Free Trade as Cultural Threat: American Film and T.V. Exports in the Post-War Period." In *Hollywood and Europe: Economics, Culture, and National Identity, 1945–95,* edited by Geoffrey Nowell-Smith and Steven Ricci, 34–46. London: BFI, 1998.

Jefferson, Bonnie S. "John Wayne: American Icon, Patriotic Zealot, and Cold War Ideologue." In *War and Film in America: Historical and Critical Essays,* edited by Marilyn J. Matelskit and Nancy Lynch Street, 25–42. Jefferson, N.C.: McFarland, 2003.

Kackman, Michael. "Nothing on but Hoppy Badges: Hopalong Cassidy, William Boyd Enterprises, and Emergent Media Globalization." *Cinema Journal* 47.4 (2008): 76–101.

Kent, John. "The United States and the Decolonization of Black Africa, 1945–63." In *The United States and Decolonization: Power and Freedom,* edited by David Ryan and Victor Pungong, 168–189. New York: St. Martin's, 2000.

King, Anthony D. *Spaces of Global Cultures: Architecture, Urbanism, Identity.* London: Routledge, 2004.

Kitses, Jim. *Horizons West: Directing the Western from John Ford to Clint Eastwood.* London: BFI, 2004.

Klein, Christina. *Cold War Orientalism: Asia in the Middlebrow Imagination, 1945–1961.* Berkeley and Los Angeles: Univ. of California Press, 2003.

Kotkin, Joel. *The City: A Global History.* New York: Modern Library, 2005.

Lefebvre, Henri. *The Production of Space.* Translated by Donald Nicholson-Smith. Oxford: Blackwell, 1991.

Lehman, Peter. "How the West Wasn't Won: The Repression of Capitalism in John Ford's Westerns." In Studlar and Bernstein, *John Ford Made Westerns,* 132–153.

———. *Running Scared: Masculinity and the Representation of the Male Body.* Philadelphia: Temple Univ. Press, 1993.

Lenihan, John H. *Showdown: Confronting Modern America in the Western Film.* Urbana: Univ. of Illinois Press, 1980.

Lerner, Daniel. *The Passing of Traditional Society: Modernizing the Middle East.* Glencoe, Ill.: Free Press, 1958. Print.

Lethem, Jonathan. "The Darkest Side of John Wayne." Salon.com, August 11, 1997. http://www.salon.com/1997/08/11/wayne/.

Lev, Peter. *The Fifties: Transforming the Screen, 1950–1959.* History of the American Cinema, vol. 7. New York: Scribner's Sons, 2003.

Levy, Emanuel. *John Wayne: Prophet of the American Way of Life.* Metuchen, N.J.: Scarecrow Press, 1988.

Lewis, Richard Warren. "John Wayne: The *Playboy* Interview." *Playboy,* May 1971.

Limerick, Patricia. *The Legacy of Conquest: The Unbroken Past of the American West.* New York: Norton, 1987.

Loy, R. Phillip. *Westerns in a Changing America, 1955–2000.* Jefferson, N.C.: McFarland, 2004.

Luhr, William. "John Wayne and *The Searchers.*" *"The Searchers": Essays and Reflections on John Ford's Classic Western,* edited by Arthur M. Eckstein and Peter Lehman, 75–92. Detroit: Wayne State Univ. Press, 2004.

Mainichi. "Huston Wants to Use Japanese Cameramen and Art Directors." May 9, 1957.

Maltby, Richard. "The Americanisation of the World." In *Hollywood Abroad: Audiences and Cultural Exchange,* edited by Melvyn Stokes and Richard Maltby, 1–20. London: BFI, 2004.

Marchetti, Gina. *Romance and the "Yellow Peril": Race, Sex, and Discursive Strategies in Hollywood Fiction*. Berkeley and Los Angeles: Univ. of California Press, 1993.

Massey, Doreen. *Space, Place, and Gender*. Minneapolis: Univ. of Minnesota Press, 1994.

Matheson, Sue. "John Ford on the Cold War: Stetsons and Cast Shadows in *The Man Who Shot Liberty Valance* (1962)." *Journal of Popular Culture* 45, no. 2 (2012): 357–369.

———. "'Let's Go Home, Debbie': The Matter of Blood Pollution, Combat Culture, and Cold War Hysteria in *The Searchers* (1956)." *Journal of Popular Film and Television* 39, no. 2 (2011): 50–58.

———. "The West—Hardboiled: Adaptations of Film Noir Elements, Existentialism, and Ethics in John Wayne's Westerns." *Journal of Popular Culture* 38, no. 5 (2005): 888–910.

McAlister, Melani. *Epic Encounters: Culture, Media, and U.S. Interests in the Middle East, 1945–2000*. Berkeley and Los Angeles: Univ. of California Press, 2001.

McBride, Joseph. *Hawks on Hawks*. Berkeley and Los Angeles: Univ. of California Press, 1982.

McBride, Joseph, and Michael Wilmington. *John Ford*. New York: Da Capo, 1975.

Meeuf, Russell. "John Wayne as 'Supercrip': Disabled Bodies and the Construction of Hard Masculinity in *The Wings of Eagles* (1958)." *Cinema Journal* 48, no. 2 (2009): 88–113.

Meyers, Jeffrey. "The Big Sleep." *Virginia Quarterly Review* 74, no. 2 (1998): 7–12.

Mirror. "John Wayne Pacifies Mob." November 19, 1957. Accessed at the Margaret Herrick Library of the Academy of Motion Picture Arts and Sciences, Beverly Hills, California.

Mitchell, Lee Clark. *Westerns: Making the Man in Fiction and Film*. Chicago: Univ. of Chicago Press, 1996.

Munn, Michael. *John Wayne: The Man behind the Myth*. New York: New American Library, 2005.

Neale, Steve. "Masculinity as Spectacle." *Screen* 24, no. 6 (1983): 2–16.

Padilla, Mark B., Jennifer S. Hirsch, Miguel Muñoz-Laboy, Robert E. Sember, and Richard G. Parker. "Cross Cultural Reflections on an Intimate Intersection." In *Love and Globalization: Transformations of Intimacy in the Contemporary World*, edited by Mark B. Padilla, et al., ix–xxxi. Nashville: Vanderbilt Univ. Press, 2007.

Pedraza, Silvia. "Women and Migration: The Social Consequences of Gender." *Annual Review of Sociology* 17 (1991): 303–25.

Pratt, Mary Louise. *Imperial Eyes: Travel Writing and Transculturation*. London: Routledge, 1992.

Rawlins, Justin Owen. "This Is(n't) John Wayne: The Miscasting and Performance of Whiteness in *The Conqueror*." *Quarterly Review of Film and Video* 27, no. 1 (2009): 14–26.

Roberts, Randy, and James Stuart Olson. *John Wayne: American*. New York: Free Press, 1995.

Robertson, Roland. "Glocalization: Time-Space and Homogenity-Heterogeneity." In *Global Modernities*, edited by Mike Featherstone, Scott Lash, and Roland Robertson, 25–44. London: Sage, 1995.

Rostow, W. W. *The Stages of Economic Growth: A Non-Communist Manifesto*. Cambridge: Cambridge Univ. Press, 1960.

Rydell, Robert, and Rob Kroes. *Buffalo Bill in Bologna: The Americanization of the World, 1869–1922*. Chicago: Univ. of Chicago Press, 2005.

Salt, John. "A Comparative Overview of International Trends and Types, 1950–80." *International Migration Review* 23, no. 3 (1989): 431–56.

Sanderson, Jim. "*Red River* and the Loss of Femininity in the John Wayne Persona." *Literature/Film Quarterly* 32, no. 1 (2004): 39–45.

Schatz, Thomas. *Hollywood Genres: Formulas, Filmmakers, and the Studio System*. Philadelphia: Temple Univ. Press, 1981.

Scheuer, Phillip K. "'Barbarian' Leaves Japan." *Los Angeles Times*, January 31, 1958.

Schwartz, Vanessa R. *It's So French! Hollywood, Paris, and the Making of Cosmopolitan Film Culture*. Chicago: Univ. of Chicago Press, 2007.

Sèbe, Berny. "In the Shadow of the Algerian War: The United States and the Common Organisation of Saharan Regions (OCRS), 1957–62." *Journal of Imperial and Commonwealth History* 38, no. 2 (2010): 303–322.

Sedgwick, Eve Kosofsky. *Between Men: English Literature and Male Homosocial Desire*. New York: Columbia Univ. Press, 1985.

Shah, Hemant. *The Production of Modernization: Daniel Lerner, Mass Media, and the Passing of Traditional Society*. Philadelphia: Temple Univ. Press, 2011.

Sharrett, Christopher. "Through a Door Darkly: A Reappraisal of John Ford's *The Searchers*." *Cineaste* 31, no. 4 (2006): 4–8.

Shaw, Gareth, and Allan M. Williams. *Critical Issues in Tourism: A Geographical Perspective*. 2nd ed. Malden, Mass.: Blackwell, 2002.

Shively, JoEllen. "Cowboys and Indians: Perceptions of Western Films among American Indians and Anglos." *American Sociological Review* 57, no. 6 (1992): 725–734.

Shohat, Ella, and Robert Stam. *Unthinking Eurocentrism: Multiculturalism and the Media*. London: Routledge, 1994.

Sklar, Robert. "*Red River*: Empire to the West." *Cineaste* 9, no. 1 (1978): 14–19.

Slotkin, Richard. *Gunfighter Nation: The Myth of the Frontier in Twentieth-Century America*. Norman: Univ. of Oklahoma Press, 1998.

Smith, Neil. *The New Urban Frontier: Gentrification and the Revanchist City*. London: Routledge, 1996.

———. *Uneven Development: Nature, Capital, and the Production of Space*. 3rd ed. Athens: Univ. of Georgia Press, 1984.

Sobchack, Vivian. "Lounge Time: Postwar Crises and the Chronotope of Film Noir." In *Refiguring American Film Genres: History and Theory*, edited by Nick Browne, 129–170. Berkeley and Los Angeles: Univ. of California Press, 1998.

Soja, Edward. "History: Geography: Modernism." In *The Cultural Studies Reader*, edited by Simon During, 113–125. 2nd ed. New York: Routledge, 1999.

Solimano, Andres, and Nathalie Watts. *International Migration, Capital Flows, and the Global Economy: A Long Run View*. New York: United Nations, Economic Commission for Latin America and the Caribbean, Economic Development Division, 2005.

Strang, David. "Global Patterns of Decolonization, 1500–1987." *International Studies Quarterly* 35, no. 4 (1991): 429–54.

Studlar, Gaylyn. "Sacred Duties, Poetic Passions: John Ford and the Issue of Femininity in the Western." In Studlar and Bernstein, *John Ford Made Westerns*, 43–74.

Studlar, Gaylyn, and Matthew Bernstein, eds. *John Ford Made Westerns*. Bloomington: Indiana Univ. Press, 2001.

Therborn, Göran. *Between Sex and Power: Family in the World*. London: Routledge, 2004.

Thomas, Deborah. "John Wayne's Body." In *The Book of Westerns*, edited by Ian Cameron and Douglas Pye, 75–87. New York: Continuum, 1996.

———. *Reading Hollywood: Spaces and Meanings in American Film*. London: Wallflower Press, 2001.

Tompkins, Jane P. *West of Everything: The Inner Life of Westerns*. New York: Oxford Univ. Press, 1992.

United Nations. *International Migration Report, 2002*. New York: United Nations, Population Division, 2002.

Wallerstein, Immanuel. *The Modern World-System*. Vols. 1–3. New York: Academic Press, 1974, 1980, 1989.

Warshow, Robert. "Movie Chronicle: The Westerner." In *Focus on the Western*, edited by John G. Nachbar, 45–56. Englewood Cliffs, N.J.: Prentice-Hall, 1974.

Westbrook, Max. "Flag and Family in John Wayne's Westerns: The Audience as Co-Conspirator." *Western American Literature* 29, no. 1 (1994): 25–40.

———. "The Night John Wayne Danced with Shirley Temple." In *Old West–New West: Centennial Essays*, edited by Barbara Howard Meldrum, 60–73. Moscow, Idaho: Univ. of Idaho Press, 1993.

Wexman, Virginia Wright. *Creating the Couple: Love, Marriage, and Hollywood Performance*. Princeton, N.J.: Princeton Univ. Press, 1993.

Wills, Garry. *John Wayne's America: The Politics of Celebrity*. New York: Simon and Schuster, 1997.

Wilson, Rob, and Wimal Dissanayake. "Tracking the Global/Local." In *Global/Local: Cultural Production and the Transnational Imaginary*, edited by Rob Wilson and Wimal Dissanayake, 1–18. Durham, N.C.: Duke Univ. Press, 1996.

Wise, Naomi. "The Hawksian Woman." In *Howard Hawks: American Artist*, edited by Jim Hillier and Peter Wollen, 111–119. London: BFI, 1996.

Wood, Robin. *Rio Bravo*. London: BFI, 2003.

———. "'Shall We Gather at the River?': The Late Films of John Ford." In Studlar and Bernstein, *John Ford Made Westerns*, 23–42.

Wright, Will. *Six Guns and Society: A Structural Study of the Western*. Berkeley and Los Angeles: Univ. of California Press, 1975.

Yoshimoto, Mitsuhiro. "Images of Empire: Tokyo Disneyland and Japanese Cultural Imperialism." In *Disney Discourse: Producing the Magic Kingdom*, edited by Eric Smoodin, 181–199. New York: Routledge, 1994.

Zhang, Yingjin. *Cinema, Space, and Polylocality in a Globalizing China*. Honolulu: Univ. of Hawaii Press, 2010.

Index

Milton Keynes UK
Ingram Content Group UK Ltd.
UKHW012109230923
429161UK00019B/451